INDIA'S FOREIGN POLICY IN THE NEW MILLENNIUM
The Role of Power

Vatsala Shukla

ATLANTIC
PUBLISHERS & DISTRIBUTORS (P) LTD

Published by

ATLANTIC

PUBLISHERS & DISTRIBUTORS (P) LTD

7/22, Ansari Road, Darya Ganj,
New Delhi-110002
Phones : +91-11-40775252, 23273880, 23275880, 23280451
Fax : +91-11-23285873
Web : www.atlanticbooks.com
E-mail : orders@atlanticbooks.com

Branch Office
5, Nallathambi Street, Wallajah Road,
Chennai-600002
Phones : +91-44-64611085, 32413319
E-mail : chennai@atlanticbooks.com

Printed in India at Glorious Printers, A-13, D.S.I.D.C.,
Jhilmil Industrial Area, Delhi-110095

Dedicated

to

My Younger Sister
Vismita (Beenu)

(1979–1995)

Contents

Preface

In today's world it is the power and power alone that counts. It may be the power of press and public opinion, power of culture, intellectual power, money power, manpower or nuclear power, political power, economic power and so on. A nation's power is the combination of all these various forms of power and of course a nation's international profile depends on its power quotient. But the exact understanding of any nation's power is far difficult because there are multiple positive and negative factors that influence national power. Besides, the absolute and relative aspect of power cannot be ignored while counting a nation's power. The book takes all these factors into consideration. It begins with the introduction, which attempts to answer all the questions that come instantly into the mind when one sees the title.

In its first chapter, the book focuses on the current global trends and developments and briefly relates the meaning of Major Power Status, including in its details the origin, components and changing configuration of power and India's search for it. The international activities of India prior to Independence, that later in the post-1947 period proved to be the very basis of India's global posture, have been examined from a distinct perspective.

As the title itself suggests, the book is a complete treatise on India's foreign policy with particular emphasis on non-alignment, world peace, disarmament and nation's support to international organisations. India's foreign policy has been analytically studied against the backdrop of global changing circumstances — rising communalism and regionalism, decline in parliamentary culture, economic reintegration, nuclearisation, women's political empowerment, secessionist insurgencies and many other recent developments on a global scale. A detailed study on the Indian subcontinent, highlighting the local as well as regional factors, sheds new light on the bilateral relations of India with China, Pakistan and SARRC contries. The concluding chapter extensively deals with India's power acquisition strategies in the new millennium and also suggests strategies best suited to India's interests.

It is hoped that the vast coverage of the book will be of great help to the policymakers and the students of Indian politics and international relations as well as the general readers who keep interest in world politics.

VATSALA SHUKLA

Acknowledgements

I shall be failing in my duty if I do not record my gratitude to all those who helped and cooperated with me in pursuit of this study. Therefore, I wish to acknowledge the individuals and organisations that helped me to make this book possible.

First of all, I shall like to record my thanks to my teacher Prof. K.K. Mishra, whose inspiring guidance has always been a source of encouragement to me, without which I would not have been able to complete this literary work. I am also highly indebted to Head of the Political Science Department, Allahabad University, Dr. Alok Pant, who provided me the necessary help whenever I needed. His encouragement acted as an energiser for me. I also owe much to all the colleagues and staff of the Political Science Department of the same university, where I studied and also started my career as a teacher.

I am also highly grateful to the officials of all libraries that I consulted in the course of collecting material. Their cooperation deserves special mention here. I am particularly indebted to the Nehru Memorial Museum and Library, Teen Murti House, New Delhi, Goa University Library, Defence Library, Department of Defence Studies, Allahabad University, Jaikar Library, Pune University, ILS Law College Library, Pune, SNDT Women's University Library, Churchgate, Mumbai, Mani Bhavan Library, Laburnum Road, Mumbai, which provided a large collection of books, periodicals, journals, newspapers etc. to me. Also, I am thankful to electronic media where a bulk of information is available on different sites of internet.

I also wish to thank Prof. Usha Thakkar, Secretary, Center for Gandhian Studies, Mani Bhavan, Mumbai; Prof. Vibhuti Patel, Head, Department of Economics, SNDT Women's University, Mumbai; Prof. Nita Ramaiya, Director, Center for Canadian Studies, SNDT Women's University, Mumbai for their latent inspiration, which became apparent in the form of chapters on women in the book. I also feel indebted to Prof. Shiv Kumar, Director, Center for Latin American Studies, Goa University; Prof. P.M. Kamat, Director, Center for International Studies, Mulund, Mumbai; Prof. Madhuri Cheeda, Director, Post-Graduate Studies and Research, SNDT Women's University, Mumbai; Dr. Mangesh Kulkarni, Head, Department of Political Science, SNDT Women's University, Mumbai and Dr. Pushpa Pai, Head, Department of Applied Linguistics, SNDT Women's University, Mumbai, for their helpful advice and continuing interest in this ambitious work.

I convey my sincere thanks to M/s. Atlantic Publishers and Distributors, especially to Dr. K.R. Gupta for speedily completing the job.

It would be injustice if I do not record my thanks to my brother, Mr. Vinayak Shukla and sister-in-law Mrs. Aabha Shukla who assisted, co-operated and spared time for me. It is because of them, that I was able to collect relevant material for the study. I lack words to express my gratitude to my parents, who have throughout been helpful to me in the pursuit of my writing, without whose co-operation, support and encouragement I could not be able to spare time for my writing. Also, I acknowledge my debt to my in-laws who have been a great support throughout the writing of the final draft of the book and all my family members and friends, who have directly or indirectly helped me in completing this work. I am very much thankful to my husband, Dr. Ravindra Katyayan, who has constantly been my guide, philosopher and friend with his able help and support. I greatly value his encouragement and support. Last but not least, the contribution of my five-year-old son Vayun in this book is also of great significance to me. My deep sense of appreciation to him.

VATSALA SHUKLA

Introduction

With the sea change in international system, the interplay of forces shaping international relations and the sources of power and influence in global polities are witnessing sweeping changes. It is vitally important for India to grasp the meaning and direction of these changes, new trends and developments and redefine its foreign policy objectives in the new millennium. The post-Cold War era demands new strategies on India's part. The strategies, which will facilitate India's search for major power status.

Part-1 presents a brief understanding of current global trends and developments and also briefly shows the meaning of Major Power Status, its origin and components, changing configuration of power and India's search for power. The second half touches upon the international activities of India prior to independence, which became the foundation and the very basis of India's global posture in the post-1947 period. Part-2 is an attempt to show the elements of India's foreign policy with major emphasis on non-alignment, world peace, development, disarmament etc.

Parts-3, 4 and 5 comprise an in-depth analysis of local, regional and global factors, respectively, affecting India's foreign policy. In local factors, the focus is on politico-economic-defence scenarios of India. Regional factors include Pakistan factor, China factor and SAARC. While the global factors comprise recent trends and developments at international flora.

The entire analysis and study has been concluded in Part-6, which deals with India's power acquisition strategies. This part tries to formulate strategies, best suited to India's interests, with the maximum utilisation of her resources, so that India could attain an optimum global posture, in global power matrix.

Power comes in many forms and sizes. While analyzing the meaning and nature of power Hans J. Morgenthau describes, "Power is a psychological relationship between those who exercise it and those over whom it is exercised. It gives the former control over certain actions of the latter through the influence which the former exerts over the latter's mind." Further, in the words of Organski, "Power is the ability of a nation to influence the behaviour of others in accordance with its own ends. Unless a nation can do this she may be large, she may be wealthy, she may even be great, but she is not powerful." Power has a key role in international affairs. In a broad sense, it exists mainly in three forms viz. political, military and economic power. With the collapse of the Soviet Union, Cold War came to an end. As a result, old world order was replaced by new one, which is still evolving. Certain features mark the emerging new world order. These are:

- **End of bipolarity.** With the disintegration of the USSR, a pole marked by Communist ideology withered away and thus the ideological division of world into two poles came to an end.
- **Emergence of multiplayer world order.** With the emergence of new centers of power, new players are coming at international flora with growing economic capability. These new major centers of power include, Japan, European Union, China, ASEAN and Russia.
- **Primacy of economic dimension of power.** It is self-evident that no country — whatever its size, population or history, can aspire to be a major power without a solid and prosperous economy. Examples of rise of Japan and Germany and fall of USSR can be seen.
- **Prominence of Geo-economics.** It is manifested by the rise and strengthening of regional economic groups, like — European Union, APEC, NAFTA etc.
- **Changing configuration of power.** As global actors became more inter-dependent, none of the major powers can now call the tune at will.
- **Prevalence of globalisation.** It means the integration of

the national with the global economy and the acceptance of international economic agreements, in a broad sense.

- **Disparity between developed and developing countries widened.** Science and technology became new tools of exploitation in the hands of developed countries, thereby North-South divisions were aggravated and further entrenched, leading to the rise of a 'New Northern Concert of Powers'.
- **Existence of the Doctrine of Different Rights or Inequality.** It was an old doctrine, which states that some people or groups — it may be the developed nations or whosoever may be on top, have the right to do things that others do no have. Whether the case of CTBT, non-proliferation of nuclear weapons, re-structuring of the United Nations, operation of international economic institutions or any other international agreement, the reflection of this doctrine can be easily seen.

India has achieved the Nuclear Power Status, true. But the international standing of India or for that matter any other power in the world will flow from its economic surplus and technological dynamism. Although because of its size and location and heavy consumer market, India will always be strategically and commercially important, but it has to build its economic strength and domestic stability (not just military strength), if India really wants to attain major power status in international affairs. This is the three-dimensional posture of power, in which economy takes central position.

Thus, in the new situation India has some difficult choices, but also a remarkable opportunity to achieve an optimum global posture. But as the challenges faced by India are quite formidable, there is every need for redefining India's priorities and discarding some of its old shibboleths. As India, not because of ambition of hers, but because of geography, because of history and because of so many other things, inevitably has to play a very important part in the world.

The search for major power status by India has its roots in

the pre-independence international activities of India that shaped the character of Indian foreign policy. With the decades of official and unofficial international activities India benefited and emerged with a clearly defined international personality and competence to engage in the complex art of diplomacy. Besides, the resolutions and statements of the Indian National Congress and the writings of its spokespersons in numerous journals, newspapers and books provide the principal sources for identifying elements of independent India's foreign policy. Next positive aspect of pre-independence international activities, was India's League of Nations experience, that enabled India to influence multilateral diplomacy in the post-independence period. Finally, the unofficial and official diplomatic activities of Indians prior to 1947, had long-term consequences in that they provided India with a preliminary pool of personnel for the establishment of its Foreign Ministry and overseas missions.

The name of Mahatma Gandhi and the method of moral persuasion to gain independence gave the country a special international standing. Furthermore, the independence of India was a watershed in human history for two important reasons. First, it signaled the beginning of the end of colonialism, thus opening the possibility of a democratic world order based on the sovereign equality of all nations. The second major development was India's articulation of an alternative world order to the one being fashioned by the rival power blocs. This alternative world order found expression in the philosophy of Non-alignment. Means, India would no longer be the camp-follower of any power. It would decide its foreign policy on the basis of its own understanding of India's national interest. Indian foreign policy is organically linked with India's struggle for development and self-reliance in the economic field. For which world peace is necessary as peace and development are inseparable. India denounced the trend towards nuclear arms race. It became a passion to plead for disarmament. 'Friendship with all and malice towards none', peaceful co-existence of nations, support to and strengthening of world organisations are the other important elements on which India's foreign policy rests. Indeed, these are the elements, which constitute the 'core values' of Indian foreign policy.

It was the ability of Jawaharlal Nehru to keep the Indian image at center stage when world crisis emerged that enabled this sub-continent to play such a significant role. India's respect was at its highest when it fearlessly followed non-aligned principles and played a sagacious role during and after the Korean War (1951-53), during the Crisis over Suez (1956). India was looked upon as the leader of the developing continents in Bandung (1955) and Belgrade (1961) and was obvious choice for the biggest UN peacekeeping operations in Congo (1960). Thus two of the most striking aspects of the Nehru era were the high visibility of India in UN efforts to intervene in international disputes and the complete dominance of Pt. Nehru himself in the formulation of foreign policy, at least up to 1962.

The Sino-Indian War damaged India's reputation, true, but it could preserve and protect the non-aligned image of India. During the Nehru era India followed the idealistic policy relating to diplomacy. But, idealism without the kernel of self-interest may sound hypocritical and hollow. The foreign policy of a nation is a complex and dynamic political course, which must include the prevailing pattern of its interests as well as principles and ideas in its conduct towards other states. Thus, the task of statesmanship lies in arriving at a balanced integration between idealism and realism. After 1962 India's global role began to recede. The post-Nehru years witnessed injection of greater realism in India's foreign policy. Indira Gandhi used non-alignment as an instrument in a manner, which reflected her positivistic thinking. During her stewardship of the nation, she has made the policy more purposeful and dynamic. Two important developments, one, the help to the liberation of Bangladesh (1971) and the other one is peaceful nuclear explosion (1974), exhibit legendary courage of Indira Gandhi and it was the courage to use power, when the nation needed it. These developments enhanced the regional image of India. At the same time, the fact of regional dominance gave India a global status and prestige.

Among the elements of India's foreign policy, the non-alignment comprises within itself all the other elements of foreign policy. It is the struggle for the removal of poverty, illiteracy, health and nutrition problems of the neglected millions, for which non-alignment is striving. It is a humanitarian approach which is much more acceptable than cutthroat competition policy approach. This campaign should continue. Thus, never before in history, the thrust of foreign policy is felt in all fields of human affairs.

The end of 20th century embarked new values, new thinking, new culture, new technology, new institutions and so on. With the great revolution in information technology, everything has changed. New developments, new trends and new forces emerged. Though, what was experienced in India was the part of worldwide phenomenon of change, like the victory of democratic institutions and prevalence of market economy, coalition culture and nuclear technology.

Since independence, Indian political scenario is full of surprises of both positive and negative kinds. Violence, caste conflict and terrorism persist in India. But in the face of all these hurdles, Indian democracy has matured and has come to age and its future seems secure. Democracy in India is a way of life and can never be changed. According to Henry Kissinger, "India has matured into a fine making democracy."[1] Professor Chia Nakana of the Tokyo University opined that "in Asia and in the world, there is no parallel to the Indian Democracy. Democracy is innately and inherently strong in India and can withstand all shocks and surprises."[2]

The foreign policy of every country is a mirror reflection of domestic co-relationship of social forces. During the 1990s, Indian foreign policy has become reactive, defensive and obliging, because political parties have fractured the Indian society on the basis of caste versus caste, community versus community, region versus region, and language versus language. The consequence of this highly fragmented political process is that political parties have multiplied to promote their sectional and sectarian group interests.

There have been five general elections between 1989 and 1999, all of which have produced a fractured mandate. With no single party able to muster a clear majority on its own, India has entered the period of coalition politics in the last decade of the twentieth century. This has had effects on the foreign policy. Besides, in order to overcome the domestic economic crisis, India opted for aid from the IMF and the World Bank in the early nineties. As a result, the process of liberalisation and privatisation got underway, which in turn brought various pressures on the Indian foreign policy. The other domestic factors, which made influence on India's foreign policy in this period, range from caste-class conflict, religious extremism, insurgencies, terrorism, decline in Parliamentary culture, fragmentation in party system, crisis of governance, to globalisation, nuclearisation and women empowerment.

The Main threat to India's future is not political, but economic. The Indian economy has been semi-closed for most of the post-World War-II period. Since independence in 1947, the Indian government has pursued a strategy of self-reliance with autonomous industrialisation at its core. The state has attempted to transform the material basis of Indian society through detailed intervention in the economy.

But, beginning in the 1980s and more recently in 1991, the government decisively moved away from an interventionist posture by drastically altering its industrial and trade policies in favor of an 'open' economy. The first phase (roughly from 1950 to 1980) is called the phase of resistance, a process by which the Indian state along with the Indian bourgeoisie attempted to resist the forces of global capitalism and foster self-reliance. The second phase (1980 onward) is called the process of reintegration with the world economy, whereby previous attempts to fend off external economic forces are substituted by a desire to participate in the world economy.[3]

Thus, globalisation, though not a novel concept, has assumed new significance since the turn of the 1990s mainly because of the changed international balance of forces resulting from the collapse of the Soviet Union, the disintegration of the world socialist system and the end of the Cold War.[4]

Globalisation means the attempt to bring the world under single domination and one system.

Further, development is not merely an economic process but a political one as well. It therefore ultimately requires a "democratisation" of political communities to give citizens a voice in important decisions made for the community. To fail in this regard, is to limit human freedom — and, by extension, the possibility for full human development.

India has broken the monopoly of the Nuclear-Five. The question is asked whether India should join the Nuclear Club and enjoy its privileges. Having pleaded for a total elimination of nuclear weapons, it would be immoral for India to join any group, which would have the privilege of increasing the nuclear arsenal. On the contrary, India should strive through the United Nations to bring about a Treaty on "No First Use" of nuclear weapons by any of the member-states. In India, in spite of India's policy *vis-à-vis* nuclear issue, being more rational, there is no consensus and not even a concerted attempt at building a consensus. Economic liberalisation is not the only liberalisation we need. If defence and foreign policy is to be receptive to world change, they must be made more in the open.

Pakistan and China are the top regional factors. India and Pakistan have been in a state of undeclared war, with varying degree of intensity, throughout their brief history as independent states. Both Pakistan and China had waged wars against India. Though both of them differ in their political systems and perceptions of several domestic and external issues, they could initiate cordial relationship in early 1960s. China remains determined to supply nuclear power technologies to Pakistan. No other nuclear relationship between two countries has been of such a long duration. The seriousness of these factors lie in the fact, that although quite a sizeable chunk of the population of India lives in pervasive ignorance of foreign affairs, but even the most ordinary citizen knows that he has to be very careful about Pakistan and China and he will not forgive any Government at New Delhi that can let these countries off the hook.

It is overwhelmingly in India's national interest to strengthen regional co-operation by harnessing the collective power of all South-Asian countries. What is more important is, an acceptance of the fact, that the Indian sub-continent is a single economic zone. Today India provides the second largest consumer market in the world. When South Asian Free Trade Area (SAFTA) is fully realised, the region will be the largest market in world. This, in turn, will enormously increase India's own importance and potential.

After the disintegration of the Soviet Union the world faced a new situation and so did India. Many of the old hypotheses had become victims of the march of history. The economic struggle had become far more crucial than before, with palpable consequences for foreign policy. United States with its overwhelming power became the chief architect of all the major decisions in the post-cold war era. US, to establish its supremacy in the world has played the dangerous game of wars. Gulf war 1 and Gulf war 2 were imposed upon the innocent people of the West Asia. Terrorism became the widespread phenomenon across the globe. Even the US could not escape from the clutches of terrorism. Worldwide expansion of technology and possession of nuclear weapons by many countries made easy accessibility of lethal weapons in the hands of terrorists. Globalisation made national boundaries irrelevant. Flow of capital did not see any barrier. Besides, the rich countries tried to marginalise the poor through the institutions of WTO, IMF and World Bank. In the era of democratic and representative institutions, there is UNO, which is pursuing the principle of hegemonism and inequality. Rich countries dominate this world body. Interdependence, competition and technology are today's ideologies.

In this atmosphere, countries have to formulate their foreign policy. For India, this task is even more challenging for the obvious reasons inherent in its history, polity and economic potential, which place it among the leading nations of the world.

A strategy is the policy design, which while considering threats and challenges, best safeguards the national interest with the maximum utilisation of power resources, within the perimeter of capabilities. In other words it is a grand policy design which functions under various compulsions namely domestic, regional and global. It is also a grand design, which is formulated after analyzing nation's capability and its place in the global power matrix, so that a nation could attain a maximum possible global posture. Thus the formulation of strategy is a matter of both absolute and relative power of a nation.

India had a strategy in the form of non-alignment, anti-colonialism, democracy, secularism, state planning and self-reliance in the Nehru era. But, unfortunately, India no longer has such an integrated conception. In the post-Cold War period, hard new world realities calls for hard new thinking on the part of India. Strategies for India, which will facilitate India's power acquisition in the new millennium, are:

- India needs to continue to maintain a balanced relationship between and among the major powers. The prospects for greater economic and commercial co-operation and India's new advances in the Information Technology and other knowledge-based industries have created a very positive environment in which Indo-US differences can now be managed with greater confidence and in a more relaxed manner. Possible, through economy both democratic countries come closer in other spheres and India and the US achieve durability of their relationship. As far as bilateral relations between India and China are concerned, the best course of action for India is an approach of constructive engagement.
- India's foreign policy has not been fixated on Pakistan, but that has been a significant preoccupation of it. India needs to re-examine this in detail. Globally, India has to move purposefully towards realizing its true dimensions — as a major civilisational state, with its own strategic autonomy and strategic space, born out of its economic and political interaction with other countries particularly in the Asia-Pacific community.

- The categorical and unambiguous commitment to no first use of nuclear weapons in case of conflict determines the contours of India's nuclear posture. India should also campaign for an international treaty banning the first use of nuclear weapons. India should have in place modest nuclear arsenals to achieve minimum and credible deterrence. With India's nuclear neighbors, nuclear arms control, as well as confidence building measures can increase transparency and reduce the dangers of an open-ended nuclear arms race.
- As India enlarges its share of world trade, its voice in world councils will also gather weight. Over the next thirty years, India must aim for growth rates of 10 to 12 per cent per annum. However, even with a far more modest growth rate of 7 per cent per annum, national income will double every ten years. Therefore, strategy should be to maintain peace and grow strong economically.
- Besides prosperity for all, India must pay attention to social cohesion as a fundamental security need for India, which is challenged by caste conflict and communal tensions. The deeper institutionalisation of political liberty and of egalitarian democratisation is the need of the hour, which means the ever-greater empowerment of ordinary people. The concept of 'humane governance', which puts people at the center of all governance policies, strategies and actions, should be adopted.

Notes

1. Rekha Saxena, *Indian Politics in Transition*, Deep & Deep Publications, New Delhi, 1994.
2. *Ibid.*
3. Anthony P. D'costa, 'The long march to capitalism: India's resistance to, and reintegration with the world economy', *Contemporary South Asia*, 1995.
4. Girish Mishra, 'Globalisation and India', *World Focus*, Oct.-Nov.-Dec. 1999.

1

India and Power

INTRODUCTION

Power is the main concept of Political Science. According to Laswell and Catlin State Science is Power Science. Elements of power reside in the government, state, sovereignty and law. In the view of Barker politics cannot be divorced from power. For McIver, as the role of money in market economy, so is the role of power in politics. Politics is thus a struggle for power — a 'lust for power'.

'Power' comes in many forms and sizes, *viz.*, economic power, nuclear power, the power of press and public opinion, power systems, power elites and so on. According to classical scholars its roots are (to be) found in Greek words, meaning both "to start" and "to rule" or to control. In his book on Metaphysics, Aristotle explained that a powerful individual or group is one "at whose will that which is moved is moved and that which changes, changes. Power is what makes things go, wheels to turn, ships to sail, men to move in particular ways. Power is the great initiator, the cosmic self-starter that starts everything else and keeps it going.[1]

Although power has become a common term in the natural sciences, its earliest, most continuous and consistent usage has been in political science. Without the ability to enforce decisions (*i.e.* laws, decrees, rules, or regulations) we cannot speak of power or for that matter of government, for government is simply the making and enforcing of decisions concerning certain kinds of behavior. As Bertrand Russell said in his book, "Power: A New Social Analysis" that power implies "the production of intended effects". Also Aristotle called man a political animal, which, is another way of calling him a power-seeking animal.[2] Power in this context means man's control over the minds and actions of other men. Other scholars like Machiavelli, Treitschke, Robert Dahl, David Easton, Weber advocated, state as a power system. According to Robert Dahl, power is "the ability to shift the probability of outcomes", means power refers to one's ability to influence the behavior of another. Schwarzenberger defines power as "capacity to impose one's will on others by reliance on an effective sanctions in case of non-compliance". While analyzing the meaning and nature of power Morgenthau describes, "Power is a psychological relationship between those who exercise it and those over whom it is exercised. It gives the former control over certain actions of the latter through the influence which the former exerts over the latter's mind."[3]

There are various elements of power. But, what determines power is the skillful use of the elements of power and not merely their possession by a state. The elements of power may be broadly classified into two categories: tangible and intangible. Tangible elements are those elements, which can, to some extent be assessed in quantitative terms, like, Geography, Raw material and Natural Resources, Population and Technology. Intangible elements, which cannot be calculated precisely, comprise, Ideologies, Morale and Leadership. Among these seven elements the first two are related to the land and its resources and last five are related to people, their ways of doing things and their ways of thinking. Besides, The Military Power and the Quality of a nation's diplomacy can also be examined for measuring the power of a state. The interdependence of all these elements is so complete that actually power is indivisible. In other words, no single factor is an absolute factor in the making of national power. Each of the factors has an influence on national power and the nature of relationship among them is rather complex.

How do we measure the power of a state? It is very difficult to answer this question in precise terms. We cannot, after all, depend upon the results of a war as a criterion of the measurement of national power. Further, the instrument of coercion cannot be equated with effective national power. For, there are various reasons why even a nation with large, well-equipped and well-commanded military forces may suffer frustration in foreign policy. Important among these are: relativity of power, changes in power, single factor determinism, the gap between the estimate and reality of power, the actual and potential power and the specificity of power. Power is never absolute. It is always to be measured in terms of the states. As in the contemporary world of nuclear deterrence, the national power is to be assessed not in terms of the capacity of first attack but in terms of the capacity of surviving retaliatory strength. Beside, power is subject to continuous change. Absolute power may change for many reasons. History is full with the examples of 'Rise and Fall' of nations. For instance, before World War-I, Britain was the mistress of sea, but close to World War-II, she reduced to second grade power, as the significance of sea warfare had diminished. Typical error in measuring the national power is giving to one single factor a decisive role to the disregard of all other factors. No one factor is absolute. Although, all factors are not of equal importance. The gap between the estimate and reality of power also makes measurement difficult. The possibility of the underestimation or overestimation of one's power and that of the opponent is always there. Further, an observer, while calculating power, must be aware of the actual and potential power of the states. Potential power is the possibility that a state possesses of developing into a powerful state on the basis of its natural resources etc. Evaluation of potential power helps in chalking out long-term plans involving commitment of power. The actual power is the power that a state really has. The measurement of this power is useful in forecasting short-term developments and in making immediate commitments of power. For the transformation of a potential power into an actual power, a state requires, capital, labor and technology. The problem of a correct appraisal of power is intimately linked with the problem of the credibility of power, which, in turn, is related to the specificity of power. That means, no particular type of power can be such that it can be applied in any form and in any condition. Even the most impressive stock of nuclear weapons will be an ineffective deterrent if the opponent thinks that those weapons will not be used, while less destructive weapons can have greater effectiveness if the opponent believes that those weapons will be used. Thus, the power of a state cannot be measured exactly, at the best, it remains a matter of conjecture.

Padelford and Lincoln, have opined that, "National power is that combination of power and capability of a state which the state uses for filling its national interests and goals."[4] Further in the words of Organski, "Power is the ability of a nation to influence the behavior of others in accordance with its own ends. Unless a nation can do this she may be large, she may be wealthy, she may even be great, but she is not powerful."[5] Nations always try to seek power, demonstrate power, use power and increase power, which makes struggle for power as the key characteristic of all international relations. In short, national power signifies the capacity of the state to exert strength, authority or influence. This capacity is never static; it is relative and changing and it cannot be measured by precision. It must be weighed with reference to other states and their positions. In itself, it is neither good nor bad, but it can be used for good causes as well as for badones.[6] It is said that weak nations always provide a temptation to the strong and powerful nations to invade them. In fact, the real cause of war, it is argued, is not the power of the powerful, but weakness of the weak. Many scholars, therefore, believe that in international relations only power counts and that power and international relations go hand in hand. Thus, it seems, power theory is the most appropriate theory for the study of international relations.

National power operates within certain limitations. These act as restriction on state action. Therefore howsoever powerful a country may be and be in the possession of as many elements of power as possible, it cannot act in an arbitrary and authoritative manner at international level. These limitations are in the form of: International morality, world public opinion, international law, balance of power, international organisation and disarmament. There may be contradictions in the acceptance and adoption of these codes, among nations, but it does not mean that it is not in existence. Yes, it is up to the will and convenience of the state to follow these set standards. But, states usually do follow these norms, to avoid unwanted circumstances, like, war, instability and change.

In a broad sense, three forms of power, *viz.* political, military and economic power, exist in international relations with the prime focus shifting from time to time. As for instance, in the post Second World war period, the focus was on military power. Subsequently nations wanted to enhance their military capability, in order to make themselves more powerful. In this power game USA and USSR were the captains, who possessed huge stockpiles of military equipments together with nuclear arsenals. But as Heraclitus (of Ephesus), observed, six centuries before Christ that nothing in the universe is constant – or, if you prefer, that the only constant thing is change itself.[7] The same is true of international relations as well. The shift in the prime focus of power enabled economy to supercede the military. It was in the eighties, that this change became visible and consequently economy came into being as the leitmotif of power in the international relations. The collapse of the Soviet Union was the outcome of this phenomenon. Though militarily she was strong enough, but weak on the economy front. As a result, USSR withered away from the world map. Earlier Mikhail Gorbachev, who came to power in March 1985, initiated reforms through his ideas of *glasnost* and *perestroika*. His "New Thinking" was aimed at reforming both political and economic systems. While *glasnost* was a political slogan aimed at democratisation and decentralisation of political power, *perestroika* was meant to restructure the Soviet economy, which was in doldrums. But his "New Thinking" could not save USSR. According to a leading Sovietologist, Dankward Rustow, Gorbachev's commitment to *glasnost* and *perestroika* was clearly motivated by his calculation that the Soviet Union could not continue to bear the burden of the arms race; presenting communism as an alternative model; supporting the regional conflicts to achieve their goal and; satisfying the expectations of its people for a better standard of living.[8]

The year 1989 was a watershed in the history of the world. In perhaps one of the most extra-ordinary turning points in modern history. Eastern Europe witnessed a bloodless revolution and opted for a western type democracy and market economy. The communist cadres in these countries deserted their party and joined the new democratic movements. Gone are the days when the Soviet armies could march into the Eastern Europe to crush any rebellion. The leaders have crafted the most ambitious economic reforms in Eastern Europe for a radical switch over to western-style democracy. While democratic and popular movements swept Eastern Europe in the Soviet Union, a silent revolution was underway. Although it was Gorbachev who initiated the reforms first in the Soviet Union, the Soviet people had to wait till the outbreak of the Second Russian Revolution in August 1991 to completely free themselves from the yoke of communism. Thus, in addition to acquiescing in the unification of Germany and the collapse of Soviet control over the Eastern Europe, Gorbachev withdrew the Soviet army from Afghanistan and other Third World countries, such as, Angola, Ethiopia and Vietnam[9] and further having realised, that the USSR was economy-wise no longer in a position to sustain itself as a world power in military terms, took several unilateral initiatives towards political solution of regional conflicts.[10]

In his book Gorbachev wrote, "I have explained on many occasions, that we do not pursue goals inimical to western interests. We know how important the Middle East, Asia, Latin America, other Third World regions and also South Africa are for American and West European economies, in particular as raw material sources. To cut these links is the last thing we want to do and we have no desire to provoke ruptures in historically formed economic ties".[11] Emboldened by Gorbachev's unabashed apologia for neocolonialist exploitation and plunder of the Third World countries, the

Soviet scholars and publicists have started raising doubts about the very existence of neocolonialism. Thus, N. Volkov and V. Popov of the Moscow Institute of USA and Canada contributed an article to the October 1988 issue of the Soviet monthly 'International Affairs' under the title "Neocolonial Epoch did not exist". These Soviet scholars tried to prove that neocolonialism, as a system of total economic exploitation of the developing countries never existed. They termed the relationship of the Western countries with their former colonies as a 'mutually gainful partnerships' in which the USSR must also jointly participate with the West,[12] while orthodox Marxists condemned it as a conspiracy hatched by imperialists in collaboration with their agent, Mikhail Gorbachev.

A leading US scholar and former policy analyst with the Rand Corporation, Francis Fukuyama, wrote in his famous article that "what we may be witnessing is not just the end of Cold War or the passing of a particular period of postwar history, but the end of history as such; that is, the end point of mankind's ideological evolution and the universalisation of western liberal democracy as the final form of human government".[13] However, as Stanley Hoffman of Harvard University remarked, the end of the Cold War was neither the end of history nor the end of ideology. At most, it might mean the emergence of a new international order replacing the old system.[14]

Off all the changes under way internationally, the most dramatic and decisive one is in the relationship between the USA and the USSR. It is so not only because their revived detente is this time enormously far reaching, but because of what is seen as their weakened power and the concomitant rise of other major power centres.[15] In the present world, relationship is undergoing a marked change with the mightiest becoming less and less effective to enforce his will on the weak. Obviously, none of the major powers can now call the tune at will. As the global actors become more interdependent, the dominant actor would further lose strength and the subordinate actors attain more and more bargaining power.[16]

The new global order is going to be an era of region-by-region disorder, a period of extra-ordinarily complicated diplomacy, where the notion of vital national interests is replaced by a shifting series of alliances and arrangements, patched together issue-by-issue.[17] There has been considerable discussion in the United States of an emerging era of co-operative diplomacy, of a national strategy based on "what we are for" as opposed to containment which was a strategy of "what we were against."[18] Further, the patterns of economic development, the subordination of ideology to practical need and, the vast uncomprehended impact of the technological revolution are crucial determinants of change. As Shafiqul Islam, an analyst at the council on foreign relations, said, that "if the Cold War was a competition driven by the race for military superiority, the quest for economic and technological domination will propel the new competition."[19] Another important feature is the prominent role of geoeconomies manifested by the emergence and strengthening of regional economic groups.[20] These include the European Union, APEC (1993), NAFTA (1993), US-Canada (1989), Pan Americana Free Trade Area, Mercosur (1991) and the dream of South Asian nations for SAFTA.

The rise of a multipolar world in place of a bipolar world dominated by the USA and the USSR is the reality of the new global order. This multipolarity emerged from the existence of significant major power (economic) centers, namely, US, Japan, Germany and in a wider sense, the European Union, China, ASEAN and Russia constitute other centers of the global power matrix.[21] But the description of the changing world, as 'the rise of multipolarity' is quite misleading. Because a pole must by definition be able to attract others to it and none of the new 'poles' show any likelihood of doing so. As it is not clear which states are going to group around Japan, China and Western Europe (which is all we really mean by the new multi-polarity') as the West did around the USA or Eastern Europe around the USSR. In fact, each of these supposed poles carry strong negative charges and will have to cope with their capacity to alienate others before they can become really major power centers. Thus the term multi-player world or polycentric world seems more appropriate instead of fashionable description 'multi polar world'. However, the multi-player rather than multi-polar world is not just a matter of semantics. Since different centers of power are emerging and new players are coming up in the international flora, these new major powers have today either great military capability or great economic capability but not both.[22]

SEARCH FOR MAJOR POWER STATUS BY INDIA: CURRENT CONTEXT

As far as the history of the existence of major powers is concerned, it goes back to the middle of 17th Century, when the Sovereign Nation State System (SSS) formally came into being, thereby, all states are recognised as being sovereign, independent and equal, despite great many diversities of all kinds. However, since the inception of the system, it has been dominated by the hegemonism of a small number of Great Powers. Only the number and identity of these Powers has changed over these three and a half centuries. The overwhelming majority of the Middle and small powers have been struggling against this Great Power hegemonism, but largely, in vain. Since international organisations came into being, particularly in the twentieth century, the Major Powers have also dominated these organisations.[23]

The concept of Great Powers, however, developed at the Congress of Vienna of 1815. Thus, it is essentially a nineteenth century concept. In the Cold War, Soviet Union and United States have not only retained their earlier great power status but have also achieved far greater superiority over the other great powers of the nineteenth century concept. Earlier the great power status of a country was in danger whenever a war broke out and the consequences of a war were not very stable, for they were always subject to further change as a result of the frequent occurrences of war. Here United States and Soviet Union are something more than mere great powers. Therefore the concept of super power evolved. While the France, Britain and China belong to the category of great powers only. The chief factor supposedly necessitating the preservance of a distinction between super powers and great powers is the accumulation of unprecedented military power, particularly the nuclear power by the United States and Soviet Union.

According to George Modelski, with the change in international values and the urgency of the problems of peace, economic development and international cooperation the old concept of great power will have to be given up. That is why, he talks not of great power status but of great power institution. By the institution of great powers he means a web of certain special rights and special responsibilities. According to the old definition, great powers only enjoyed rights, inasmuch as they tried to expand their spheres of influence and improve their economies at the cost of smaller states. But in the twentieth century, these rights have lost their significance in the wake of the emergence of new states and the recognition of their right to development by the world public opinion in general. The view, which now prevails, is that the more powerful nations of the world have a great responsibility towards the development of less developed nations and towards the maintenance of international peace and security. This idea was first enshrined in the covenant of the League of Nations and then further strengthened by the United Nations Charter. The various development programmes being carried on under the United Nations are directly or indirectly based upon this notion of the great power responsibility towards the development of the new nations. In any case, the fact remains that even the modern concept of great power is what Modelski calls a "pre-modern" or "feudal" concept. For, by assigning the special role to certain powers in the realm of maintaining peace and guaranteeing peace, the supporters of the idea of great powers deny this role to the small powers which theoretically are also capable of playing significant role in the maintenance of peace and in ensuring stability in the world. The idea of the modernisation of the world order is based upon the principle of not merely decolonisation but also of sovereign equality of states. While the concept of great power goes against the modernisation of world order, it cannot be denied that all states of the world cannot claim equality in terms of their resources, economic development and military power. Nor are all states in a position to play a similar role in world affairs. It would, therefore, be wrong to presume that the idea of great power is absolutely irrelevant. What is being stressed here is the fact that the special role which certain nations are able to play in matters relating to the entire international system because of their rich resources and great military strength should not be a justification for the undue interference of the so-called great powers in the affairs of the small states. We must distinguish between the special role in upholding the world order and the right to impose one's will on others as a price for playing that special role.

The recognitions of major global power status by other nations, traditionally, came as a result of alleged or real contribution in large scale wars-in-arms or diplomacy. That was what happened in the congress of Vienna in 1815, the Paris peace conference 1918 and most recently, Yalta conference 1945 and the UN conference (San Francisco, 1945) on the creation of the United Nations. This circumstance is unlikely to occur again. World wars have become too destructive and dangerous — thanks to the invention/possession of weapons of mass destruction. Since the end of the Second World War, the possession of nuclear weapons has been, in effect, a qualification for a major global power status in world affairs including permanent membership of the Security Council. For many years, India has been opposed to these weapons — until in May 1974, India demonstrated its technical nuclear capability by a peaceful nuclear explosion. Nevertheless, India observed self-restraint in not going in for weaponisation for 24 long years and still opposing the proliferation of the weapons. However, there was hardly any positive response from the existing nuclear weapons powers.[24]

Although India entered into nuclear hibernation after the 1974 Pokhran test, but the Chinese-US proliferation to Pakistan from the eighties left India with no choice but to develop its deterrent. Thus India, perceiving a threat to its security, carried out five successful nuclear weapon tests, in May 1998, in effect preparing for nuclear weaponisation. India (and Pakistan too) thus became undeclared weapon power, but the existing nuclear weapon powers have declined to accept India's (and Pakistan's) new status. But then, India in effect has become a nuclear weapon power — one last formal *de facto* qualification of the existing nuclear weapon powers.[25] After India has successfully conducted nuclear tests, Prime Minister A.B. Vajpayee said that the greatest meaning of the tests is that they have given India 'Shakti' (power), they have given strength, and they have given India self-confidence.[26] India has achieved the nuclear Power Status, true. But the traditional prescriptions of power as primarily based on military strength are shattering. In fact, the international standing of India or for that matter any other power in the world will flow from its economic surplus and technological dynamism.[27] The growing power of the nations like Japan and Germany proves this. Although because of its size and location and heavy consumer market, India will always be strategically and commercially important, but it has to build its economic strength and domestic stability (not just military strength), if India really wants to attain major power status in international affairs.[28] This is the three-dimensional posture of power, in which economy takes the central position.

For India, to get this status, is essential for the very reasons embedded in its history and geography, such as:

- India has had a history of foreign dominations for centuries. We had a prolonged struggle to get our independence. With this memory we could not afford to remain defenseless and helpless in the kind of security environment around us.[29]
- Moreover the geographical partition of Indian sub-continent resulted in the formation of two hostile nations (*viz.* India and Pakistan) and the emergence of dispute over Kashmir.
- A neighbor like Pakistan stands in the western border of India while a nuclear powered China surrounds India's northern territory.
- Besides living in this security environment, India has a population over 100 cr. whose security had to be assured so that people could go about peacefully developing the country's economy.

The question related to this is, 'Has not India introduced a dangerous element and a race for nuclear arms in the Indian subcontinent and would this not open the way to others to follow the same path?' The then President of India said in this regard that "as far as the subcontinent is concerned, I feel and it is my belief that now that India, as well as Pakistan, have acquired a minimum of nuclear weapons, just as it happened in Europe and elsewhere, we will also realise in the subcontinent that it is necessary for us to resolve our disputes, our differences by peaceful means and not by war.... A war between India and Pakistan, not to speak of a nuclear war, is now unimaginable. Thus I think negotiated peaceful settlements of disputes in the subcontinent have become inevitable."[30] The similar thoughts were presented by John Vincent in 1975 in his Paper that 'there is clearly a relationship between military power in being and political impact on its environment.'[31] The point about latent military power is that it can allow political relations to develop without violence.[32] However, India has already declared "No first Use" of nuclear weapons, seeking only a minimum nuclear deterrence and also no more nuclear tests. There is also an assurance that India will not use nuclear weapons against non-nuclear powers. This is on the top of India's commitment not to transfer nuclear weapon technology to any one. It has also, successfully, urged the United Nations to take steps to prevent miscalculations and accidental use of nuclear weapons. All this shows that India has set a limit to its nuclear weapon development and that India is prepared to do what is necessary for nuclear control and denuclearisation in the world. But there has been little reaction from the other nuclear weapon powers.

Besides, being a leading non-aligned nation India has to take lead in several global issues of importance. The emphasis on economics and the process of globalisation marginalised the post-colonial states shrinking both their political and economic space. North-South divisions were aggravated and further entrenched, leading to the rise of what has been conceptualised by A.P. Rana as a New Northern concert of Powers.[33] In International law there was a Doctrine of Different Rights or inequality. India witnessed the operation of this doctrine throughout the British rule. The essence of this doctrine of Different Rights is that some people or groups—it may be the developed nations or whosoever may be on top— have the right to do things that others do not have. India's struggle for independence, her foreign policy, had in it a challenge to this concept. Shortly before India had become independent, Jawaharlal Nehru called an Asian Relations conference in New Delhi. He declared at this conference that for too long, we had been the playthings of other powers, but that chapter was now over. However there is a talk of universal human rights today. But the Doctrine of Different Rights not only existed in those days, but a quintessential residue of this doctrine of inequality can even be seen today in international relations.[34] Whether it is CTBT, United Nations structure, international economic institutions or other international agreements, the law of differential rights can be seen reflected in them. While the principle of equality and participative democracy enshrining all over the world, the persistent hegemonism of nuclear powers in the permanent membership of United Nation's Security Council entails the idea to reform its structure, so that it could allow greater, equitable representation to major regions (including Asia) of the world and its actions can become more legitimate and effective. Asia was the cradle of major human civilisations; its influence in shaping the political and strategic events beyond the confines of the continent has been part of recorded history. This largest continent accounts for nearly 60 per cent of the global population and it remains the most under-represented region. Moreover, given their size, present performance trends and future potentials, a few Asian countries such as China, Japan and India are reckoned as the giants in the twenty first century. Given all these characteristics, it would only be rational that the Asian countries have a proportionate presence in the Security Council. India is the only country to have offered its candidature officially since 1994, for the permanent seat proposed for the developing countries in Asia.[35] India's strong points are:

– India is the largest democracy in the world, with

ancient civilisational values and attainments and a worldview based on universal inspiration, participative governance, respect for diversity and pluralism, as well as the readiness for constructive engagement in the world's affairs, India becomes an obvious choice.[36]

– Member countries elected India six times so far to serve as a non-permanent member of the Security Council, a distinction not achieved by any other developing country in Asia.

Developing countries with about 80 per cent of world's people have little representation and influence in global economic institutions and decision-making processes within them. Global governance is highly centralised and there is hardly any possibility of breaking the monopoly of the rich in this context. F. Braudel observed that under the globalisation regime, MNCs have replaced the colonial states and their tools of exploitation are knowledge and technology.[37] Globalisation is proceeding largely for the benefit of the dynamic and powerful countries. In international commerce, it has increased the subordination of the developing to the developed world.[38] Thus as globalisation progresses economic disparity deepens and it seems to be more appropriate to say — globalise and perish, rather than today's slogan globalise or perish. Competition must be there, but among equals. Nations of the developing world, need more time for preparation so that local industries, commerce and the financial markets can meet the challenges in the face of unequal competition that has suddenly been thrust on them.[39]

All this, is the reality of new world order, which exhibits the very presence of the doctrine of inequality even today, in the form of New Northern Concert of Powers. Thus the hard new world calls for hard new thinking and hard work on the part of India.

When other nations were advocating the use of coercive power, India was addressing international problems in terms of consensual power. The balance-of-power approach in international relations is unlikely to help any major power which would like to dominate the international system.

Realizing the challenges of new epoch, India is accomplishing a major programme of economic liberalisation and is well on the way to becoming a vibrant economy like several other growing and powerful Asian economies which have all come into a new focus in the post-Cold War world. There is some truth in the statement that India is a tiger which has got out of the cage but still imagines that it is inside and hence refusing to be a first runner.[40]

The most marked political development of the contemporary world is the rising position of Asia and India can play an adequate international role as an Asian power even at present, because

- India is now a major player (with nuclear weapons capability and sustained economic growth) in the global scenario and
- The Indian ethos are not burdened by the legacies of Stalin, Mao, Hitler or of Japanese militarism, but is naturally tuned into global citizenship in the best sense of the term.
- Both the Indian free market and democracy are dynamic forces, which can help to harmonise state sovereignty and interdependence in a *suigeneris* manner.
- India, therefore, has an indispensable role in setting the pace for evolving global norms as a major player in the global system and more so if it becomes a permanent member of the United Nation's Security Council.
- The great Indian democratic experiment is especially relevant to conflict and peacemaking in all multiethnic societies. There is no need for any country to play the role of world policeman, but the United Nations should deal with ethnic tensions.[41]

At the home front, too, India has a very hard work to do, as far as India's existing socio-political milieu, is concerned. Conditions will have to be made conducive to channelise the fruits of modern science and technology for the benefit of the common man. Stress will have to be placed on pursuing a development strategy that encompasses growth with equity and social justice to meet the basic needs of people, such as food, clothing, shelter, education, employment and safe drinking water.[42] As Dr. Amartya Sen, the Nobel Laureate, points out that economic take off requires an educated, healthy and socially secure population. Without investments in human capital, investments in every other form of capital fail to yield optimal results. Human capital is the link with the future and so is central to growth and development and also the very heart of the typical modern economy.[43]

Thus, in the new situation India has some difficult choices, but also a remarkable opportunity to achieve an optimum global posture. But as the challenges faced by India are quite formidable, there is every need for redefining India's priorities and discarding some of its old shibboleths. "Our size, situation, status plus the circumstances of the world we have lived in, as well as our own fitful efforts, have all enabled India to count in the international world," Pt. Nehru used to point out that we might be poor, weak, good or bad, but "India counts".[44]

Furthermore, as regards strategic location of India, Pt. Nehru said, "When we talk of Asia, remember that India, not because of ambition of hers, but because of geography, because of history and because of so many other things, inevitably has to play a very important part in Asia. And not only that, India becomes a kind of meeting ground for various trends and forces and a meeting ground between what might roughly be called the east and the west.... Whether it is a problem of defense or trade or industry or economic policy, India cannot be ignored. She cannot be ignored; because I said her geographical position is a compelling reason."[45]

INDIA'S PRE-INDEPENDENCE INTERNATIONAL ACTIVITIES

Even prior to independence, India made its presence in international affairs, to some extent. During the nationalist struggle the Congress leaders expressed their views on almost all international issues. Pt. Nehru was the chief spokesman of the Indian National Congress in external affairs from late 1920s. Nationalist leaders in the freedom struggle never allowed themselves to remain insulated from developments surrounding

India. During the post First World War era they showed great keenness about developments in Europe. Jawaharlal Nehru helped the Congress to define its stand on world affairs. He viewed India's Struggle for freedom as part of a worldwide movement against colonialism and imperialism.[46] Ever since the AICC session of 1921, the party projected its definite opinion on foreign affairs. Thus, by the time India achieved independence there had developed a distinct, Indian outlook on world affairs and this became the foundation of India's foreign policy.[47]

With an organised and articulate movement for independence in place by the 1880s, a sophisticated leadership that engaged in frequent international travel, opportunities afforded to Indians for many years prior to 1947 to work in various departments of the British Indian Civil Service that touched on matters of an international character and with Indians attending sessions of the League of Nations and Imperial (Commonwealth) conferences, a variety of means were available to them to gain experience at the international level over an extended period prior to independence.[48] Although before 1947 India had no foreign policy, for in relation to every country, it was determined by the British Government. Yet the leaders of thought during the Period of the British hegemony reacted to external events and sometimes these reactions were expressed in the resolutions of the Indian National Congress. It was during World War-l, that matters of foreign policy seriously engaged the attention of the Indian leaders whose primary concern continued to be dislodging the foreign rulers. At the end of the war, India signed the Treaty of Versailles and became an original member of the League of Nations. India's participation in the League activities was regular and the Indian delegations to Geneva invariably contained non-official representatives. India had already been admitted to the membership of the Imperial conference in 1907 and she was duly represented at the Imperial war conference. India held a permanent seat on the Governing Body of the International Labor Organisation and in 1931; Atul Chandra Chatterjee was elected chairman of the Permanent committee of the ILO. Beside ILO, another agency that provided an opportunity for diplomacy more in tune with nationalist India was the International Committee on Intellectual Co-operation, on which India was represented from 1931 to 1939 by the illustrious Dr. Sarvapalli Radhakrishnan. India also participated actively in the social and humanitarian activities of the League. She took part in important International conferences like the Washington conference (1921), the World Economic Conference and the Disarmament Conference (1932).[49]

India's participation was at both official and unofficial level, in world's diplomatic activities. As early as 1889, the newly founded Indian National Congress established an associated agency in England to present to the British public the views of nationalist India and win favor for the programme of the Congress.[50] Subsequently, efforts were also made to organise nationalist Indian propaganda centers in Germany, France, Japan and especially the United States where expatriate Indians founded a number of information agencies and publications during the period before and after World War I. [51] In addition, late in the nineteenth and early in the twentieth century, the numerous journeys of Indians to England continental Europe and North America were also of importance in promoting knowledge abroad and interest in the Indian political struggle. Indeed, even such distinguished Indian travelers in this period as Swami Vivekanand and Dr. Rabindranath Tagore, who were not directly involved in the national political movement, unconsciously became a part of its unofficial diplomatic effort, for in the eyes of their foreign hosts they were regarded as representatives of the new, renascent India[52] and hence, by their own eminence they raised the stature of nationalist India in the international community.

From the late 1920s, the intensified, unofficial diplomatic efforts had essentially four components: the establishment of a foreign department by the Indian National Congress; the encouragement of Congress — affiliated and other pro-independence agencies abroad; the participation by nationalist Indians in various non-governmental international conferences and travel abroad by Indian leaders that entailed giving lectures and media interviews.

Thus, perceiving that the domestic Indian problem of subjection was only part of the world problem of imperialism and that it was, therefore, perilous for nationalist India to remain isolated from the outside world, since political developments elsewhere affected the Indian struggle, just as it in turn affected events in other dependent countries,[53] the Indian National Congress in 1928, established a Congress Foreign Department. The object behind the establishment of foreign department was of getting "into touch with all such organisations and all such peoples" as were in the same position as India so that they "might as far as possible co-operate with each other to combat... Imperialism".[54] This initial effort at establishing a kind of congress "Foreign Ministry" was, however, relatively paltry and short-lived. In May 1936, a new Congress Foreign Department began functioning with Dr. Rammanohar Lohia as its head. By the end of 1936 it was in touch with a total of over 400 individuals, journals, political, cultural and Indian organisations throughout the world. Until the outbreak of the Second World War, the foreign department persisted with the same programme.[55] Beside, although, the Government of India Act, 1935 recommended for the creation of a separate External Affairs Department and this was done in 1937 which became an integral part of the Central Government under the Governor General in council. The Governor General was also a member for External Affairs in the Executive Council. But, "the external affairs department functioned more or less like an overseas branch of the British foreign office as far as vital matters of international policy were concerned. It only implemented the decisions taken at Whitehall. Indians had no influence in the conduct of foreign affairs, which remained in the hands of the Governor general.[56] However, with the formation of the interim government in the pre-independence British India on 2 September 1946, there was a structural change in the department. Jawaharlal Nehru became vice president and member for external affairs and commonwealth relations in the Governor-General's new Executive Council.

In so far as the operation of overseas nationalist Indian bureaus was concerned, the Britain, the United States and the Germany were deemed as the important loci for nationalist Indian information activities. In June 1928, some 60 Indians resident in London met under the chairmanship of the Congress leader Srinivasa Iyengar, to form an organisation to provide more active support for the nationalist cause.[57] Moreover, the commonwealth of India League, (initially established by the theosophist leader, Dr. Annie Besant, as the Indian Home Rule League) at that time, was already actively engaged in publishing pamphlets, supplying information to interested parties and producing *The India News*. In addition, it had organised 27 branches throughout England.[58] After V.K. Krishna Menon assumed the secretaryship of the League in 1929, it began to work with the congress branch, adopted the congress demand for complete independence for India and accordingly, changed its name to the India League.[59] The League attracted to itself a number of prominent Britons, including Bertrand Russell, Harold Laski and Kingsley Martin, who gave it greater publicity and no doubt helped to augment attendance at its public meetings. Likewise in 1928, unofficial bureau of the Congress in New York,[60] and in 1929, the Indian Information Bureau, associated unofficially with the Indian National Congress, in Berlin, were established.[61] An unofficial Congress committee was also formed in Kobe, Japan in 1928. Guided by A.M. Sahay, it held regular meetings and published a monthly newspaper — *Voice of India* — in both English and Japanese. During the 1930 Non-co-operation movement, the branch raised money, which was remitted to India for national political work.[62]

Next component of unofficial diplomatic activity was participation by nationalist Indians in various non-governmental international conferences. One of the first prominent conclaves of this nature was the congress of oppressed Nationalities, held in Brussels in February 1927 and attended by Jawaharlal Nehru. Some 175 delegates from 37 countries participated.[63]

Nehru used the meeting essentially as a platform to publicise Indian grievances against the British rule and win assistance from sympathetic organisations. Nationalist India was next represented at an international conference the Anti-war Congress in Amsterdam in August 1932. The conference was attended by the venerable congress leader Vithalbhai Patel. In September 1933, two congress leaders — Subash Chandra Bose and Bhulabhai Desai attended an International Conference on India at Geneva. The Geneva Conference was the mouthpiece of the International Committee on India, which had been established by Europeans in 1932. It had as its object the dissemination of authentic news about the Indian situation to counteract alleged misrepresentation of Indian affairs by the British Government and the international press in the West. The Geneva Conference, attended by representatives of affiliated organisations of the international committee on India in eight countries, passed a number of resolutions pertaining to Indian affairs, on of which, *inter alia,* declared India's right to complete independence.[64] The Indian National Congress was also represented at the Brussels World Peace Congress in September 1936 and at the subsequent meetings of the International Peace campaign, the permanent organ of the Brussels meeting. Once again, Congress attendance was used to raise the issue of Indian subjection, as Krishna Menon's speech to the gathering focused on the relationship between the liquidation of imperialism and the creation of world peace.[65] Further, in July 1938 along with Pt. Nehru, Menon attended the Paris conference on the bombardment of open towns organised by the Peace campaign. Apart from these, over several decades prior to independence, Indians actively participated in a number of regional non-governmental conferences designed in one way or another to promote the notion of Pan-Asian unity, especially in the struggle against imperialism. Some of the earlier such gatherings included the Soviet organised Baku conference of 1920, the first Pan-Asiatic congress at Nagasaki in 1926 and the Pan Asiatic conference at Shanghai in 1927.[66] Later on, several meetings were a result of specifically Indian initiatives, like the All-Asia Education conference at Benares in December 1930; the All-Asian Women's conference at Lahore in January 1931; the Pan-Asiatic Labor congress at Colombo in May 1934; and finally the Asian Relations conference, held in New Delhi in 1947 on the eve of Indian independence.[67] All these unofficial international activities of India, show, the diplomatic skill and involvement of India in world affairs, prior to independence.

Perhaps of greater importance than any of the above activities in attracting international attention to the Indian situation were the individual trips abroad of prominent Indian leaders. Among those of particular significance, in the late 1920s were visits by Pt. Motilal Nehru, Vithalbhai Patel (1932-1933), Dr. Rabindranath Tagore (1930), Srinivasa Iyengar, Sarojini Naidu[68] (1929), Mahatma Gandhi[69] (1931), Subhas Chandra Bose[70] (1933-1935) and Chaman Lal (1936) to Europe and North America. Especially noteworthy over the latter years before the outbreak of World War-II was the unofficial diplomacy of Pt. Jawaharlal Nehru. He paid visits to London and continental Europe in the year 1936 and 1938.[71] In Asia also, Pt. Nehru began to play a diplomatic role in the late 1930s, visiting Burma and Malaya in 1937 and Ceylon and China in 1939.[72] Pt. Nehru did not, however, confine himself to winning support for Indian independence, but also expressed emerging nationalist Indian views on international questions in general, thereby a global outlook entered in Indian politics.

Thus, Indians involved in the independence movement attached greater importance to the non-governmental organisations, in which the voice of nationalist India could be fully heard. Nevertheless, in several modest ways official Indian participation in the League of Nations and the Commonwealth reflected national Indian opinions and concerns and presaged elements of independent Indian diplomacy via such bodies as the United Nations and the commonwealth.

Beside these official and unofficial level international activities, India reacted against each external event in the inter-war period. When Japan attacked Manchuria in 1930-31, Italy invaded Ethiopia in 1934-35 and Germany and Italy intervened in Spain in 1936-38, the Congress condemned the aggressor in an unqualified manner. In 1937-38, when Japan committed aggression in China, the Congress condemned the brutal imperialism of the Japanese and decided to send a medical mission to China as a token of its sympathies with the Chinese people. India was in favor to use ethically correct means to achieve right ends.[73]

Thus, it can be legitimately asserted that in inter-war period, India had achieved a position of some importance in international affairs. With its pre-independence international activities, India gained experience and emerged from colonial rule with both a reservoir of diplomatic talent and an incipient orientation for its diplomacy, including a range of general foreign policy goals.[74] It was thereby better prepared than perhaps any other country which acquired its independence after World War II to take a prominent place on the global stage quickly and forcefully and to influence the diplomacy of other countries that were in time to constitute the Third world.

Notes

1. E.V. Walter, "Power and Violence", *American Political Science Review*, June 1964.
2. Peter H. Odegard, *Political Power and Social Change*, Oxford & IBH Publishing Co., New Delhi, 1969.
3. Morgenthau, H.J., *Politics Among Nations*: 'The Struggle for Power and Peace', 6th rev. Ed. New York: Knopf, 1985.
4. H.D. Ghoshal (Ed.), *International Relations*, Unique Publishers, 1996.
5. *Ibid.*
6. M.G. Gupta, *Indian Foreign Policy — Theory and Practice*, Y.K. Publishers, Agra, 1985.
7. Peter H. Odegard, *Political Power and Social Change*, Oxford & IBH Publishing Co., New Delhi, 1969.
8. Dankward A. Rustow, "Democracy — A Global Revolution?" *Foreign Affairs*, Fall 1990, Vol. 69, No. 4, pp. 79-91.
9. A.G. Naidu, 'India and the New World Order', in K. Raman Pillai (Ed.): *Indian Foreign Policy in the* 1990s, Radiant Publishers, New Delhi, 1997.

10. Devendra Kaushik, "India and the Changing World Scenario in the 1990s", in R.S. Yadav (Ed.): *India's Foreign Policy Towards 2000 A.D.*, Deep & Deep Publications, New Delhi, 1993.

11. Mikhail Gorbachev, "Perestroika: New Thinking for Our Country and the World", Russian edition, p. 185.

12. R.S. Yadav, (Ed.) *India's Foreign Policy Towards* 2000 *A.D.*, Deep & Deep Publications, New Delhi, 1993.

13. Francis Fukuyama, "The End of History", *National Interest*, Summer 1989, pp. 3-18.

14. Stanley Hoffman, *Foreign Affairs*, Vol. 69, No. 4, Fall 1990, pp. 115-22.

15. K. Shankar Bajpai, "We and the World" in Verinder Grover (Ed.): *International Relations and Foreign Policy of India*, Deep & Deep Publications, N. Delhi, 1992.

16. Andrew M. Scott, *The dynamics of inter-dependence*, North Carolina University Press, 1982, p. 40.

17. Stephen P. Cohen, "India's Role in the New Global Order: An American Perspective", *Indian Journal of Asian Affairs*, Vol. 6, No. 1-2, 1993.

18. Quote from a member of the US Policy Planning Staff, see also current work on "cooperative diplomacy" being done at a Harvard/ Stanford Brookings consortium.

19. Shafiqul Islam, "Capitalism in Conflict", *Foreign Affairs*, Vol. 69, No. 1, pp. 172-82.

20. Shanta Varma, 'Global Transformation and India's Foreign Policy' in M.P. Singh & Rekha Saxena (Ed.): *Ideologies and Institutions in Indian Politics*, Deep & Deep Publications Pvt. Ltd. 1998.

21. *Ibid.*

22. Verinder Grover (Ed.), *International Relations and Foreign Policy of India*, Vol. 1, Deep & Deep Publications, New Delhi, 1992.

23. M.S. Rajan, "India as a Global Power in the Next Millennium", World Focus, *The New Millennium — Agenda For India*, Vol. 19, Oct. Nov. Dec. 1998.

24. *Ibid.*

25. *Ibid.*

26. Quote from the *Sunday Times*, 24.5.98.

27. Jagat S. Mehta, "Forty Years of Foreign Policy", in Verinder Grover (Ed.): *International Relations and Foreign Policy of India*, Vol. I, Deep & Deep Publications, New Delhi, 1992.

28. R.S. Yadav (Ed.), *India's Foreign Policy Towards* 2000 *AD*,' Deep & Deep Publications, New Delhi, 1993.
29. Based on a talk delivered by the President of India, K.R. Narayanan, at the German Society of Foreign Affairs in Bonn.
30. *Ibid.*
31. John Vincent, 'Military Power and Political Influence', Adelphi Paper No. 119, London, *International Institute for Strategic Studies*, 1975.
32. Lawrence Freedman, 'Military Power and Political Influence', *International Affairs*, Vol. 74, No. 4, 1998.
33. M.P. Singh & Rekha Saxena (Ed.), *Ideologies and Institutions in Indian Politics*, Deep & Deep Publications Pvt. Ltd. 1998.
34. K.R. Narayan, 'India and the World Today', *World Focus*, Oct.-Nov.-Dec. 1998.
35. C.S.R. Murthy, 'Reforming the UN Security Council—An Asian View', *South Asian Survey*, Vol. 5, No. 1, 1998.
36. I.K. Gujral's statement in the General Assembly of UNO, *UN News letter* (New Delhi), Vol. 52, No. 39, 27 September, 1997, p. 4.
37. T.K. Oommen, 'Deepening Disparities', *The Times of India*, 9 Dec. 1999, p. 10.
38. Jyoti Basu, 'Challenges of the Twenty First Century', Mr. Jawaharlal *Nehru Memorial Lecture*, 1998.
39. *Ibid.*
40. M.L. Sondhi, 'Reshaping India's Agenda in the U.N. System in the Post-Cold War Era', *India Quarterly*, July–December 1997, No. 3 & 4.
41. *Ibid.*
42. Jyoti Basu, 'Challenges of the Twenty First Century', Jawaharlal Nehru Memorial Lecture, 1998, *World Focus*, Oct.-Nov.-Dec. 1998.
43. *Ibid.*
44. Dorothy Norman (Ed.), *Nehru — The First Sixty Years*, New York, 1965, p. 462.
45. John Mellor (Ed.), *India: A Rising Middle Power*, Westerview Press, Boulder, Colorado, 1979.
46. K. Raman Pillai, *India's Foreign Policy*, Meerut, 1969, p. 2.
47. S.N. Mishra, *India — The Cold War Years*, South Asian Publishers Pvt. Ltd., New Delhi, 1994.
48. T.A. Keenleyside, 'Diplomatic Apprenticeship — Pre-independence Origins of Indian Diplomacy and its Relevance for the Post-independence Foreign Policy'. Verinder Grover (Ed.) : *International*

Relations and Foreign Policy of India, Vol. 1, Deep & Deep Publications, New Delhi, 1992.

49. M.G. Gupta, 'Historical Background and Sources of India's Foreign Policy', in '*Indian Foreign Policy*, Y.K. Publishers, Agra, 1985.
50. For details of the establishment of the British committee, see *Report of the Fifth Session of the Indian National Congress*, Bombay, 1889, p. 73.
51. For further details see M.V. Kamath, *The United States and India — 1776–1976*, Washington; Embassy of India, 1976.
52. When Vivekanand visited the Chicago Parliament of Religions in 1893, was described as a "missionary from India to America", suggesting that Americans identified him with the whole of awakened India. See the Rev. C.C. Everett in Prabuddha Bharata, Calcutta, August, 1896. Tagore, during his 1924 trip to China, was given the name "Chu Chentan", meaning " Thundering Morning of India", a reflection of how the Chinese associated Tagore and his ideas with renascent nationalist India. See *The Far Eastern Times*, 10 May, 1924.
53. See for example, *Indian Quarterly Register*, Calcutta, 2, 1927, p. 373; J.L. Nehru, "India and the Need for International contacts", New Era, Madras, Vol. 1, No. 1, Oct. 1928, p. 23; J.L. Nehru, "Whither India?" *The Leader*, Allahabad, 14 October 1933.
54. *Report of the 43rd Session of the Indian National Congress*, Calcutta, 1978, p. 91.
55. Although, at that time, with the imposition of press censorship and the resignation of Dr. Lohia the department became inoperative.
56. K. Raman Pillai, *India's Foreign Policy*, Meerut, 1969, p. 1.
57. See *Hindu Weekly*, 21 June and 12 July 1928.
58. *Indian Affairs*, London, July 1931, p. 46.
59. *The Leader*, 7 December 1931.
60. *Modern Review*, 47, No. 3, March 1930, p. 399. For the branch's activities see also *The New York Times*, 16 February 1930.
61. *Congress Bulletin*, No. 3, 1931.
62. For accounts of the operations of the Japanese branch, see *Modern Review*, 52, No.1, July 1932, p. 101; A.M. Sahay, "India and Japan," *Hindu Weekly*, 20 Aug. 1933.
63. *Labour Monthly*, London, 9 March 1927, pp. 179-85.
64. *Indian Annual Register*, 2, 1933, pp. 372-74.
65. T.J.S. George, Krishna Menon, N. 18, pp. 109-11.
66. For details of these conferences, see Vasudeo B. Metta, "The Pan-

Asiatic Movement: A study," *The Hindustan Review*, July-Aug. 1938, pp. 479-80; *Indian National Herald*, 10 Jan, 25 Dec. 1927, 7 June 1928; *Indian Quarterly Register*, 1, 1928, pp. 378-79.

67. For details see *Indian Annual Register*, 2, 1930, pp., 387-90; 1, 1931, p. 375; 1, 1934, pp. 351-54; Asian Relations, *Report of the Proceedings and Documentation of the First Asian Relations Conference*, New Delhi, March-April, 1947, (New Delhi: Asian Relations Organisation, 1948).

68. See *The Leader*, 7 Jan., 6 May, 28 July 1929; *Indian Quarterly Register*, 1, 1929, p. 143; 2, 1929, p. 257.

69. D.G. Tendulkar, *Mahatma: Life of Mohandas Karamchand Gandhi*, Bombay, 1951-54, Vol. 3, p. 179.

70. S.C. Bose, "Passing Through Cairo", *Modern Review*, 57, No. 4, April 1935, pp. 430-31.

71. J.L. Nehru, 'India and the world', London, 1936, p. 210; *The Manchester Guardian*, 28 June, 7, 16 July 1938; *The Times*, London, 24 June, 12 July 1938.

72. *Nehru: An Autobiography*, No. 37, p. 608; *Indian Annual Register*, 1, 1937, p. 235; *Indian Review*, 40, No. 8, August 1939; *Report of General Secretary of the INC*, March 1939, Feb. 1940, pp. 13-15.

73. M.G. Gupta, 'Historical Background and sources of India's Foreign Policy' in *Indian Foreign Policy*, Y.K. Publishers, Agra, 1985.

74. S.R. Mehrotra,"The Development of the Indian outlook on world affairs before 1947", *The Journal of Development Studies*, London, Vol. 1, No. 3, April 1965, p. 291.

2

India's Foreign Policy — Core Values

India is an old civilisation, but a new state. With freedom, India changed from being an object of world politics to the status of its creator. Thus free India was reasonably imagined to be a maker of world peace and prosperity, if not its prime creator.[1]

Geo-physically, India forms 1/41 portion of the Earth with an area of 3.3 million square kilometers out of Earth's total area of 133.9 million square kilometers. It is a part of the landmass called the continent of Asia.[2] In fact foreign policy is never original, it is determined by a certain order of facts, geographical, historical and economic. "One characteristic of our foreign policy", Jawaharlal Nehru once said, "is that it is not foreign".[3] What he was emphasizing was that India's foreign policy (and for that matter the foreign policy of any country) is rooted in the domestic determinants — history, traditions, culture, geography, economic resources, level of economic development, military strength, political institutions — and of course the international milieu at a given time. The foreign policy aims of the British rule were neither a guide nor relevant to India's needs and status after 1947. Moreover, the partition of the country had created a new set of problems. Therefore the foreign relations, that India had to forge after independence were essentially to be evolved in a new setting and the process was one of learning by making mistakes or avoiding them.[4]

Prior to the transfer of power, Jawaharlal Nehru, who was already a factor in world politics could organise an Asian Relations conference in March 1947. In his address he observed: "For too long have we of Asia been petitioners in the Western courts and chancelleries. That story must now belong to the past."[5] He declared that after independence it would be India's task... to chart a new course in world politics for all states which wished to join in breaking with political alignments centering on the established great powers. He had the vision of an independent India playing its rightful role in Asia and the world.

Besides, India's historical experience is too long and too varied and therefore, in the making of India's foreign policy the Indian leaders were deeply influenced by the philosophy and traditions of their ancient civilisation. In this regard the two most influential streams of thought in the country were of great importance — the positivistic philosophical framework of Kautilya and the moralistic philosophy enunciated and practiced by Buddha and Ashoka. Of these two, the latter — the moralistic philosophical tradition — had a deep impact on a whole lot of India's nationalist leaders, including Jawaharlal Nehru, whose role in shaping the country's international behavior was singularly important.[6] However, the foreign policy of a nation is a complex and dynamic political course, which must include the prevailing pattern of its interests as well as principles and ideas in its conduct towards other states. Thus, the task of statesmanship lies in arriving at a balanced integration between idealism and realism as represented by the above two streams of thought.[7] Furthermore, "the central message of India's philosophical tradition, dating from Buddha has revolved around the rejection of absolutes and extreme positions; on the contrary, it has stressed philosophical relativity, intellectual Catholicism and coexistence of good and evil; in short the golden middle path of compromises and tolerance of opposites."[8] This philosophical tradition has yielded "the idea of the independence of the two power blocs in making up her own mind as to the rights and wrongs of a given problem, the use of methods that relax inflexibility and counter-flexibility."[9]

The international environment also influences foreign policy considerably. The pre-Second World War era had a different story. Foreign policy then was largely a matter of military strength and alliances.[10] But India's problem of under-development, poor per capita and poverty situation were the compulsions, which avoided the luxury of defense spending slicing away from funds meant for economic development. As far as political institutions are concerned India adopted the parliamentary form of government of the British type with which the ruling political elites in India were familiar and they were trained in that system too.[11]

The name of Mahatma Gandhi and the method of moral persuasion to gain independence gave the country a special international standing. Furthermore, the independence of India was a watershed in human history for two important reasons. First, it signaled the beginning of the end of colonialism, thus opening the possibility of a democratic world order based on the sovereign equality of all nations. In fact, India is the first of such nations that cast away their shackles of colonial slavery. With the independence of India started the process of decolonisation on a global scale. The implications of this development are far reaching. It brought a new element in the concept of foreign policy of every nation — it could no longer be confined to the exclusive club of monarchs and caucuses. Foreign policy has become a matter of interest and concern for the people, the new nations suddenly emerging into freedom. Diplomacy could no longer be confined to the well-groomed diplomats; it had to take into account the urges and aspirations of the demos — both on a world scale and within every country. It is unthinkable today that a government — even if it is not democratic — can follow a foreign policy without taking into consideration the mood and outlook of the people in a country, because the common people provide the ultimate sanction for any foreign policy. On a global scale, too, the arrival of this element could be felt with the emergence of what is called the Third World, which commands overwhelming majority in the United Nations.[12]

The second major development was India's articulation of

an alternative world order to the one being fashioned by the rival power blocs. This alternative world order found expression in the philosophy of Non-alignment. Means, India would no longer be the camp follower of any power. It would decide its foreign policy on the basis of its own understanding of India's national interest. In other words, the transfer of power from the British to Indian hands meant clearly that this country would no longer be guided by the Foreign policy of Britain.

In this politico — military — economic, historical, geographical, cultural and international environment, elements of independent India's foreign policy were evolved. These elements were/are: pursuit of non-alignment, maintenance of world peace, pacific settlement of disputes, peaceful coexistence of nations of diverse social/political/economic systems (especially cooperative relations with immediate neighbors); opposition to the remnants of colonialism (since largely vanished) and neo-colonialism; anti-Apartheid; promotion of both its own economic development (and that of other Third World countries); development of an 'Asian-identity' and intra-Asian co-operation; working for disarmament; and support to, strengthening of, international organisations — the United Nations in particular. These elements reflected not merely "official policy"; they represented the foreign policy of the people of India as such.[13]

Indeed, these are the elements, which constitute the 'core values' of India's foreign policy.

There are very few countries in the world, which have displayed such a degree of consistency, coherence and tenacious loyalty to the elements (ideals) underlying their respective foreign policies, as India has done. There has not been a single major instance when India has deviated from the core values of her foreign policy.[14]

India commanded admiration when it defied the Cold War hypothesis. India's respect was at its highest when it fearlessly followed non-aligned principles and played a sagacious role during and after the Korean War (1951-53), during the Crisis over Suez (1956). Although, it was the ability of

Jawaharlal Nehru, to keep the Indian image at center stage when world crisis emerged, that enabled this sub-continent to play such a significant role. India was looked upon as the leader of the developing continents in Bandung (1955) and Belgrade (1961) and was obvious choice for the biggest UN peacekeeping operations in Congo (1960).

As a visionary Nehru looked into the post-war environment with full involvement. He understood that the problems of the underdeveloped countries could not be solved on a regional basis. "Nor could they be solved only by the pushing back of imperialism. Their solution required that the paramount question of global confrontation be tackled. He also understood that with the power distribution in the world, the two blocs could only engage in mutual destruction and this, in turn, would mean the destruction of the entire human race."[15] The lack of communication between the two sides of the Cold War at its inception provided India with an opportunity to provide good offices in conflict and crisis situations. In fact, Nehru advocated non-aligned technique to tackle Cold War situations. His techniques included dialogue, discussion, negotiation, compromise and respect for other's point of view. Peacekeeping took India to the Congo, Cyprus and the Middle East. Thus, two of the most striking aspects of the Nehru era were the high visibility of India in UN efforts to intervene in international disputes (*viz.* Korea, Suez, Congo and so on) and the complete dominance of Pt. Nehru himself in the formulation of foreign policy, at least up to 1962.[16]

"If Mahatma Gandhi stood for the self-respect of individuals, Pt. Nehru asserted the self-respect of people"[17] Though India was economically and industrially backward and could be rated as middle power throughout 1950, yet it could be pushed to the front rank of nations because it could exhibit self-respect and rational and constructive attitude in international politics. The Gandhian message that India should have certain mission in the world prompted the Indian administration to avoid entanglement in the conflicts of big powers and at the same time play a major role in world affairs. As an outcome of the dual urge the policy of Non-alignment was given high priority in foreign policy formulations. Thus India played a serious global role in the fifties.[18]

Despite, Nehru era was not above criticism. "The constant desire to adhere to general principles without realizing the difficulty of applying them to practical situations, was indeed a general weakness running through the entire gamut of India's policy under Nehru."[19] India refused to accept military assistance, which was available from both the groups. The Indian leadership thought that by accepting the assistance the policy of Non-alignment adopted by India would be questioned. Even Marshal Tito and Col. Nasser, the other champions of Non-alignment could make their countries militarily strong by receiving external military aid. Had India been militarily strong China would not have dared a military action in 1962. In the same vein when India appealed for military help in 1962 it became a laughing stock. Again the principles of 'panchsheel' covered the Chinese deeds in Tibet. Too much of adherence to the principles was not good. It prevented the Indian leadership to assess Chinese mood and ambitions. Further, the Goan episode damaged the reputation of India of India. Since Prime Minister Nehru had always given importance to peaceful settlement of disputes without taking resort to forcible means. Thus when force was used, the whole world was practically shocked and condemned India.[20]

The Sino-Indian war damaged India's reputation, true, but it could preserve and protect the non-aligned image of India. Failure of Non-alignment in India would have invited death to a cause, a mission and a technique.[21] Idealism without the kernel of self-interest may sound hypocritical and hollow. The foreign policy of a nation is a complex and dynamic political course, which must include the prevailing pattern of its interests as well as principles and ideas in its conduct towards other states. Thus, the task of statesmanship lies in arriving at a balanced integration between idealism and realism. After 1962 India's global role began to recede. The post-Nehru years witnessed injection of greater realism in India's Foreign Policy. Indira Gandhi used Non-alignment as an instrument in a manner, which reflected her positivistic thinking. During her stewardship of the nation, Indira Gandhi has made the policy more purposeful and dynamic. Her realisation was that India was on the threshold of becoming a great world power and had to survive and play its due role in making the globe safe for humanity to survive and struggle in. It was the pursuit of this goal that brought her into conflict with the US and to a friendship and co-operation treaty with the Soviet Union. She linked the march of our country to its great world power status with world peace and development.[22] Two important developments, one, the help to the liberation of Bangladesh (1971) and the other one is peaceful nuclear explosion (1974), exhibit legendary courage of Indira Gandhi and it was the courage to use power, when the nation needed it. These developments enhanced the regional image of India. At the same time, the fact of regional dominance gave India a global status and prestige.

In 1976, the US Agency for International Aid organised a seminar on the re-examination of the US policy towards India. Participants were of the view that:[23]

"India has made substantial, perhaps even extra-ordinary progress. India left its colonial era poorly equipped to preserve its national integrity and freedom of action in a difficult and hostile world environment. Since then India has built a domestic base of political, economic, technological and trade capabilities consistent with a large and growing international role. The first 30 years of independence saw India laid the foundation for its goal of growth to major power status. The second 30 are likely to see that aspiration realised." The participants spoke highly of the development of science and technology in India and of the fact that India now had the third largest pool of scientific and technologically trained manpower.[24]

However, in concise, the policy pursued by India in her external affairs has injected a moral tone in world politics. Nehru, Shastri and Indira Gandhi firmly believe that, however, deep the crisis and however obstinate the opponent, the doors of negotiation, peaceful parleys and conciliatory approach should never be closed. In this respect India herself set an example, with regards Pakistan, in spite of her bellicosity, aggression and terrorist activities, India never broke diplomatic relations with Pakistan, but continued her talks with her in a spirit of accommodation. On both the occasions in 1965 and again in 1971, Pakistan received the conquered territory back. In 1972, India even returned 5000 square miles of territory in Sind to Pakistan. In 1965 conflict, India restrained its victorious march to Lahore, so as to spare Pakistan a further humiliation. In her hour of victory, India displayed generosity with a view to lay down the groundwork of conciliation. Pt. Nehru in 1948 was conciliatory to Pakistan and Shastri readily agreed to Tashkent Agreement; Indira Gandhi displayed statesmanship and spirit of generosity in 1972 and concluded the Simla Agreement. The same may be said about China when both countries were engaged in hostilities in October-November 1962. Since 1972 the process of normalisation between China and India has gained momentum.

Among the elements of India's foreign policy, the Non-alignment is the one, which comprises within itself all the other elements of foreign policy. It is the struggle for the removal of poverty, illiteracy, health and nutrition problems of the neglected millions, for which Non-alignment is striving. It is a humanitarian approach which is much more acceptable than cutthroat competition policy approach. This campaign should continue. The issues of the New Economic Order, an equitable relationship between the needs for environment and development, a comprehensive understanding of the place of human rights in vulnerable societies, terrorism etc., call for the articulation of our positions in forceful language. Here Mikhail Gorbachev's sound suggestion that the chairman of NAM must always be a member of the Security Council by virtue of his position is quite valuable and NAM ought to insist that its chairman must be on par with the delegates of the other five permanent members.[25]

Thus never before in history, the thrust of foreign policy is felt in all fields of human affairs. "Men learn slowly" wrote Donald G. Bishop, "but one lesson that they should have learned in the 20th Century is that foreign affairs are infinitely the most important branch of politics.[26]

PURSUIT OF NON-ALIGNMENT

The polarised post-war politics of the Cold Warriors had no attraction for the newly emergent nations. The ideological strife and the struggle for hegemony were alarming for them. It was opulence for the powerful nations. The free but militarily weak nations viewed the expensive power game as anti-peace and destruction-oriented. The strong nations also tried to carve out the political support of the newly independent nations of Asia and Africa by persuasion, cajolery, threat and temptation. "Thus, the most remarkable feature of international politics when these new nations were toddling into world scene was the crystallisation of the Cold War into polarised struggle for power between two blocs."[27] The international environment provided difficult choices for the new nations, which were emotionally charged with their concern for economic development. They were interested to pursue foreign policies, which would ensure international peace and internal development. Their economic development was dependent upon foreign assistance. Therefore, in this type of international environment, the rational choice paved way for the policy of non-alignment.[28]

Specific Meaning of Non-alignment

"Non-alignment is the courage of true independence", said Indira Gandhi, in the Colombo Non-aligned summit conference (1976), "it was the only practical policy for the preservation of newly won independence of many countries. To us, choice between one military bloc and another seemed irrelevant and unreal. Our choice was between independence and dependence, between progressing through co-operation and perishing through confrontations."[29] Thus for India, non-alignment not only meant maintenance of independence, sovereignty and equality in foreign policy and relations; it also meant certain specifics: opposition to division of the international community into blocs/groups of any kind — political, economic or ideological; opposition to Great Power hegemony and the Cold War between and among them and their allies; freedom of foreign policy and relations, consistent with the increasing interdependence among nations; refusal to accept the stationing of foreign military forces or bases or facilities on one's territory, since they impinge on one's freedom of policy/action ; and peaceful coexistence of nations of different political, economic and social systems. In general, non-alignment meant avoiding any dependence on other nations for large-scale economic and/or military assistance, except on the basis of capability and mutual interest.[30] Moreover, 'non-alignment' has generally been used in two distinct though related senses. In its first sense it is a worldview or ideology concerning how the global state system should function. It purports to describe a broad movement, the third world Non-Aligned Movement (NAM), which initially sought to play the role of an international buffer between the two Cold War blocs. Non-alignment as a normative principle undoubtedly had a certain moral cast. It was supposed to represent an alternative to 'balance of power' and 'alliance' politics'.[31] In its second and more important sense, it is a description of the specific foreign policy orientation of a particular non-aligned country. As such, it becomes a loose synonym for the traditional policy of effective pursuit of national interest through the expansion of national power.[32]

When India became independent, Jawaharlal Nehru declared, that since India coveted nobody's territory nor had claims against any foreign land, India would remain aloof from all the conflicts and wars that arose only from such claims. This was a doctrine, which happened also to suit a rather under-developed and ill-armed country, which though vast in size was yet to emerge as a state with material resources and armed forces of any significance.[33] However, although India pioneered the policy, it was not done solely to serve India's interests. It was, from the beginning, conceived as also serving the interests of world peace. That would explain why the policy was opted for by many other nations also. In this connection, Prime Minister Morarji Desai remarked, "it is recognised by other commonwealth nations, that the policy of non-alignment, as enunciated, and practiced by India not only serves our interests, but makes India a coveted partner in their own network of relationships and their views of a stable world order".[34]

Characteristic Features of Non-alignment

The basic characteristics of non-alignment, as evolved by India, though not codified into a charter, they are openly practiced in inter-state relations and approach to international issues[35] —

(1) Non-alignment stands for a plurality and democratic equality within international community. It affirms faith in self-determination and total end of colonialism. It opposes all forms of pressures and outside interventions in the internal policies of a nation. It stands for international co-operation and functional relationship in an interdependence world.

(2) It opposes all forms of racialism and discriminations and it champions the cause of fundamental human freedoms. Economic and social justice is the motto of Non-alignment.

(3) "Non-alignment through its ideological agnosticism in determining international relationships, stood for the freedom of nations to determine their own internal socio-political philosophies. It upheld the validity of differing and opposing socio-economic concepts and opposed the imposition of an external ideology. In effect it argued that a nation must have the right to evolve from its own civilisational roots and economic circumstances."[36]

(4) Non-alignment rests on the presumption that the national security is linked with national strength. It negates the validity of military power in ensuring internal legitimacy; even less is it prudent to surrender to outside protection.

(5) Lastly one of the major characteristics of non-alignment is that it asserts, that international peace is an inalienable prerequisite for accomplishing national aspirations and the exercise of sovereign independence. It therefore pleads for peaceful coexistence and avoidance of confrontation that will lead to international strife. In the face of weapons of mass destruction and the

potentialities of nuclear war, it pleads for the peaceful resolution of international disputes.[37]

India pushed the non-aligned concept into an international doctrine in the Bandung Conference in 1955 and had stuck to these basic postulates since her Independence.

Policy of Non-alignment — Origin

However, this is nothing new. The United States and Britain followed such a policy for long and then only they could manage the heavy task of nation building and overhauling of their economy. Until these complex tasks were accomplished, USA kept herself in complete isolation from the rest of the world. Thus it was non-alignment with neutrality or isolationist policy.[38] It is only after, that they managed to become a completely developed nation; they followed the policy of engagement in world affairs.

In India this policy is not merely a creation of Jawaharlal Nehru, but 'it flows from our historical as well as our recent past.' As Jawaharlal Nehru, in his unique style and imbued with humility, once said, "I have not originated the policy of Non-alignment. It is a policy inherent in the circumstances of India, inherent in the past thinking of India, inherent in the whole mental outlook of India, inherent in the conditions of the Indian mind during our struggle for freedom and inherent in the circumstances of the world today. I came in by the mere accidental fact that during the few years I have represented that policy as Foreign Minister, I am quite convinced that whoever might have been in charge of the foreign affairs of India and whatever party might have been in power in India, they could not have deviated very much from this policy. Some emphasis might have been greater here or there because, as I said, it represents every circumstance that goes towards making the thought of India on these subjects."[39] Indeed, Indian spokespersons were in the habit of emphasizing the indigenous roots of the pôlicy,[40] while the beginnings of Non-Alignment can be traced to Afro-Asian resurgence — a reaction against European colonial system (1919-1945) and even prior to that in the struggle of small and weak states against the hegemony of great European powers since the birth of the sovereign nation system in the middle of the seventeenth century Europe. These oppressed, suppressed and dominated states struggled hard for freedom from colonialism, imperialism and great power domination to choose their own path in internal development and external policies.[41] Their common commitment to world peace, justice, security and co-operation, to the elimination of imperialism, colonialism and neo-colonialism, to the eradication of apartheid, racism and all forms of foreign domination, aggression, intervention, occupation and pressures, to the acceleration of the process of self-determination of peoples under colonial and alien domination and the consolidation of the national independence, sovereignty and territorial integrity of states and to the social and economic development of their peoples, constitutes an irreversible factor in world history.[42] The Non-alignment with its emphasis on independent judgment, independent decision-making and independent action provided them a suitable foreign policy alternative. Again the Cold War as a dominant theme of post-World War II international politics certainly influenced and shaped the emergence of Non-alignment, but it was by no means the cause of that emergence, because it was just a coincidence that when these countries began to gain independence (in 1940s) they found themselves in a bipolar world.[43]

Non-alignment — A Need

However, the policy of Non-alignment does not imply pacifism or isolationism. Jawaharlal Nehru, summing up his attitude in 'The Discovery of India' said, "it is surprising how internationally minded we grew in spite of our intense nationalism. The policy of Non-alignment was not isolationism, but rather a condemnation of the powerful countries and their policies of imperialism and wars."[44] Besides, the Herculean task of building up a country of 360 millions, as India then was, with its legacy of poverty and the worldwide nature of war, could not allow India to follow U.S.-line non-alignment with the policy of isolation.[45] India was comparatively backward and economically weak country at that time. She had yet to stabilise her economy. Its agriculture and industries were in the early stages of development. Thus India was in urgent need of foreign aid in building up her economy. She has to build up her strength in peace and under the condition of Non-alignment. The basic rationale of Non-alignment was that a climate of peace was necessary to optimise development, which was desperately urgent after centuries of foreign rule and retarded progress. Therefore, India followed Non-alignment with the policy of co-operation and has established diplomatic relations with almost all the independent states[46] and welcomed aid from all quarters — USSR, UK, USA, Germany and Japan. India commanded respect in the West for embarking on a massive social and economic transformation through the democratic political system. As a consequence, for almost three decades, in spite of India's 'irritating' non-aligned positions, India was the biggest recipient of economic aid from the West.[47]

Furthermore, India's policy of Non-alignment rests on 'Panchsheel', which is a set of five principles. Since a guarantee, which says, that there will be a war, except in your country, has no meaning today when war is worldwide. Therefore the guarantee must be to avoid war and going a step further to avoid interference with any country.[48] Dr. Sukarno, addressing the Investigating Committee for Preparation of Independence on 1 June 1945, referred to the 5 rites of Islam, five fingers and the five Pandavas. The five principles of international conduct were first included in the preamble of Sino-Indian Agreement on Tibet on 29 April 1954.[49] These are: mutual respect for each other's territorial integrity and sovereignty; non-aggression; non-interference in each other's internal affairs; equality and mutual benefit; and peaceful coexistence. Jawaharlal Nehru introduced the term "Panchsheel" into the domain of international relations on 23rd of September 1954 at a banquet given in honor of the Prime Minister of Indonesia. The Bandung Conference held in April 1955 and attended by countries of Asia and Africa, further elaborated and reinforced these principles.

Crisis Situation and India's Non-alignment

In a conflict situation during the Cold War era,[50] the peaceful negotiation of a non-aligned nation had some meaning. The nation conducted negotiation free from pressure. The diplomatic technique adopted by India in crisis situations provided ample testimony to that effect. Through peaceful negotiation a desirable solution might not be arrived at. But Non-alignment helped to establish an attitude and approach that made those solutions possible. "It is not our intention to be a part of ... a third bloc, or to tell the world how to establish peace," asserted a leader of the Indian delegation to the General Assembly; "In our circumstances, in light of our history and in the great traditions of the man who made our national independence possible, we think it is always necessary to talk to one's opponent and to seek the basis of reconciliation and negotiation becomes necessary."[51]

Korean Crisis

The Korean crisis was a legacy of the Second World War and its post-war military occupation. The military understanding developed at the Potsdam Conference decided the future of Korea, which was previously under Japanese occupation. Japan surrendered. Korea was divided at the 38th parallel. The artificial division of the country and the military occupation of both the parts by the Superpowers, who had already entered into a phase of Cold War in the Eastern Europe, gave birth to several problems. The US-USSR rift forced the Americans to place the matter for discussion in the UN Agenda. On 14 November 1947 the General Assembly passed a resolution, which recognised the right to independence of the Koreans. It further established a UN Commission for Korea (UNCOK) for facilitating a programme for that country having a national government and withdrawal of all occupying forces. The Soviets reacted sharply to the resolution and called that illegal. It refused to accept the UN proposals. Ultimately, the war in Korea broke out on 25 June 1950. The North Korean forces crossed the 38th parallel. This action of the North Korea led to a serious apprehension that the tension might lead to Superpower confrontation in the Far East.[52]

Korea was treated by the USA as a test case for the so-called domino theory, that if the UN/USA allowed the USSR/China to overcome Korea, this would lead to other countries like Vietnam to fall into Communist hands.[53] The North Korean attack upon the South Korea was under the active Soviet support, which was trying to test the firmness of the American policy of containment.

From the beginning of the conflict the Indian position was quite distinct from those of two Superpowers. Both of them were dictated by the Cold War considerations. The sole objective of the Indian policy was to help maintain world peace and reduce international tensions. As per the Indian action it recognised neither North nor South Korea. Thus, it had not taken a partial view of the situation. India had voted in the Security Council branding North Korea as the aggressor and asking it to withdraw behind the 38th parallel and to cease hostilities.

The Truman Administration had enough faith in the institution of the United Nations as an instrument of international action during the war in Korea. While India had an experience of the United Nations which was able to arrange a cease-fire between India and Pakistan over Kashmir in 1948-49, but was not successful in enforcing the vacation of the Pak-occupied areas of Jammu and Kashmir State as a preliminary to holding a plebiscite. Therefore, when President Truman appealed to the United Nations to organise an international force under the UN flag to oppose the invasion, India did not offer to send any troops, India sent a Red Cross contingent to work among the UN forces in South Korea.[54] The diplomatic action thus taken was to keep the options open. India was interested to get out of the situation once large-scale conflict got in. "India from the beginning wanted to localise the conflict and that in case of its spread she wanted to be out of it."[55]

Thus despite India's public condemnation of the aggression by North Korea, it stood outside the US camp. Because of this attitude and action it was also accessible to the other bloc. "A major declaration of its aloofness from the western position regarding the conflict came by way of its withdrawal from the sponsorship of the Eight Power Resolution of the General Assembly which established the UN Commission for the Unification and Rehabilitation advocating unification by force, if necessary."[56] The Indian decision to abstain from voting was based upon reason. It had all faith in the UN. In the Korean crisis how could UN take resort to force to unify the two Koreas and that to the action supposed to be taken against North Korea, which had crossed the 38th parallel with the same intention of unifying both the Koreas. Further the UN action might invite PRC to intervene. This would have resulted in the extension of the conflict in the region. India was careful not to preempt the UN forces from crossing the parallel until all other possibilities had been exhausted.

The Indian apprehension came true. The crossing of the 38th parallel by the UN Forces immediately provoked the armed action by PRC. The Chinese forces crossed the Yale River from Manchuria to aid North Korean forces and the war in Korea developed into a serious conflict between China and the USA. Attlee, the Prime Minister of UK came to USA to advise Truman that instead of relying on the domino theory, the USA should negotiate with China on the assumption that China would behave like Yugoslavia and might be weaned off the alliance with the USSR. This advice was not heeded.[57]

India advocated peaceful negotiation to diffuse the tension. It tried its best to arrange for a cease-fire without publicly denouncing the Chinese action. It piloted a draft resolution along with twelve Asian nations for the constitution of a ceasefire group and presented the proposal to the UN First Committee. It also appealed to both China and North Korea to declare that they had no intention to cross the 38th parallel. The appeal was rejected by China and the Soviet Union. The Indian piloted draft resolution was presented to the First Committee of the General Assembly on 11 January 1951 and was accepted on 13 January 1951 with overwhelming support. The proposal had five principles[58] enclosed to settle the crisis. The PRC rejected these principles. The Chinese action was treated as a total defiance of the UN by the USA. The situation was further aggravated by a UN resolution on 1 February 1951 branding China an aggressor. India, Burma and the Communist bloc strongly opposed the resolution. The American action for a military settlement was resented in the Western world. An opinion was created that it was undesirable to defeat China. This resulted in the historic decision taken by President Truman in dismissing Gen. Mac Arthur, the Commander of the UN Forces from his post. Both USA and USSR then agreed for a ceasefire negotiation, which commenced from July 1951.[59]

India's role in the war in Korea was her first assay in international affairs. But China and the USA used the Indian Ambassador in Beijing for negotiations and passing on messages and warnings to each other since they had no other mutually acceptable contact. An Indian proposal regarding the repatriation of the Prisoner of Wars (POW) was accepted. The Armistice Agreement was signed on 27 July 1953. India was made a member-chairman and executive agent of the Neutral Nations Repatriation Commission (NNRC) consisting of India, Czechoslovakia, Poland, and Sweden as members and Switzerland as Chairman. Despite several bottlenecks and controversial developments General Thimayya, of India, did a marvelous job and finally succeeded to persuade both the groups to accept the procedure for repatriation. The prisoners were given the right to exercise their choice whether they wished to be repatriated to the Communists or stay in South Korea. India won all-round praise for carrying out this difficult task with impartiality.[60]

Thus during the Korean crisis it was evident that India pursued a neutralist track, but it was positive and not elusive in character. It never gave support to just one side and opposed the other side forever. India followed an independent policy that was by and large independent of the decisions of the other powers. Jawaharlal Nehru always insisted on taking 'decisions on merits'. India always gave importance to the solution. Mahatma Gandhi had told in order to arrive at good end you must adopt good means. The Indian diplomacy in the Korean crisis just reflected the Gandhian way of settlement of disputes.

Moreover, in 1954, France arranged a nine-power conference in Geneva to deal with the question of the successors of France in Vietnam and to arrange the modus vivendi between North Vietnam held by HO Chi Minh and South Vietnam. Krishna Menon played an active role at the Conference as a "tenth power".

Suez Crisis

In the Suez crisis, India played both visible and invisible role. The Suez Canal, 101-mile long canal, extends from Port Said to Port Suez. On 30th November 1854, the then Khedive (Viceroy) of Egypt gave a concession to a Frenchman Frendinand de Lesseps to establish an international company under the name Universal Company of the Maritime Canal of Suez to build a canal. It was leased out for 99 years and after the completion of the leasing period the canal was to be handed over to Egypt. The construction of the canal started in April 1859 and the completion of the work took nearly ten years. The canal was opened to traffic in November 1869. The canal was within the Egyptian territory. But it was an international waterway, built and owned by an international company.[61]

Prior to that due to financial crisis the Khedive had sold the shares of the Suez Company to Britain in 1875. That brought in the British to begin its dominance in the region. In 1882 Britain temporarily occupied Egypt in order to ensure 'Stability and Peace' in the region and to protect her share in the Company. The temporary occupation developed the tendencies of taking permanent character and continued up to 1922 when Egypt was granted independence. Despite this new development the British forces stationed there continued. In 1936 Britain imposed a Treaty upon Egypt by which Egypt gave the British people the right to defend the Suez Canal. The Treaty came to an end in 1951 by the unilateral abrogation by Egypt. The abrogation of the Anglo-Egyptian Treaty followed great changes in Egypt leading to the military supremacy.[62] The Britain agreed to withdraw its forces by 1956. The British withdrawal process was initiated. But meanwhile a Baghdad Pact was signed which brought the Anglo-American forces nearer to the Egyptian soil. Israel was already an enemy of the Arabs. To counter the military developments, General Gamal Abdel Nasser, the then Army Chief of Egypt, made arms deal with Czechoslovakia and Russia. In July 1956 USA abruptly broke off negotiations with Egypt, which was expecting big finance from USA for its ambitious project, the Aswan Dam that was second largest in the world. Nasser countered by expropriating the shares of the Suez Canal Company and asserting Egypt's sovereign right to operate the canal itself. The objective was also to raise additional sources of revenue to finance the dam. However, the main purpose of the nationalisation was indeed to find money for the dam. But, nonetheless, it did affect the power equations in the area and the world.[63]

The US Administration's withdrawal of economic aid from Egypt had caused the nationalisation. Egypt also refused to take part in the US inspired alliance system in the region (Middle East Defense Organisation). Of the Western powers Britain and France, who were also members of NATO, were visibly upset by the steps taken by Gen. Nasser. Both of them were erstwhile controlling parties of the Suez Canal Company. The Suez crisis was thus initiated which experienced the Superpower involvement and UN intervention.[64] India played a crucial role. Its participation was active and extensive. Britain and France were the allies of USA. Naturally the US reaction could not be as sharp as non-aligned India's.

Israel attacked Egypt on 29 October 1956. The inevitable happened when Franco-British forces launched a military attack on Egypt. Along with India the two Superpowers denounced the Franco-British military action on Egypt.

Factors behind India's Stand

Its basic attitudes and interests dictated the Indian stand in the Suez crisis.

(a) It was against colonialism. Jawaharlal Nehru denounced the attack as a "flagrant case of aggression by two strong powers against a weaker country."[65]

(b) India was determined to support a neutral country in its attempt to make the nearby region of its own country a Cold War free zone.

(c) It was also interested in supporting progressive Arab nationalism as practiced by Egypt as a means of minimizing the danger of unqualified Muslim support for Pakistan and an anti-Indian course.[66]

(d) The most important single factor attributable to India's stand with regard to Suez was "the inclusion of Pakistan in the Baghdad Pact, which aroused the fear that the Cold War had been brought close to her door."[67]

(e) In the words of V.K. Krishna Menon, the then Minister without Portfolio: "India was concerned in the Suez Canal as a life line in her economy...76 per cent of her exports pass through the Canal. The fulfillment of India's Five Year Plans depended upon traffic through it. India did not approach the problem in a legalistic way but with a full sense of the reality of the importance of the canal for many countries of the world who used it."[68]

The Security Council could not take any positive step due to Anglo-French veto. Both the Superpowers demanded immediate cessation of hostilities. Yugoslavia suggested convening of the General Assembly under 'Uniting for Peace Resolution'. The Assembly met on November 1956. The British Premier Anthony Eden charged India for its clandestine role to present the proposal through Yugoslavia. "India and Canada, both suspicious of the motives of the two Superpowers and fearful that simple ceasefire may not be enough, proposed, that there be an International Emergency Force, under the UN, to be constituted of the willing contribution of small powers only."[69] It was at that point that India came to play a role in the UN for the first time with regard to the issue. A ten member (including India) International Force was formed on the basis of resolution adopted on 5th November 1956. On November 6 Britain declared that it would be willing to order a ceasefire from the midnight. But it was a victory for Arab nationalism as the proposal put an end to Anglo-French imperialism-colonialism.

In essence, the Indian stand was a novel kind of neutralism. It never helped either of the party, but could put a check on both. It checked the growth of colonialism. Further it encouraged the Afro-Asian nations to pursue neutralism. India also secured the support of a Muslim State in its future conflicts with Pakistan. Egypt also joined the Indian mission for the Non-alignment cause. Sarbadhikari observed: "India's stand during the crisis therefore measured up with the principles guiding her foreign policy in that area. Her efforts towards the withdrawal of foreign troops stemmed both from her anti-colonial policy and the fear that the intervention of the Great Powers, which was in the logic of events, would spark off a major war. The impact of the crisis in strengthening the non-aligned policies of some Arab governments, such as Egypt and paving the way for others to follow suit, such as Iraq, was a success for India's rationale, that neutralism was the most logical policy for the developing states. Moreover, the support of a secular India for a Muslim State on the basis of colonial intrusion was an acute embarrassment for Pakistan, wedded as she was to Western alignments; it revealed that diplomacy on the basis of religion was unsuited to modern relations of States."[70]

Hungarian Crisis

At this very time, the Hungarian crisis also emerged. The revolution in Hungary was against the Soviet occupation by stationing Russian troops in that country. The revolution occurred about the same time as the nationalisation of the Suez Canal. The revolt was fierce and the measures taken by the U.S.S.R. were ruthless. Pt. Nehru had been outspoken about the Suez Canal issue, but kept his own counsels in regard to the events in Hungary. This was taken note of by the liberal elements both in India and abroad, who felt that Nehru had shown discretion to be the better part of velour where. Russia was concerned. The silence of Pt. Nehru was also adversely commented upon by the Western powers that pointed out that the liberation movement in Hungary was a test for those who stood for liberty and freedom and India had failed in that test. Nehru had spoken out in favor of Egypt against the USA, but not for Hungary against the USSR.[71]

Congo Crisis

In the Congo Crisis, India's position was anti-colonialist. The second part of the 20th century experienced awakening in Africa. Africa was the unfortunate scene and example of the arrogance of the Western countries. Exploitation in Africa knew no limits. Colonial powers adopted the policy of racial discrimination (apartheid). It was observed through physical and cultural segregation of the Black community. Congo, situated in tropical Africa was under the Belgian control for decades. Belgium ruled over Congo in a paternalistic-colonial way and had not cared much for the welfare and real interests of the people of that country. Rather it was busy to exploit the land commercially, which had rich mineral resources. Meanwhile, the two developments stirred nationalistic sentiments in Belgian Congo (Leopoldville). One, the neighboring French occupied Congo (Brazaville) attained independence and the other was, in Accra All African People's Conference was held and urged for the end of Colonial system.[72] In the Round Table Conference between Belgian government and the Congolese leaders between January to March 1960 the demand for immediate freedom was accepted and 30th June 1960 was fixed for the commencement of Congolese sovereignty.

Joseph Kasavubu and Patrice Lumumba assumed offices as the President and Prime Minister of Central Republic of Congo respectively. But within hours after independence, a wave of unrest began sweeping across the country. There was another competitor for power, Moise Tashombe who was the Premier of the Province of Katanga. The region was rich with minerals. Without Katanga's financial support Congo could not think of progress. But on 11th July 1960 Katanga announced its secession from Congo and form a new state allied with Belgium.[73] Prior to that P.M. Lumumba had asked the Belgians to vacate Congo. On July 12, 1960 the Belgian troops from Katanga, had already marched into Leopoldville. The situation became chaotic. "Faced with that kind of circumstances Lumumba looked for assistance from President Eisenhower, Premier Khrushchev, as well as to Beijing and on 12th July sent urgent appeal to the UN Secretary General for the UN assistance in maintaining the national integrity of his country against the aggression being hatched by foreign interests."[74] The Secretary General Dag Hammarskjoeld took the matter immediately to the Security Council. The Secretary General threw the resources of the UN into his effort to save the Congo from becoming an East-West battleground.

The Congolese crisis took a new turn when President Kasabuvu dismissed Premier Lumumba and the latter did the same to the former. Seeing an opportunity, pro-Western Colonel Joseph Mobutu took command of the armed forces through a coup, thus making it possible for the Belgians to return to Congo, as unofficial advisers. Both the superpowers reacted sharply. As expected the USA supported Kasabuvu-Mobutu faction for their claim to have legitimate government and the Soviets gave moral and material support to Lumumba. Both the superpowers remained adamant on their stand. "This helplessness was mitigated to a degree by the action in the emergency session that followed it of an overwhelming majority including India, which supported the US position; and therefore the Secretary General's position...."[75]

An irritated Khrushchev presented his Troika Proposal, which would have three-man committee replacing one Secretary General who shall be representing three worlds (both the Superpowers and the third world). India opposed the Troika proposal, but suggested for the reform of the Secretariat by having an advisory Committee from different geographical areas. In December, India along with seven non-aligned nations asked for immediate convening of the Congolese Parliament. In a debate on this resolution Indian representative Krishna Menon emphatically observed, "that his government considered the Kasabuvu regime as unvarnished, unashamed and unconstitutional dictatorship".[76]

The death of Patrice Lumumba in a mysterious situation shocked the conscience of the world. The Soviet Union demanded that Gizenga, who was Lumumba's deputy, be the head of the lawful Congolese government. But later on the Soviet Union had to change its stand and supported the UN decisions. For this P.M. Nehru played a significant role.[77]

India took leadership with Afro-Asian members passing a resolution calling upon Belgium to accept its responsibility as a member of the UN and the proposal demanded the withdrawal of all military and non-military personnel from Congo. That led to a UN resolution rejecting Katanga's claim as a sovereign nation and authorised the Secretary General to take all possible steps to make the area free from foreign action.[78]

In the Congolese crisis apart from the support or opposition to proposals in the UN, India had a share of 5600 strong force in a 30-nation pool of 20,000 forces. It also contributed $ 105,000 to UN Fund for Congo. Rajeshwar Dayal, an Indian diplomat, served as Secretary General's personal representative in Congo. He was instrumental in bringing the UN to a stage for strong action through his reports. India's military contribution was politically important for the UN.[79]

As per the views of a researcher, the Secretary General who was accused as the agent of the Western colonialism could function strongly because he received the support of the neutral powers and India was one of the prominent supporters.[80] Another observer said that the successful conclusion of the UN operation in Congo depended to a large extent on two powers — India and USA.[81] "In a real sense India and the USA were two countries the UN operation most depended upon, both for political support in New York and for military in Congo. Despite some differences in interpreting the mandate, the US India partnership remained solid throughout the Congo drama. The Congo operation would probably have collapsed if either New Delhi or Washington had withdrawn its support before the integration of Katanga."[82]

Crisis in Goa

Immediately before the third general election in India (1961), the Indian forces entered Goa, drove out the colonial Portuguese regime and incorporated Goa, Daman and Diu into the Indian Union. Since Portugal and South Africa were the only powers to display obstinacy and intransigence. The Portuguese imperialism refused to retreat from Goa. At first India fought the costly litigation in the International Court of

Justice at The Hague for six years from 1955 to 1960. When Portugal refused to abide by the advice of the World Court, then India resorted to police action in 1961 under the effective guidance of Krishna Menon.[83] The forcible liberation of Goa was perfectly justified as the final step in eliminating colonial rule in India, but it further eroded the moral credibility of India and P.M. Nehru as apostles of non-violence.[84]

Border War With China

India's China policy popularly known as *Hindi-Chini Bhai-Bhai* folly was not successful. In 1962 there was a thirty-one day border war with China in which India suffered a humiliating defeat. Its forces had to withdraw in the Northeast. In the north, China managed to advance still further beyond Aksai Chin region, which it had occupied earlier. The Indian authorities sought aid from the USA and the UK. At this moment the Chinese withdrew in the north-east beyond the McMohan line and announced a ceasefire unilaterally. India's Non-alignment had been exposed as a non-workable basis for international relations.[85] Nevertheless, China's humiliation of the Indian armed forces in the border war, did not cause India to abandon non-alignment, though it forced it to seek active support from the West (particularly the USA), to give up the wider global pretensions of the Nehru era and to pay much more attention to developing its own military powers.[86] Henceforth, strengthening Indian Non-alignment would mean strengthening the Indian capacity to pursue its national interest. This shift away from international preoccupations also meant a sharper definition of Indian 'interests', which were now seen to be essentially, indeed almost entirely, regional in character. Non-alignment was still a valid framework for policy-making because it was still the only approach compatible with the effort to make India an independent and respected power in the region.[87]

Following the humiliation suffered by India at the hands of the Chinese in October-November 1962 when they pushed back the Indian forces in Himalayas, it began to be pointed out that the nation's relatively unarmed foreign policy had failed to ensure the security of the country and that the policy of Non-alignment, though based on noble idealism, was no substitute for realism. What was more obvious the reverses suffered by India's armed forces had damaged India's military establishment and its image abroad.[88] The Indian foreign policy became a policy of double alignment when India began to take military aid from both the Super powers.[89] To compensate for the Sino-Indian imbalance, India sought support from the USA, USSR and Western Europe. Its great success story was its developing link with the USSR.[90] In 1963 US President Johnson sent General Maxwell Taylor to India regarding India's needs for defense aid. After this trip Taylor recommended a five-year $ 500 m programme for India for the defense plan drawn up by the Indians. The US had given supersonic aircraft F-104s to Pakistan; they were denied to India. Six Indian mountain divisions were to be equipped with better communications, transportation and air defense, for the defense of the northern frontier.

As the U.S. refused to provide F-104s, the Indians took up a Soviet alternative. The USSR agreed to provide 45 MIG-21st and to set up factories to assemble another 400.

War with Pakistan

Another shock was yet to come and it came in 1965, when the nation's much smaller neighbor, Pakistan, considered itself strong enough to mount an attack on India. Though, then India was three times the size of Pakistan and the Indians numbered five times as many as who were then Pakistanis; and though since 1962, India had been engaged in improving its defense capabilities by spending more and more on defense and by acquiring sophisticated weapons from wherever the country could get them, yet militarily, the outcome was a stalemate. But politically it represented a victory of sorts for India.[91] The Pakistani assumption that the war would spark off a rebellion in Indian-occupied Kashmir was belied. Indian Non-alignment had resulted in the USSR providing aid to India and the USA remaining neutral.

Although, Lal Bahadur Shastri succeeded in teaching Pakistan a salutary lesson in 1965, yet due to lack of political will, India surrendered her military and political gains at the Tashkent Conference.[92] The Soviet role during the war and at the Tashkent Conference, January 1966, made it clear that India no longer enjoyed a privileged position in Moscow's South Asia policy. In fact, since 1963, the Soviet leaders had been working towards achieving a balance in their policy between India and Pakistan and had achieved some success in improving their relations with Pakistan.[93] On the other hand, Pakistan's membership of the SEATO (it withdrew after the 1965 war) got it nothing. With the USA increasingly bogged down in Vietnam, it was the USSR that emerged as a truce-maker. The Soviet Prime Minister Kosygin offered his good offices in arranging talks between the Indian Prime Minister Lal Bahadur Shastri and President Ayub Khan of Pakistan. Ayub Khan accepted the position and Lal Bahadur Shastri decided it would be in the long term interest of their mutual relations to give up the two important positions it had wrested in the operations, *i.e.* Haji Pir Pass and Tithwal. The agreement was signed on January 10, 1966 and unfortunately Lal Bahadur Shastri died on January 11, 1966.[94] One of the paradoxes of the Indian misfortune in 1965 was that none of the Super Powers was willing to accord even the position of a predominant regional power.[95]

Nevertheless, one lesson that was not lost on Washington or Moscow was that the Indian military performance (in contrast to 1962) suggested that the country would soon emerge as the dominant power in South Asia. In the last years of the Johnson administration such a realisation was beginning to dawn and was expressed in policy re-examination in the State Department. The 'no arms' policy to both India and Pakistan embodied the new perception.[96] The two wars had weakened India considerably and had thus increased its dependence on others. However, the major source of foreign aid had dried up when the United States and Britain suspended both military and civilian aid as soon as the 1965 war began.

Thus, Indira Gandhi assumed the office of the Prime Minister on 24th January 1966, she not only faced serious economic problems and shortage of food grains but also the fact that both Washington and Moscow considered India a power of little consequence, a "play-thing of circumstances" which could be controlled by the big powers and "harassed by smaller countries."[97] Therefore, in the beginning of her rule, she at first tried to strengthen bonds of friendship with the US (1966 Indira-Johnson Joint statement, branding China as a threat to peace and supporting the US position in Vietnam ; 1966 devaluation of the Indian rupee etc.). But later, the compulsions at home (to defeat the rival Congress-group through leftist slogans and with communist help) and the US continued support to Pakistan, induced her to tilt her foreign policy towards the USSR.[98] In the 1968, Czechoslovakian crisis when the Russian armed forces went into action against the people in Prague, India remained quiet.

At home, the steps taken (like the bank nationalisation) and promises made, like *garibi hatao* (abolish poverty) in 1969-70 to bring about the needed socio-economic changes won her the support of the people who rallied around her in the March 1971 election. The result was that the Congress Party won 350 out of 518 Lok Sobha seats. By this time Congress was back in power in most states. Political uncertainty thus came to an end and it appeared that India had found in Prime Minister Indira Gandhi a leader who was tactful, forceful and effective enough to carry out the promised social and political reforms.[99]

These events and what happened in Pakistan between 1969 and 1971[100] made Moscow realise that the assumptions on which it had adopted the policy of equating Pakistan with India were wrong. The happenings in Pakistan made it abundantly clear that the reported Soviet view that Pakistan was more stable politically and sounder economically than India[101] had proved to be wrong. On the eve of the Bangladesh crisis, therefore, India was back in favor in Moscow.

Bangladesh Crisis

In the wake of the gruesome events in East Bengal, refugees started pouring in from all parts of East Pakistan. They literally flooded the adjoining states of Assam, Tripura and West Bengal. By the end of May 1971, 335 camps had been set up; and the refugees continued to pour in at the rate of sixty thousand a day. This created a tremendous strain on India.[102] Indira Gandhi told Parliament:

"So massive a migration, in so short a time, is unprecedented in recorded history. About three and a half million people have come into India from Bangladesh during the last eight weeks. They belong to every religious persuasion—Hindu, Muslim, Buddhist and Christian. They come from every social class and age group. They are not refugees in the sense we have understood this world since partition. They are victims of war who have sought refuge from the military terror across out frontier".[103]

The growing burden of the refugees put intolerable strain on India's meager resources. The Indian economy could not bear the burden indefinitely, nor would the people tolerate inaction for any length of time. The Opposition pressure for strong action daily mounted. However, attempts were made by Pakistan to give the tragic happenings a communal turn. Despite the emotional strain and provocations from Pakistan, India presented a picture of absolute national unity. Communal Harmony was maintained throughout the country.[104] Gradually the world opinion began to turn against Pakistan. Jayaprakash Narayan was deeply moved by the happenings in East Bengal and came out of his Sarvodaya "shell". He organised a World Conference on the issue of East Bengal in New Delhi that played an important part in moulding international opinion. Further, his tour abroad evoked good response.[105] Ultimately, Indira Gandhi assured Parliament that the Government would be guided by its own "independent assessment of the situation."[106]

Besides, there was a threat from President Nixon to the region when he ordered Kissinger to "tilt" the US actions towards Pakistan. Resentment of India's Independent attitude particularly over war in Vietnam was the cause. In this situation, India and the U.S.S.R. signed a treaty of friendship to come to the aid of each other in case either country was attacked by another.[107] Nixon's action was in contrast to

Russia's role at Tashkent in 1966 when Kosygin had maintained an equanimity and patience, which brought about peace. On the other hand, Nixon in 1971 created a threat of enlarging the risk and scope of a war by ordering the carrier Enterprise to move to the Bay of Bengal. Nixon had thus tried to use the massive armed strength of USA for a show of force.[108]

Despite political stability, increased production and healthy economy made it possible for Prime Minister Indira Gandhi to face the Bangladesh crisis with courage and determination.[109] As a result, she handled the situation tactfully—refused to be rushed into premature recognition or to be pressurised into accepting U.N. observers all along India's frontier with what was then East Pakistan; ensured Soviet support by concluding a 20-year treaty of peace, friendship and co-operation in August 1971 and led the country to victory some four months later.[110]

The emergence of Bangladesh as an independent nation has been described as "a second liberation for India", for it made the nation "more secure than it ever was"[111] and shattered all Pakistani hopes of achieving parity with India, at least in economic strength and military might. Additionally, many countries praised India's diplomacy and capability demonstrated in 1971. New Delhi was thus able to rehabilitate India's image in Asia where it began to be recognised as a great power.[112]

Following the liberation of Bangladesh, one of the major aims of Indian diplomacy was to improve India's relations with its neighbors and to make South Asia free from outside interference. For this, it was necessary to assure the sub-continent nations that India did not have expansionist designs, though it had become the dominant power in the region.

Testing Time for India's Non-alignment

By concluding the 1971 Indo-Soviet Treaty of Friendship, India's Non-alignment was put to severe test. As the August 1971, 20 year Treaty of Peace, Friendship and Co-operation with the Soviet Union initially raised many questions at home and abroad, about India's continued Non-alignment.[113] But

India managed to push aside any Western doubts and anxieties. First India had managed to insert a particular provision in the Treaty (Art. 4), which ensured the Soviet Union's continued respect for India's policy of Non-alignment. Second, the Art. IX, which provoked suspicion about the Treaty being a de facto military alliance, was treated in practice as an enabling provision for mere "consultation" in the event of a threat to the security of either nation. Third, the Treaty provided substantially for continuing economic and scientific co-operation between the two nations.[114]

Another test for India's Non-alignment came, when U.S.S.R. President Brezhnev spoke about the Soviet proposal of an Asian Collective Security system, to Members of the Indian Parliament in November 1973. Obviously, India could not have accepted such a proposal, largely because it involved a political and/or military alliance among Asian nations, including the Soviet Union, during the Cold War period. It was also the India perception, that the proposal was directed against China and the United States. The Indian response not only avoided a straight answer, it was also a highly constructive one.[115] Said Swaran Singh:

"Our own thinking is that an adherence to such principles as renunciation of the use of force, peaceful coexistence, respect for sovereignty of all countries, non-interference in internal affairs and broad development of economic and other co-operation on the basis of equality and mutual benefit will assist such a peoples".[116]

Once again, India triumphed over the suspicions and anxieties of other states and critics who thought that India had compromised its non-alignment by an alleged military alliance with a Super Power. India remained a genuinely non-aligned nation, as before.

Allegations against India's Non-alignment

Throughout the Cold War years, India was persistently buffeted by allegations, both domestic and external, that it was tilting either towards the United States, or the Soviet Union; Western propaganda was especially insistent that India was friendlier, at least towards the Soviet Union (and Warsaw Pact countries) than towards Western bloc states. In response to these criticisms, Prime Minister Indira Gandhi asserted that friendship with the Soviet Union would not be at the cost of India's friendship with any other country (the United states?).[117]

Some months later, she told the Commonwealth Conference, "it is absolutely ridiculous to suggest that we (India) are under Soviet or any other influence. We have been scrupulously trying to keep out of power rivalries and we feel that a country of our size and background cannot be in anybody's orbit."[118]

Beside, the fact of the matter was that[119]:

(1) Soviet bloc countries followed foreign policy postures parallel to India's in some respects, such as anti-colonialism, anti-racialism and promotion of economic development of the so called "Third world" and developing countries.

(2) They were very helpful to India commercially, especially by supplying military stores and sophisticated technology.

Despite this, India never conceded any favors to the Soviet bloc countries, which would compromise its non-aligned stance. Indeed, it is fair to say that it remained throughout an exemplar of Non-alignment, as it was a pioneer of policy.[120]

When Soviet military forces invaded Afghanistan in late 1970s, India was again criticised for not making a harsh reaction against the Soviet Union. The Minister for External Affairs, P.V. Narasimha Rao, told Parliament that the Government was "deeply concerned and vitally interested" in the security, independence and territorial integrity of this "traditionally friendly neighbor" (Afghanistan). "We are against the presence of foreign troops and bases in any country. We have expressed the hope, that Soviet forces would withdraw (soon) from Afghanistan." This was consistent with the policy of non-alignment.[121]

Tasks in the New Millennium and India's Non-Aligned Policy

Non-alignment, by definition, represents a global, universalist policy and outlook. It is true that some of the parameters of Non-alignment developed during the Cold War period, but it would be misplaced to think that Cold War or block politics was its sole reference point.[122] The policy of Non-alignment as formulated by Jawaharlal Nehru in 1946 was primarily meant to serve the Indian national interests and security. It is only after the July 1956 Brioni Island Conference (Yugoslavia) that the non-aligned movement as launched by Pt. Jawaharlal Nehru, Marshal Tito of Yugoslavia and Col. Gamal Abdul Nasser of Egypt and institutionalised at the Belgrade summit in 1961, was conceived in the context of the Cold War. From India's point of view the Belgrade Summit was pleasant and useful but not vital. Individual countries like India without the necessary backing of a movement could effectively pursue the non-aligned policy.[123] However, Indian leaders were quick to realise that in case a war broke out, the chances of the domestic development of their poor and backward societies would become further distant. Hence, Cold War and bloc politics were considered anti-thetical to their hopes and aspirations of better conditions of living for their people. In this way there was established an organic link between promotion of national interests and international peace. On the other hand, the policy and movement of non-alignment are enduring factors in the conduct of international relations, while Cold War and détente are transient factors. These transient, superficial vagaries of the international system and of super power relations do not affect the continuing validity and relevance of the policy and movement of Non-alignment.[124]

Beside this, what is equally significant is that, the scope of non-aligned movement's concerns has greatly expanded; they now cover practically the whole gamut of international affairs (somewhat like that of the United Nations).[125] While the other view is that the end of the Cold War and the disintegration of the Soviet Union have serious repercussions for Third World countries and, for that matter, for non-aligned movement. In fact, the end of the Cold War is a fatal blow to some Third World nations, which used to get economic and military aid either in the name of containing communism or opposing imperialism.[126] Today NAM summit meetings have been reduced to mere rituals where resolutions are adopted which have no relevance to the emerging international situation. As usual, the leaders of these countries indulge in high eloquence and empty rhetoric. Their membership has been swelling as though it is a United Nations of Third World country.[127] Even during its heyday, the non-aligned movement achieved nothing except for making some noise against imperialism, colonialism and neo-colonialism. P.M. Jawaharlal Lal Nehru, Marshal Josef Tito and President Abdul Nasser the high priests of the non-aligned movement were quick in their condemnation of both imperialism and colonialism. At the same time, they remained silent when the Soviet Union intervened and crushed democratic movements in Hungary, Poland, East Germany and Czechoslovakia. Peaceful settlement of disputes has been a major tenet of the NAM and yet, failure to comply with this tenet (and of UN Charter obligations too) on the part of some members and blatant use of force against each other (for example, Iran and Iraq) have brought a bad name for the movement. Thus its efforts to promote peaceful settlement in some cases (for example, Iran-Iraq war) have been a demonstrable failure. When hostilities broke out between India and China, the non-aligned movement remained a silent spectator. In effect, Non-alignment and the NAM have remained irrelevant to the security of non-aligned states. Therefore, a major failure of the NAM is its inability to ensure some security in all its three senses — politically, militarily and economically. When Soviet troops marched into Afghanistan, a loyal non-aligned nation, NAM did not raise a finger. The non-aligned nations had conflicts among themselves.[128]

Despite, many of the seeming failures cannot altogether be placed at the doors of the NAM. They are also the failures of the world organisation and the international community generally.[129] Just as we all desire the continuing functioning of the World Organisation, despite its limitations, so should we desire the continuance and effectiveness of the largest inter-governmental organisation next only to the World Organisation in size and in similarity of objectives. Further, the NAM can at least claim that it is the only active movement having as its regular agenda the promotion of many of those proposals and constantly urging their implementation. If they have not been achieved (or at least fully), they are not due to lack of its efforts, but some other reasons, including the international environments in which the movement has to operate unavoidably. Therefore, the future of the NAM depends only partly on its own success/failure; it depends on many other factors outside its control.[130] There is one other consideration that needs to be taken into account is assessing the future of the NAM. Many of the important objectives/demands of the NAM are of a long-term nature, such as establishing the New International Economic Order (NIEO), disarmament and the true democratisation of the international system and its functioning and so their non-fulfilment appear to be failures. Surely, no one can expect the achievement of these large, worldwide objectives in the foreseeable future. But they are worth fighting for and waiting for![131]

Rajiv Gandhi, in an address to the Ninth Non-aligned Summit at Belgrade (1989), opined, that an end to dominance was what we sought, an end to the outdated belief, that it was in any way legitimate for nations with muscle to impose any kind of hegemony-military, political or economic-other nations. We set out to persuade the world to change its worldview by bringing to a close the dangerous and ultimately self-destructive pursuit of military domination, by ending "policies of pressure in the economic sphere," and by working towards an international order in which there is no "intimidation, interference or intervention."[132] Our endeavors began in the human mind, for it is the human mind that is at once the repository of the detritus of the past and the engine of change for the future."[133] In Belgrade, at the time of first NAM summit in 1961, Jawaharlal Nehru said:

"The power of the nations assembled here is not military

power or economic power; nevertheless it is power. Call it moral force."[134]

There have been successes. There have been setbacks and the path ahead is strewn with problems.

Critical Global Issues

There is nothing legitimate about a system, which mortgages the long-term interests of all to the short-term gains of some. There is nothing legitimate about a system, which marginalises the developing countries in the management of the global economy. There is nothing legitimate about a system, which cannot offer the prospect of rapid development to the developing countries.[135] The major economic powers are determined to perpetuate their dominance over the global economy. That is not acceptable. It is the developing countries that suffer most the deleterious consequences of the structural imbalances, which afflict the world economy. They must be party, therefore, to decisions, which affect the world economy. International security rests not only on disarmament, arms reduction and confidence building. Ultimately, it must rest on the elimination of the real scourges of humankind: hunger, disease, illiteracy, poverty, exploitation, conflict and war. There is no lasting security to be found in a world segmented into the rich and the poor, the developed and the developing, North and South.

Furthermore, there are certain global problems, which are not only serious and urgent, but the rich and the industrialised nations alone cannot tackle them and they must seek the co-operation of the developing countries. These comprise the threats presented by the massive increase in international drug trafficking, environmental destruction, the regional crisis and the increase in terrorism (also state sponsored).

In concise, in the new millennium, task for a non-aligned country like India, is manifold. These are:

(a) Non-aligned movement must give substance to the political sovereignty through true economic sovereignty.

(b) Continuous struggle against domination, exploitation, war, poverty, illiteracy and women subjugation.

(c) Commitment to one world and one humanity translates into a struggle to end the iniquities of a system in which the prosperity of the prosperous is pursued in disregard of the problems of the poverty of the poor.

(d) Struggle for the establishment of a system of international economic relations based on the interdependence of the global economy, a system in which the common interest of all prevails, as much the interest of those who fall within the charmed circle of the developed countries as of those who fall without.

(e) Call for revolution, but revolution of a different kind — not to bring down those who have climbed the ladder of economic success but to enable those who remain at the bottom to climb the rungs of opportunity.

DEVELOPMENT AND SELF-RELIANCE IN ECONOMIC-FIELD

Before we can play a significant role in world politics, we have to make the home front very strong and sound, both physically and economically.[136] As Pundit Nehru has remarked that "he was in spite of his being Minister in-charge of External Affairs, interested in external affairs so much as in internal affairs, because external affair would follow internal affairs; but there was no basis for external affairs if internal affairs were wrong."[137] It is for the most part due to British imperialists, that India is so industrially backward. They have left us in a pitiable economic position. Therefore, the first and foremost problem is of economic development. To devise ways and means, to improve the living standard of teeming millions.

"Nobody can bear our burdens for us; we have to bear them ourselves," this is what, we understand by the term self-reliance, said Jawaharlal Nehru. It means paying our own way, standing on our own feet,[138] we hold ourselves responsible for our own development. At the other hand self-reliance does not mean autarchy; it does not mean isolation from the international community or the global economy. That is why we have willingly sought — and given — economic and technical co-operation. We have stressed that such co-operation can only be on terms compatible with our honor as a nation, our independence as a State and our self-reliance as an economy.[139] Thus it was realised that if India was to find her rightful place in the family of nations, she had to reduce her dependence on aid from abroad. And by the 1960s, India had achieved considerable success in its own economic development enabling it to, in turn, help other, less developed countries of the Third World. This was of course, partly due to the fact, that most of the less developed Third World countries realised that the Indian experience and intermediate technology were more relevant to their economic conditions than the experiences of developed countries using advanced technology. Thus beginning from the 1960s, India developed extensive economic co-operation with both the developed and the developing state-of-course, at different levels and in different directions; by and large, it was a beneficiary of the former as the latter was of India.[140] "This approach to our foreign policy has already paid some handsome dividends in as much as it has greatly increased the goodwill, friendship and trade between us and a large number of countries of Africa and Asia".[141] India gave extensive financial, economic and technical assistance to a large number of Asian, African[142] and other countries, including the smaller neighbors.

India played a leading role in international forums (especially in the "Group of 77", the UNCTAD and NAM Conferences) in persistently making proposals and putting forward ideas and suggestions for promoting economic co-operation between the developing and the developed countries and among the developing countries themselves. While recognizing the essential interdependence of the economies of the world, Jawaharlal Nehru described enlightened self-interest, as realizing that if some parts of the world do not progress, remain backward, they have an adverse effect on the whole economy of the world and they tend to drag down those parts that are at present prosperous.[143]

MAINTENANCE OF WORLD PEACE

Since independence, it has been India's conviction that its plans for economic development raising the living standards of its people and fulfilment of the people's aspirations cannot be achieved without both world and internal peace. Thus the maintenance and promotion of world peace became India's primary objective in world affairs. Beside, India has been an old and persistent opponent of nuclear weapons, their proliferation and all that these new weapons of mass destruction represent. This applies not just to the conduct of war but also to the maintenance of international peace and security. Nearly forty-six years ago in 1954, India's Jawaharlal Nehru was the first to bring the problem of proliferation of nuclear weapons to the attention of the world and also of the World Organisation. India was opposed to both horizontal and vertical proliferation.

Not only does India strongly and persistently oppose nuclear weapons and their proliferation, while rejecting the nuclear weapons option for itself, for years it persistently urged the development of nuclear energy for peaceful, non-military purposes. It took seriously and sincerely the propagation, by the major nuclear weapon powers themselves, the idea of developing Peaceful Nuclear Explosion (PNE) technology for use for economic and medical purposes. Nor did India object to PNEs being made by the nuclear weapon Powers.

While explaining the rationale and significance of the Indian PNE, Sardar Swaran Singh made a statement in Parliament, that, it was "a step forward" on the road to peaceful uses of nuclear energy for the welfare of the Indian people, an important landmark in the development of nuclear technology for peaceful purposes.[144]

Since India took a global view with respect to foreign policy and relations, it naturally viewed the security of the world as indivisible. It is this larger perspective that determined India's approach to peace zone proposals. It backed the UN resolution on the "Indian Ocean as a Peace Zone", because it covered and affected the large number of states on the periphery of the ocean, which had Great Power military presence. Further, India conceived of "Peace", not only in the conventional political/military senses, but also and perhaps especially, in its economic and social dimensions.[145] Peace cannot coexist with violence and tyranny, or when justice is trampled upon. The one real threat to the maintenance of peace is the problem of poverty and economic under-development.... The problem is that two-third of the human race living in areas well-endowed with natural resources and populated very often by people inheriting ancient culture and high technical skills, are wallowing in extreme poverty, while one-third of the humanity has become rich through a misdistribution of the wealth of this world.[146] The social dimension of international peace visualised by India, relates to maintenance and promotion of human rights and fundamental freedoms, in particular racial equality. India firmly believed in the equality of all human beings.

Thus, India was concerned not only with the obvious causes and symptoms of non-peace, but also with deeper, potential causes poverty, violation of human rights, racial discrimination, narrow national interests, non-commitment to the Purposes and Principals of the UN Charter and other sources of international conflict.

India regularly reiterated the need for peaceful settlement of disputes and conflict situations; avoidance of confrontation between nations; pursuit of co-operation in order to obviate the use of force by any of the parties concerned. It particularly urged, as it did in the Delhi Declaration with the Soviet Union,[147] the creation of a non-violent and non-nuclear world. The new approach to international relations enunciated in the Delhi Declaration requires a change of doctrines, policies and institutions to build and sustain a nuclear weapons free and non-violent world. This needs demilitarisation, democratisation and humanisation in international relations.[148] It expounds the new world order, which India at least envisages in the post-Cold War era.

Furthermore, peace demands and end to the fanning of conflicts by proxy. Peace means an end to terrorism, whether by States or individuals. Peace requires the diversion of resources from armaments to development. Peace needs a world freed of the menace of drugs. Peace demands a wholesome environment and the conservation of nature's gifts to life on planet Earth.

WORKING FOR DISARMAMENT

Indian foreign policy was based on non-violence and truth, as enunciated by Mahatma Gandhi and Jawaharlal Nehru. These, of course, are moral principles that when translated into political terms, mean disarmament and open diplomacy.[149] For years, India has been in the forefront of the campaign for general and complete disarmament, both in India and in many forums abroad — the United Nations, the NAM conferences, the Commonwealth forum and so on. For years, it has repeatedly expressed dissatisfaction with the poor progress in any international disarmament measure; while, on the contrary, the armaments race was constantly spiraling upwards, with grave consequences to world peace and economy.[150] The NPT had failed to arrest the growth of nuclear armaments either qualitatively or quantitatively. In addition, India has been opposed for years to the development, production and stockpiling of chemical weapons. India has also been for years urging the holding of a World Disarmament Conference.

DISARMAMENT: MEANING

In a general sense, it connotes the idea of the limitation or control or reduction of armaments. It acquires a definitive meaning only when some adjective is added to it. For disarmament may be unilateral/multilateral, general/local, total/partial, and controlled/uncontrolled.

- *Qualitative disarmament.* This refers to the limitation or prohibition of only certain types of weapons.
- *Quantitative disarmament.* This refers to the control of the weapons of all categories.
- *eneral disarmament* . When all or most of the great powers participate but not necessarily with a commitment to do away with all types of weapons.
- *m re ensive disarmament* . This refers to the control or prohibition of all armaments of all categories. It is also called total disarmament .
- *tal disarmament* . It implies the ultimate achievement of a world order in which all human and material

instrumentalities of warfare will have been abolished. There will be no weapon of any kind whatsoever. Armies would be completely disbanded. Military training centers, war ministries and ordnance factories will also be closed.

Therefore, it is clear that in a generic sense, disarmament may mean anything from a simple limitation to complete abolition of armaments. But it is to be noted that disarmament is concerned with the reduction or abolition of only existing weapons. And weapons technology is always on the move and this movement is likely to lead to the development of new types of armaments. The criterion of reduction/abolition cannot be applied to those weapons, which may be developed in future. In fact the term disarmament does not cover control of the weapons of the future. This control is designated by the expression — arms control. Therefore, disarmament refers to the control of existing weapons and arms control to that of future weapons. In other words, disarmament seeks to control armaments, while arms control tries to check arms race.

From the point of view of international peace, disarmament and arms control are complementary to each other. As the mere reduction or abolition of existing weapons would not serve the basic purpose of peace if nations are allowed to acquire new and improved types of weapons in future. The purpose of disarmament is to deprive nations of the very instruments of fighting. The only direct cause of war admissible in disarmament approach is the existence of armaments. Armaments cause war, while disarmament leads to international peace.

Quincy Wright has, however, a different opinion, in this regard. He says disarmament probably tend to increase the frequency of war. For, if states are lightly armed, they may regard war as a manageable instrument of policy. What led to First and Second World War was not the armament competition, but the lack of it.

Arguments in favor of disarmament:

(1) It promotes international security and reduces international tension.

(2) It promotes economic prosperity.

(3) It promotes moral objective.

In theoretical terms, there can be conflict between the security, economic and moral objectives. For, there can be a disarmament policy, which guarantees economic prosperity and is in conformity with moral principles but which may not ensure security. Further, the concept of national security, national prosperity and national morality differs from nation to nation. But today the prime need is international peace and disarmament is viewed as a step in that direction. Therefore, primary basis of disarmament is the concern for avoidance of war. Human survival is much more important than economic prosperity and moral values. Disarmament has to be accepted at least as an element of the solution of the problem of war and as a necessary condition of the evolution of a peaceful international order. Armaments cause war, not that war is caused by armaments. Disarmament can prevent wars that arise from armaments but other ways would be required for preventing wars emanating from other sources. Since peace is a matter of avoidance of all kinds of wars, disarmament is only a partial solution of the problem of war.

Disarmament: Different Ways

Disarmament can be done in three ways:

(a) Gradual disarmament in agreement with other nations.

(b) Total disarmament in agreement with other nations.

(c) Total disarmament by a single nation (Unilateral disarmament).

On one hand unilateral disarmament may pave the way for others to follow suit, on the other it may also mean national suicide. Actually the idea of unilateral disarmament is linked to the idea of non-violent defense. For a nation disarming unilaterally will have to take care of the problem of how to deal with aggression. The problem of non-violent defense is the problem of finding out an alternative to war that could replace war as a means of defending freedom and as a way of life against tyranny and aggression. This alternative has to be capable of providing the necessary protection without military armaments. In fact, unilateral disarmament does not ignore the problem of defense, but insists that defense should be sought by a non-military policy. Therefore, what the world needs today is not only disarmament but also what Theodor Ebert calls 'transarmament' by which is meant a complete change from a military defense system to a non-military defense system. This is what Gene Sharp calls a 'third approach'. However, a complete strategy of non-violent defense is yet to be developed. In any case, unilateral disarmament has to be logically followed by transarmament.

Major Steps towards Disarmament

More serious and consistent efforts for disarmament were made after First World War. The important function of League of Nations was 'the reduction of national armaments to the lowest point consistent with national safety'. In Paris Peace Conference 1919, disarmament was declared to have been one of the 'war aims' of the Allies. Which means to apply the principle of disarmament effectively to the states defeated in the war. Under the treaty of Peace, Germany, Austria, Hungary and Bulgaria accepted an immense reduction and rigid limitation on their armed forces. The forcible disarmament of the vanquished by the victors was not new. In 1808 Napoleon had also compelled Prussia to limit her army to 42000 men for ten years. But in 1919 it was carried out more completely than ever before.

World Disarmament Conference was organised in 1932 and was attended by representatives of 61 states. Germany withdrew from Conference and also from League of Nations. Conference met intermittently for sometime. But in 1934, UK acknowledged that disarmament was not practicable and that she would increase her own armament. However, efforts for naval disarmament outside the framework of League also continued. Washington Conference held in 1927, was a success in bringing about a limitation in battleships and battle cruisers. There was London Agreement in 1930. But with the withdrawal of Germany from the League and the failure of Disarmament

Conference, Europe slide back to the pre-war days of unrestricted arms competition.

After Second World War, hopes, however again rose about general disarmament. Great powers agreed on the basic principle for disarmament. Provisions for disarmament were written into the UN charter signed on 26 June 1945. On 11 January 1952, UN Disarmament Commission was established by General Assembly. In 1960 Ten-Power Conference, consisting of 5 western powers and 5 members of Soviet bloc, was convened, but Soviet delegate broke up the conference. Then Disarmament Commission was expanded by General Assembly in 1961 from 10 to 18 nations, to include 8 non-aligned nations, like-Brazil, India, Ethiopia, Mexico, Nigeria, Sweden, and United Arab Republic. In 1969, the membership of disarmament commission increased from 18 to 26, in order to ensure better geographical and political distribution. It was renamed, Conference of the Committee on Disarmament.

The protracted post-war disarmament negotiations produced a limited agreement in 1963. It was signed by US, Soviet Union and Britain. They sought to prohibit the nuclear tests and as such, this treaty came to be known as the test ban treaty. Apart from three principal powers India was among the first countries to sign this treaty. 8 NAM countries of the Disarmament Commission made a notable contribution to the conclusion of test ban treaty. The 'principal aim' of treaty was the speediest possible achievement of an agreement on general and complete disarmament under strict international control. Preamble to the treaty acknowledges the fact that nuclear tests contaminate man's environment by radioactivity. Para-2 of Article 1 imposes an obligation on each of parties "to refrain from causing, encouraging or in any way participating in the carrying out of any nuclear weapon test explosion or any other nuclear explosion." It, however, permits the underground explosion, but with certain limitations. Underground explosions are permissible only if they do not cause radioactive debris to spread outside the territorial limits of a state. Therefore, theoretically speaking, the treaty permits the continuance of underground tests.

The disarmament negotiations after 1963 treaty have shown that world powers are interested more in nuclear non-proliferation than general and complete disarmament. US advocated a program for nuclear non-proliferation and a draft of Non-Proliferation Treaty (NPT) was submitted to UN in 1968. India had been opposed to this treaty because it did not specify any guarantee for her security against China — a nuclear power and it would prevent India from developing nuclear energy for peaceful purpose for which she was sufficiently equipped because of her being in an advanced state of nuclear research. NPT was open for sign in 1968 and came into force in 1970. Besides, efforts have been made to control the use of nuclear and conventional weapons through Strategic Arms Reduction Treaties (START).

With India's initiative, a meeting of the heads of states/ governments representing Argentina, Greece, Mexico, Sweden, Tanzania and India was convened at New Delhi on 28 July 1985. This meeting attended by, among others, the distinguished African statesman and former Tanzanian President, Julius Neyerere, launched what came to be known as the Six-Nation-Five-Continent Initiative on Nuclear disarmament. The Initiative, urged the nuclear weapons states to halt testing and to conclude an early comprehensive test-ban treaty. It also called for prohibition of development and use of all weapons in space. It urged that outer space must be used for the benefit of mankind as a whole — not as a future battleground.[151] Later on, regular meetings took place on nuclear disarmament in different places. Even while pursuing multilateral effort, bilaterally India and Soviet Union urged the need for "a Nuclear-Weapons-free" and non-violent world order. In Delhi-Declaration (1986), specific and immediate action for disarmament was spelt out.

Beside, with the efforts of Rajiv Gandhi a time-bound Action Plan for general and complete disarmament, was submitted to the Special Session on Disarmament of the United Nations General Assembly. The essential features of the Action Plan are:

- *First*. There should be a binding commitment by all nations to eliminating nuclear weapons, in stages, by the year 2010 at the latest.
- *Second*. All nuclear weapon States must participate in the process of nuclear disarmament. All other countries must also be part of the process.
- *Third*. To demonstrate good faith and build the required confidence, there must be tangible progress at each stage towards the common goal.
- *Fourth*. Changes are required in doctrines, policies and institutions to sustain a world free of nuclear weapons. Negotiations should be undertaken to establish a comprehensive Global Security System under the aegis of the United Nations.

The heart of the Action Plan is the elimination of all nuclear weapons, in three stages.

In 1996, comprehensive test ban treaty (CTBT) came into existence. But India refused to sign it, on the ground of its being discriminatory.

Thus, we see that, although disarmament is one of those phenomena of international politics, which are mooted as solutions to problems but became problems themselves. As the efforts made in this direction show how difficult has been the achievement of a state of disarmament.

PEACEFUL CO-EXISTENCE OF NATIONS

An inevitable corollary to Non-alignment is non-interference. A nation, which does not belong to a multi-military alliance, usually does not wish to interfere in affairs of other nations and, in turn, this attitude generates mutual tolerance. This leads to Co-existence and when nations co-exist for some time they begin to display an element of dynamic co-existence. By dynamic so-existence is meant that nations take active steps to forge co-operation first in non-political matters such as trade, commerce and cultural exchanges and later on this blunts the edges of political differences.[152]

This element of India's foreign policy has consistently

remained the same in all the years since independence. In a sense, the pursuit of this element was/is unavoidable for a country like India. Both politically and in other respects, India has remained a highly pluralistic society and therefore its external policy as well as the domestic one calls for harmonisation of the outlook and interests of its diverse population. This is not only a desirable policy, but also unavoidable in an interdependent world — self-isolation no longer being a foreign policy option for the vast number of states. As both Pt. Jawaharlal Nehru and Indira Gandhi used to say, 'the alternative to peaceful co-existence among nations is co-destruction.[153]

"Unless there is genuine acceptance of the principle of peaceful co-existence, the desire to live and let live and the determination to convert Cold War confrontation into competitive co-operation, the process of detente will not show the desired results,"[154] observed Indian Foreign Minister.

Thus in the Indian view, peaceful co-existence compels tolerance of differing perspectives. "In a world of great diversities, it is obvious that tolerance of differing view points and understanding of each others perceptions could alone constitute the general basis for amicable relations and co-operation among nations" — in an increasingly interdependent society.[155]

Asian Identity

One of the issues, intermittently raised with respect to India's foreign policy/relations (usually at a non-official level), is India's possible role in promoting an intra-Asian forum through which an "Asian identity," and intra-Asian co-operation is established.

In this regard, the question of India doing something about developing an "Asian identity" was raised in Indian Parliament in April 1975. The then Minister for External Affairs Y.B. Chavan, acknowledged the absence of institutional arrangements for consultations among Asian countries to promote their interests and said that they were "exploring various avenues to foster a sense of identity." But, he added, "you cannot force the pace; there are certain regional and internal contradictions", which cannot forcibly be solve.[156] India, too, like other Asian nations, has not made any serious effort to pursue this larger objective.

Regionalism

India has always been a votary of regional co-operation in South Asia. The Bangladesh proposal for a South Asian regional organisation was welcomed by India. At the inauguration of the South Asian Association for Regional Co-operation in New Delhi in August 1983, Prime Minister Indira Gandhi stated that India, as a matter of policy, did not want to interfere in the affairs of its neighbors, she stressed that whatever happened in any country within the region would affect the affairs of other countries, either individually or collectively. She emphasised that our co-operation in no way limits each others freedom of judgment. The co-operation was only aimed at development and strengthening of the economies of its members. India was not, she said, oblivious of differences among the nations of the South Asian region; these ought to be resolved by peaceful means.[157]

SUPPORT TO, AND STRENGTHENING OF, INTERNATIONAL ORGANISATIONS

The United Nations

India has been a founder member of most of the international organisations, especially the United Nations and its Specialised Agencies (as it was earlier of the League of Nations). Consequently support to, and strengthening of the World Organisation is an important element of India's foreign policy. The principal purpose of India's foreign policy *vis-à-vis* the United Nations is to pursue three closely related goals:[158]

(1) A significant role in the shaping of international relations in 21st century.

(2) A movement towards a non-violent and humane international system and

(3) The promotion of conditions for a sustainable and relatively equitable pattern of international development.

Like most others, India has had its share of disappointments and frustrations regarding the functioning of the Organisation, its limitations and the constraints under which it operates. It has learnt to recognise these from its own, rather bitter, experience with respect to the handling of the Kashmir question by the Organisation since 1948. Other disappointments have been the way the Organisation handled the Hyderabad question in 1948, the Goa question in 1961, even the 1971 Bangladesh question and the Ganga water dispute with Bangladesh in 1974.

Despite all this, India has remained a steadfast supporter of the United Nation and its family of institutions.

India's, Vijayalkshmi Pundit was elected, President of the UN General Assembly as early as 1953. India is one of the few countries, which got elected six times as a non-permanent member of the UN Security Council. It sought to prevent the World Organisation from being misused as an instrument of Great Power politics. India played a notable role in the peaceful settlement of many disputes and conflict situations. India was for years a major participant in UN Peace-keeping operations.[159] India became first chairman of the Committee on Decolonisation (1962). India played a leading role in the promotion of colonial self-determination of peoples. Also India was the first chairman of the Economic and Social Council (ECOSOC). Further, securing a permanent seat in the Security Council is the easiest way for India to expand its influence within the UN system. It is also clear that the expansion of the Security Council will not be easy and even if it happens, India will not be an automatic choice.[160] Japan, Germany, Brazil, Nigeria are also there. India has always been in the forefront of reforming the UN system in order to strengthen it and to make it more effective.

The reason for India's continuing support to the organisation, despite disappointments and frustrations, is that the Purpose/Principles of the Organisation broadly reflect the goals and objectives of India's foreign policy.

The Commonwealth

India has been a founder member of the Modern Commonwealth of Nations since 1949. It is because of India's decision to become a Republic on 26 January 1950 and its desire to still continue association with the Commonwealth,[161] that the modern Commonwealth ceased to be a British entity, and became a multiracial, multicultural, independent association of nations.

Despite intermittent changes in the composition and functioning of the Commonwealth association, and India's non-aligned role in world affairs (and domestic political changes too), India maintained its Commonwealth membership. It remained for India, a supplementary forum for playing an appropriate role in world affairs and for promoting the goals of India's foreign policy (and in the relations of other members of the Commonwealth, including India's neighbors, Pakistan,[162] Bangladesh, Sri Lanka and the Maldives). India, for instance, regularly used the Commonwealth forum for carrying on its crusade against South Africa's apartheid. Membership of the Commonwealth also helped India maintain with the United Kingdom some (attenuated) old, historical pre-independent) links of affinity and links of advantage.

Beside, these explicit elements in India's foreign policy, there are some implicit, innate elements, embodied in India's tradition, values, culture and civilisation, that constitute foundation stone and are inner values of India's foreign policy. The continuity of Indian civilisation has been based on an implicit recognition of the entire gamut of values comprised in the single word "non-violence." The roots of the Indian concept of non-violence lie in the philosophy of the Buddha, further developed by Indian civilisation over the last 2500 years. The philosophy of non-violence originated in Indian civilisation as a moral precept for individual conduct. That is the reason why India represented a new point of departure in history. This was the first time ever that history had seen non-violence used successfully as a political instrument. Further the continuing theme of Indian civilisation has been synthesis, that is, the fusing of numerous cultures into a composite culture, where individual identities are retained while common traits are shared. It has bred in our thought processes a sense of **tolerance.** While, more than any other single factor, it is the

Indian tradition, which has enabled her to face contemporary challenges.

In a broadcast made during a visit to the United States, Jawaharlal Nehru said:

"I have become more and more convinced that so long as we do not recognise the supremacy of the moral law in our national and international relations, we shall have no enduring peace. So long as we do not adhere to right means, the end will not be right and fresh evil will flow from it. That was the essence of Gandhiji's message."[163]

While Nehru's vision of India encompassed India's millennial past and looked out to a millennial future. It was not conditioned by immediate problems and immediate concerns. Rather, it drew its inspiration from the essential continuities of India's civilisation. When Nehru looked to the future, he visualised resurgent India as giving the moral leadership to the world, of leading the world in thought and philosophy, in culture and the arts, in science and technology, in equality and justice, in human dignity and human rights, in morality in public life and probity in personal conduct.[164]

Notes

1. Ram Manohar Lohia, 'India's Foreign Policy' in Verinder Grover (Ed.): *International Relations and Foreign Policy of India*. Vol. 1, Deep & Deep Publication, New Delhi, 1992.
2. R.P. Saraf (Ed.), *Political and Social Realities in Modern India*, Indian Bibliographics Bureau Co-Publisher Balaji Enterprises, Delhi, 1990.
3. K.P. Saksena, *India's Foreign Policy: The Decision making process, International Studies*, Vol. 33, No. 4, 1996, Sage Publications, New Delhi.
4. Sahdev Vohra, 'India's Foreign Relations Part-I', *U.S.I. Journal*, Vol. CXXVI, No. 525, July-Sept. 1996.
5. For details see *Asian Relations Conference*, 1947, Inaugural Address.
6. *World Focus*, 'India at Forty', Vol. 8, No. 11-12, Nov.-Dec. 1987.
7. Khilnani, Niranjan M., *New Dimensions of Indian Foreign Policy*, Westvill Publishing House, New Delhi, 1995.
8. Sachidanand Murty, *Indian Foreign Policy*, Calcutta, 1964, pp. 197-200.

9. K. Shridharani, "The philosophical Bases of India's Foreign Policy", *India Quarterly*, XIV, 1958-II, p. 197.
10. J. Bandyopadhyaya, *The Making of India's Foreign Policy*, New Delhi, 1980.
11. S.N. Mishra, *India — The Cold War Years*, South Asian Publishers Pvt. Ltd., New Delhi, 1994.
12. Nikhil Chakarvarty, "Evolution of Foreign Policy", in *World Focus* Nov-Dec. 1987.
13. See N.D. Tiwari, *Foreign Affairs Record*, New Delhi, Vol. 33, 1987, p. 167.
14. Khilnani, Niranjan M., *New Dimensions of Indian Foreign Policy*, Westvill Publishing House, New Delhi, 1995.
15. Mohit Sen, "Non-alignment and Non-bloc Politics," *World Focus*, 1989.
16. K.P. Misra, 'Foreign Policy Planning in India', in K.P. Misra (Ed.) : *Foreign Policy of India*, Thompson Press, New Delhi, 1977 and S. Tharoor: "Reasons of State", Vikas, New Delhi, 1982.
17. S. Gopal, 'Crusader for world peace', *World Focus*, 1989.
18. Geography and history, however, ensure that regional affairs receive priority in the affairs of most nations. Since the sixties India has found this true.
19. M.S. Rajan (Ed.), *India's Foreign Policy during Nehru Era*, Asia, 1976.
20. S.N. Misra, *India — The Cold War Years*, South Asian Publishers Pvt. Ltd. , New Delhi, 1994.
21. *Ibid.*
22. Mohit Sen, 'Indira Gandhi's Role,' *World Focus*, Nov.-Dec., 1987.
23. Girish Mathur, 'NAM and South-South co-operation,' in *World Focus*, Nov.-Dec., 1986.
24. *Ibid.*
25. Inder Malhotra, 'Harare To Belgrade,' in *World Focus*, June 1989.
26. Khilnani, Niranjan M., *New Dimensions of Indian Foreign Policy*, Westvill Publishing House, New Delhi, 1995.
27. Urmila Phadnis, 'Non-alignment as a factor in Ceylon's foreign policy', *International Studies*, April, 1962, p. 425.
28. C. Muraleedharan, 'Non-alignment at the summits,' *Kerala Journal of Political Studies*, Vol. I, 1986, p. 55.
29. *Foreign Affairs Record*, Vol. 22, 1976, p. 238.

30. M.S. Rajan, 'The Goals of India's Foreign Policy', *International Studies*, Vol. 35, No. 1, 1998.
31. A.Z. Rubinstein, 'Does Non-alignment have a future?', *The Non-Aligned World*, July–September 1984, p. 396.
32. Achin Vanaik, "The Painful Transition, Bourgeois Democracy in India", Verso, London, 1990.
33. Sahdev Vohra, "India's Foreign Relations Part-I", *U.S.I. Journal*, Vol. CXXVI, No. 525, July–September, 1996.
34. *Foreign Affairs Record*, Vol. 23, 1977, p. 97.
35. S.N. Misra, *India — The Cold War Years*, South Asian Publishers Pvt. Ltd., New Delhi, 1994.
36. Jagat Mehta, 'Non-alignment — A spent force', *Seminar*, July 1983, p. 59.
37. *Ibid.*
38. Compare from India which followed Non-alignment with the policy of co-operation.
39. Khilnani, Niranjan M., *New Dimensions of Indian Foreign Policy*, Westvill Publishing House, New Delhi, 1995.
40. *Ibid.*
41. H.D. Ghoshal, *International Relations*, Unique Publishers, 1996, p. 202.
42. M.G. Gupta, *Indian Foreign Policy — Theory and Practice*, Y.K. Publishers, Agra, 1985, pp. 106.
43. H.D. Ghoshal, *International Relations*, Unique Publishers, 1996, p. 202.
44. Sahdev Vohra, 'India's foreign Relations Part-I', *U.S.I. Journal*, Vol. 126, No. 525, July–September, 1996.
45. *Ibid.*
46. Besides, she has cultural and commercial relations on a very wide scale. She is one of the most enthusiastic members of the U.N. She is part of the Commonwealth of nations. She is one of the five Colombo Powers and plays a major role in the Afro-Asian organisations. She is the acknowledged leader of NAM. The solid basis of all this is not isolationism but co-operation.
47. Jagat. S. Mehta, 'Forty Years of Foreign Policy' in Verinder Grover (Ed.): *International Relations and Foreign Policy of India*, Vol. 1, Deep & Deep Publication, New Delhi 1992.
48. M.G. Gupta, *Indian Foreign Policy — Theory and Practice*, Y.K. Publishers, Agra, 1985, pp. 95-96.
49. *Ibid.*, p. 97.

50. The Cold War era began immediately after the II World War. Charles O' Lerche, an analyst of the Cold War era, had divided the period into four distinct phases and each phase had distinct crisis situations having all the requirements to usher in a global confrontation –- (1). Berlin Blockade of 1948 (2). Korean War (1950) (3) Suez Crisis, (1956)(4) Congo Problem (1960). Since India was a new entrant into the world scene in the late 1940. The Berlin Blockade was not a problem effecting India's Immediate interests. That was a peripheral issue.
51. *The Hindu*, Madras, 23.10.1956.
52. S.N. Misra, *India — The Cold War Years*, South Asian Publishers Pvt. Ltd., New Delhi, 1994.
53. *Journal of the United Service Institution of India*, Vol. 126, No. 525, July–September, 1996.
54. K.P. Karunakaran, *India in World Affairs*, New Delhi, 1958, p. 102.
55. J.S. Kundra, *Indian Foreign Policy*, 1950-54, Groningen, 1955, p. 128.
56. S. Bhattacharya, "Pursuit of National Interest through Neutralism", Calcutta, 1968, p. 83.
57. *U.S.I. Journal*, Vol. 126, No. 525, July-September, 1996, p. 347.
58. See *Year Book of the UN*, New York, 1952, pp. 209-10.
59. S.N. Misra, *India – The Cold War Years*, South Asian Publishers Pvt. Ltd., New Delhi, 1994.
60. Blema Steinberg, 'The Korean War — A Case Study in Indian Nationalism', Orbis VIII, Winter, 1965.
61. S.N. Misra, *India — The Cold War Years*, South Asian Publishers Pvt. Ltd., New Delhi, 1994.
62. J. Dasgupta and J.K. Ray, *The Web of International Relations*, Calcutta, 1961.
63. S. Bhattacharya, "Pursuit of National Interest through Neutralism", Calcutta, 1968, p. 90.
64. F.L. Schuman, *International Politics*, New York, 1962.
65. *Lok Sabha Debates*, Vol. 9, Pt. II, No. 3, Cols. 260-267.
66. W.F.V. Eckelen, 'India's Foreign Policy and the Border Dispute with China', *The Hague*, 1964, p. 71.
67. Bahman Amini, India's Foreign Policy with Particular Reference to Asia and Africa (unpublished thesis), cited in S. Bhattacharya: 'Pursuit of National Interest through Neutralism', Calcutta, 1968, p. 93.
68. *Asian Recorder* (I), 1956, 994-95.

69. S. Bhattacharya, 'Pursuit of National Interest through Neutralism', Calcutta, 1968, p. 98.
70. P.R. Sarbadhikari, *India and Great Powers*, Calcutta, 1962, p. 44.
71. Sahdev Vohra, 'India's Foreign Relations Part-I,' in *Journal of the United Service Institution of India*, Vol. 126, No. 525, July–September, 1996.'
72. S.N. Misra, *India — The Cold War Years*, South Asian Publishers Pvt. Ltd., New Delhi, 1994.
73. *Ibid.*
74. Marc Lee, "The United Nations and World Realities", London, 1965, p. 119.
75. S. Bhattacharya, "Pursuit of National Interest through Neutralism", Calcutta, 1968, p. 108.
76. *Ibid.*, p. 110.
77. S.N. Misra, *India — The Cold War Years*, South Asian Publishers Pvt.Ltd., New Delhi, 1994.
78. *Ibid.*, p. 244.
79. *Ibid.*
80. E. Lefever, 'Crisis in Congo: A UN force in Action', Brookings, 1965.
81. *Ibid.*, p. 107.
82. *Ibid.*
83. Khilnani, Niranjan M., *New Dimensions of Indian Foreign Policy*, Westvill Publishing House, New Delhi, 1995.
84. Achin Vanaik, *The Painful Transition — Bourgeois Democracy in India*, Verso, London, 1990.
85. Sahdev Vohra, India's Foreign Relations Part-I', *U.S.I. Journal*, Vol. 126, No. 525, July-September, 1996.
86. Achin Vanaik, 'India in the World' in *The Painful Transition*, Verso, London, 1990.
87. *Ibid.*
88. Vijay Sen Budhraj, 'Indian Foregin Policy' in Verinder Grover (Ed.) : *India's Foreign Policy and International Relations*, Vol. 1, Deep & Deep Publication, New Delhi, 1992.
89. R.P. Saraf (Ed.), 'Indian Diplomacy-cum-Defence', in *Political and Social Realities in Modern India*, Indian Bibliographies Bureau, Delhi, 1990.
90. Achin Vanaik, 'India in the World', *The Painful Transition*, Verso, London 1990.

91. *Ibid.*
92. Khilnani, N.M., *New Dimensions of Indian Foreign Policy*, Westvill Publishing House, New Delhi, 1995.
93. Vijay Sen Budhraj, 'Indian Foreign Policy — The Indira Gandhi Era', in Verinder Grover (Ed.) *India's Foreign Policy & International Relations*', Vol.1, Deep & Deep Publication, New Delhi, 1992.
94. Sahdev Vohra, 'India's Foreign Relations Part-I', in *U.S.I. Journal*, Vol. 126, No. 525, July–September, 1996.
95. Even for this India had to wait for six years, when in 1971 both the US President Richard Nixon and his versatile Secretary of State Henry Kissinger recognised India as a regional power and thus made her the custodian of peace and stability in the region of South Asia.
96. Achin Vanaik, *The Painful Transition*, Verso, London, 1990, p. 239.
97. Vijay Sen Budhraj, 'Indian Foreign Policy — The Indira Gandhi Era', in Verinder Grover (Ed.): *India's Foreign Policy & International Relations*, Vol. 1, Deep & Deep Publication, New Delhi, 1992.
98. Madhu Limaye, "Problems of India's Foreign Policy", Edited by Dr. N.C. Mehrotra, Atma Ram & Sons, Delhi, 1984.
99. Vijay Sen Budhraj, 'Indian Foreign Policy — The Indira Gandhi Era', in Verinder Grover (Ed.) *India's Foreign Policy & International Relations*, Vol. 1, Deep & Deep Publication, New Delhi, 1992.
100. Anti-Ayub Khan demonstrations in Pakistan in 1968-69 which ultimately led to his decision to step aside on 25 March 1969, in favour of General Yahya Khan, imposition of martial law, the results of the first general election held in December 1970 and the decision of the military junta to crush the demand for autonomy in March 1971 in what was then East Pakistan.
101. For details, see Vijay Sen Bhudhraj: "Soviet Russia and Hindustan Sub-continent", Bombay, 1973, pp. 189-90.
102. Madhu Limaye, 'Problems of India's Foreign Policy', Edited by Dr. N.C. Mehrotra, Atma Ram & Sons, Delhi, 1984.
103. *The Years of Endeavour: Selected Speeches of Indira Gandhi*, p. 526.
104. Madhu Limaye, "Problems of India's Foreign Policy", Edited by Dr. N.C. Mehrotra, Atma Ram & Sons, Delhi, 1984.
105. *Ibid.*, p. 116.
106. *Ibid.*, p. 118.
107. Sahdev Vohra, 'India's Foreign Relations Part-I', *U.S.I.* Journal, Vol. 126, No. 525, July-September, 1996, p. 350.
108. *Ibid.*
109. Vijay Sen Budhraj, ' Indian Foreign Policy: The Indira Gandhi Era', in

Verinder Grover (Ed.): *India's Foreign Policy and International Relations,*' Vol. 1 Deep & Deep Publication, New Delhi, 1992.

110. *Ibid.*, p. 346.

111. Pran Chopra, 'India's Second Liberation', Delhi, 1973, pp. 3-4.

112. Vijay Sen Budhraj, 'Indian Foreign Policy; The Indira Gandhi Era' in Verinder Grover (Ed.): *India's Foreign Policy & International Relations*, Vol. 1, Deep & Deep Publication, New Delhi, 1992.

113. See Appadorai and Rajan, *India's Foreign Policy and Relations*, New Delhi, 1988, p. 250.

114. M.S. Rajan, *The Goals of India's Foreign Policy in International Studies*; 35, 1, 1998, Sage Publications, New Delhi.

115. For details, see A. Appadorai and M.S. Rajan: *India's Foreign Policy and Relations*, New Delhi, 1988, pp. 569-74.

116. *FAR*, Vol. 19, 1973, pp. 512-13.

117. *FAR*, Vol. 20, 1974, p. 52.

118. *FAR*, Vol. 21, 1975, pp. 116-18, See *FAR*, Vol. 24 ,1980, p. 191, See also A.P. Thornton: "The security of South Asia: Analysis and Speculation", in Stephen Cohen (Ed.): *The Security of South Asia*, New Delhi, 1987, p. 218. Rajeshwar Dayal, "The Super Power and India," Seminar, New Delhi, Feb. 1980, pp. 12-17, says he : "India's relations with Super Powers have been rather like those of a capricious and reluctant damsel towards the jealous lovers the one impetuous and immature, the other ardent exigent," p. 12.

119. M.S. Rajan, *International Studies*, 31, 1, 1998, p. 79.

120. *Ibid.*, p. 80.

121. See. *FAR*, Vol. 24, 1980 p. 19.

122. *World Focus*, May 1990.

123. A.K. Damodaran (Ed.), 'NAM: The Road Ahead,' In Indian Foreign Policy, Vol. 1, *FSI*, New Delhi, 1997.

124. *World Focus*, May 1990.

125. *World Focus*, June 1989.

126. A.G. Naidu, India and the New World Order,' in K. Raman (Ed.): *Indian Foreign Policy in the* 1990s,' Pillai, Radient Publishers, New Delhi, 1997.

127. *Ibid.*

128. *Ibid.*

129. M.S. Rajan, 'NAM—Still Very Relevant, *World Focus*, May 1990.

130 . *Ibid.*

131. *Ibid.*

132. M.K. Rasgotra (Ed.), *Rajiv Gandhi's Worldview,'* Vikas Publishing House Pvt. Ltd., 1991.
133. *Ibid.*
134. *Ibid.*
135. *Ibid.*
136. T.B. Mukherjee, 'India's Foreign Policy' in Verinder Grover (Ed.) : *Introduction to India's Foreign Policy & International Relations*, Vol.1, Deep & Deep Publication, New Delhi, 1992.
137. *Modern Review*, March, 1948, p. 184.
138. M.K. Rasgotra (Ed.), *Rajiv Gandhi's Worldview*, Vikas Publishing House Pvt. Ltd., 1991.
139. *Ibid.*
140. M.S. Rajan, "The Goals of India's Foreign Policy", *International Studies*, 35, 1, 1998.
141. *FAR*, Vol. 19, 1973, p.165.
142. In 1983, India gave to African countries assistance of about Rs. 570 crores.
143. M.K. Rasgotra (Ed.), *Rajiv Gandhi's Worldview*, Vikas Publishing House Pvt. Ltd., 1991.
144. M.S. Rajan, 'The Goals of India's Foreign Policy', *International Studies*, 35, 1, 1998.
145. *Ibid.*
146. *FAR*, Vol. 23, 1977.
147. *FAR*, Vol. 32, 1986, pp. 380-82.
148. *FAR*, Vol. 34, 1988, p. 382.
149. Hugh H. Smythe, 'Nehru and Indian Foreign Policy, in Verinder Grover (Ed): *Introduction to India's Foreign Policy & International Relation*, Vol.1, Deep & Deep Publication, New Delhi, 1992.
150. See, for example, the lengthy statement of Ambassador P.K. Banerjee to the *Conference of the Committee on Disarmament*, Geneva, 12 Apr. 1973, *FAR*, Vol. 19, 1973, p. 150.
151. Text in *FAR*, Vol. 31, 1985, pp. 8-10.
152. Khilnani, N.M., *New Dimensions of Indian Foreign Policy*, Westville Publishing House, New Delhi, 1995.
153. M.K. Rasgotra (Ed.), *Rajiv Gandhi's World View*, Vikas Publishing House Pvt. Ltd, 1991.
154. *FAR*, Vol. 24, 1978, pp. 124-25.
155. *FAR*, Vol. 28, 1982, p. 208. Excerpts from P.V. Narasimha Rao's *Speech to Parliament* on 13 Aug. 1982.

156. *FAR*, Vol. 28, 1975, pp. 138-39
157. Asian Recorder, Vol. 29, 1983, p. 17316.
158. Amitabh Mattoo, 'India and the United Nations', in *Indian Foreign Policy*, Vol. 1, 1997.
159. However, Paul Diehl, an American scholar has recently identified 16 different types of interventions under the rubric of "Peacekeeping" in "A Taxonomy of Peacekeeping", a lecture delivered at the School of International Studies, Jawaharlal Nehru University, Feb. 3, 1997.
160. Although even in the *UN Conference at San Francisco*, 1945, some other nations raised the issue of making India as permanent member of the Security Council.
161. See M.S. Rajan, "India and the Commonwealth," New Delhi, 1990.
162. Pakistan left the Commonwealth in 1972 and rejoined in 1990. Again in 1999 after the military coup, Pakistan was threatened by Commonwealth, and it is only after the assurance given by army chief that very soon state of democracy will be restored, that the membership of Pak continues.
163. M.K. Rosgotra (Ed.), "A Vision of India", in *Rajiv Gandhi's World View*, Vikas Publishing House Pvt. Ltd, 1991.
164. *Ibid.*

3

Changing Circumstances and India's Foreign Policy

Policy-making is a quiet complex matter. As foreign policy is never uniquely determined by anyone factor, or a set of factors but is the result of the interplay of a large number of factors that affect the formulation of policy in different ways in different circumstances. The end of 20th century embarked new values, new thinking, new culture, new technology, new institutions and so on. With the great revolution in information technology, everything has changed. New developments, new trends and new forces emerged. Though, what was experienced in India was the part of worldwide phenomenon of change, like the victory of democratic institutions and prevalence of market economy, coalition culture and nuclear technology.

Since Independence, Indian political scenario is full of surprises of both positive and negative kinds. There is a slow but gradual evolution of political consciousness from election to election. The operation of rational and irrational forces in the electoral processes from one stage to another affect the health of democracy. Violence, caste conflict and terrorism persist in India. But in the face of all these hurdles, Indian democracy has matured and has come to age and its future seems secure. Democracy in India is a way of life and can never be changed. According to Henry Kissinger, "India has matured into a fine making democracy."[1] Professor Chia Nakana of the Tokyo University opined that "in Asia and in the world, there is no parallel to the Indian Democracy. Democracy is innately and inherently strong in India and can withstand all shocks and surprises."[2]

Foreign policy is expected to be dynamic—making constant adjustments with changing circumstances, internal as well as external. The framework of Indian foreign policy began to change in a subtle but definite way in the 1990s. A combination of domestic and external factors shaped these changes.

Internal Forces

The foreign policy of every country is a mirror reflection of domestic co-relationship of social forces. During the 1990s, Indian foreign policy has become reactive, defensive and obliging, because political parties have fractured the Indian society on the basis of caste versus caste, community versus community, region versus region, and language versus language. The consequence of this highly fragmented political process is that political parties have multiplied to promote their sectional and sectarian group interests. The Indian foreign policy has lost its initiatives of the 1950s, 1960s, 1970s and 1980s, because regionalists, castiests, communalists along with propertied classes have created social conditions for the weakening of the Indian state. An internally fragile, unstable, fragmented coalitional political process cannot face the new challenges of the emerging global capitalism of the 21st century. Likewise, a temporary Prime Minister cannot provide leadership, while dealing with powerful Western countries and global institutions.

There have been five general elections between 1989 and 1999, all of which have produced a fractured mandate. With no single party able to muster a clear majority on its own, India has entered the period of coalition politics in the last decade of the twentieth century. This has had effects on the foreign policy. Besides, in order to overcome the domestic economic crisis, India opted for aid from the IMF and the World Bank in the early nineties. As a result, the process of liberalisation and privatisation got underway, which in turn brought various pressures on the India foreign policy. The other domestic factors, which made influence on India's foreign policy in this period, range from caste-class conflict, religious extremism, insurgencies, terrorism, decline in Parliamentary culture, fragmentation in party system, crisis of governance, to globalisation, nuclearisation and women empowerment.

CULTURE OF COALITION POLITICS

Five decades after independence coalition politics has become a fact of life in Indian politics because no single political party on its own seems to be in a position to muster majority in the Lok Sabha elections. Since the first general elections in 1952 the Congress managed to walk away with a majority of Lok Sabha seats without even getting fifty per cent of total votes polled, except once in 1984. In fact it is an irony of electoral system of India that the seats won by a political party in an election at both the union and the state levels are disproportionate to the share of votes polled by it. With less than fifty per cent votes, the Congress party managed to win two-third seats in Lok Sabha. At the state level, there are examples where the party has won the majority seats with mere thirty per cent of vote share.

After independence Gandhi's advice to disband the Congress and convert it into a social organisation went unheeded by ambitious and power-hungry leaders of the party. But the Congress operated, mostly, as a coalition itself. It worked as a centrist party (except in 1977-80). In 1989 came the end of the Congress hegemony. The non-Congress political parties discovered the joy of putting together a post-election alliance. V.P. Singh was Prime Minister for 11 months, Chandra Shekhar for 4 months, Narasimha Rao for five years by purchasing loyalties of MPs, Deve Gowda for 10 months, Indra Kumar Gujral for six months and Atal Behari Vajpayee for 13 months. Not only this, even during their short, temporary and tension ridden regimes all the Prime Ministers were on tender hooks because of their quarrelsome coalitional partners. Also the weak and unstable coalition governments at the Centre are finding it difficult to face the new international order based on the hegemony of the western capitalist countries and in accordance with that, to formulate the foreign policy of India.

In 1996 it was the turn of non-BJP parties to come together to keep the BJP out of power. However, BJP joined hands with the other like-minded parties to form the National Democratic Alliance and fought the 1998 elections and after the early dissolution of the Lok Sabha 1999 elections securing majority in the house. With all these started the era of coalition politics in India.

A widespread concern is discernible in the public discourse over the coalitions in the country. And the concern is almost recent while the phenomenon is not new and is in fact very much inherent in the parliamentary form of government itself. Coalitions have been in existence in many of the European democracies and elsewhere. In India too the formation of coalitions precede independence and the first coalition government in a state came in existence as early as in 1937 in PEPSU and in many of the states the process was institutionalised much before the phenomenon surfaced at the Union level. The phenomenon till it was limited to the states was perhaps not a matter of great concern, it was only after the 'menace' spread to the center, it became the cause of concern. The stability is the biggest cause of concern. There is another dimension of the perceived crisis, its moral aspect. It is said that miniscule parties bereft of public mandate form immoral alliances in order to get into governance, particularly post-poll alliances are seen with much disdain in this regard and the biggest cause of concern being conspirational alliances formed to topple a sitting government and to form a new one.

Despite, the situation today reveals that no single party would gain majority and excessive worry over a so-called hung Parliament suggests an innate distaste for coalitions. This is unwarranted.[3] Coalitions are legitimate and can be purposeful and long lasting. There seems to be an irrational prejudice in India against the coalition pattern.[4] Superficially the argument against coalition appears convincing but the facts speak differently. It is very easy to access and know the reality but the general prejudices prevent people to reach the right conclusions. First is the issue of national development, which is the first exhortation of every Indian. The basic fact about coalition is that it leads to instability and an unstable government hinders the process of development. As has been stated earlier that coalitions have existed in the developed countries of Europe and that did not push those countries towards poverty. Coalitions did not adversely affect their developed status. On the other hand in many Third World countries stability, which in many place was jealously ensured by the military juntas, hardly helped them to overcome their wretched existence. India is not a different case. It was the minority government of P.V. Narsimha Rao, which initiated reforms in the country, and which has been sustained by the coalition government thereafter. India achieved the status of the second fastest growing economy of the world only in this era of coalition governance. In short, coalition government is in no way a factor adversely affecting the economic development of the country.

Besides, the given political scenario underlines the dire need that a coalition government at the center as inevitability in the existing equation of political parties in the Lok Sabha and it is the only alternative to the traditional one-party rule mode in the multi-party situation obtaining in our country. It is wrong to hold the opinion that the coalition model cannot work successfully at the centre.[5] For the success of this model, there should be mutual respect, tolerance and approval of time-bound common action plan between different constituents. India has witnessed disastrous experiences of coalition governments[6] at the center because of the heterogeneous character and outside support.

At the same time to believe that India is ripe and ready for coalition governments is to give too much credit to political actors and to their many ad hoc justifications for seeking power. It undermines the urgency to articulate developmental issues and overvalues, instead, the preservation and protection of specific interests. Given the vast disparities in living conditions in India, coalitions have the dangerous potential of exaggerating these painful diversities even further. Sometimes, of course and electoral verdict leaves no option other than a coalition government, but there is no need to make a virtue of necessity.[7]

While in many western democracies, coalition governments are hardly exceptional nor do they signal something abnormal or disagreeable. But, in contrast to the developing world, western societies possess one exceptional feature that allows them to function effectively with coalition governments: these countries have a large middle class and an overwhelmingly uniform pattern of consumption and lifestyles. This not only accounts for the similarities between parties in Europe and North America, but also marginalises the significance of developmental issues in their politics. In fact, many western scholars have commented on the post-modern exhaustion of experience where nothing new can be added in substantive terms. What is left is but to play with commodities. As Planning for the future has no allure in such societies, western democracies provide congenial settings for coalition governments.[8] The situation is vastly different in an old-new, rich-poor, multi-cultural country like India. Masses of poverty and a fragile middle class make development programmes a primary concern here. As Indian public is far from being homogenous and uniformly prosperous, it is only through developmental programmes that the existing heterogeneity of groups and interests can be realistically addressed. The Indian electorate still regards social development as a desirable goal. This is probably why every time a coalition has fallen.[9]

Two other issues related to coalition, which cause consternation, are immorality and disregard for ideology. Crass opportunism is said to be the bottom-line of coalition politics and which ironically is the reality. But the end result is positive. The coalition politics has a moderating effect on extremist party lines. There has evolved and has got institutionalised a system of checks and balances which takes care of several ills that many of our political parties suffer from. The situation has changed considerably from earlier times. The ideology as it is, stands negated in today's world. With the disintegration of the erstwhile Soviet Union in early 1990s, no one talks of ideology anymore. In an era of liberalisation and globalisation ideology has taken a back seat and fierce economic competition is the bottom line today.

In fact the above arguments which are only illustrative, not exhaustive are only meant to show that the coalition politics does not reflect any crisis or decline in the political order. Problems are there but they have been there even during the earlier times of stability. It's only a new edition of the earlier system but with positive features as its character is nearer to the spirit of the cabinet system, as the member of the cabinet have among themselves a relationship of relative equality. Moreover the coalition politics is essentially reflective of the ongoing democratisation of public life in India. Democracy essentially relates to the political order but in order to be vibrant it must permeate the public psyche and the social fabric. The Indian society is witnessing such permeation. And this process is bringing in different sections hitherto marginalised to the main stream of politics. This is the democratic federalisation of the country rather horizontally. The 'littles' not only want their voice heard but also want to be there, at the hubs of activities, at the center of decision making processes, in the limelight of attention and above all want the share in the spoils of the governance. On the other plane the mega nationalist unified party-system had left little scope for dignified representation of regional identities. Democratisation process led to the demand for further federalisation both vertical and horizontal even by these regional identities. The vertical federalisation was reflected in demands for creation of smaller states, autonomy and devolution of more powers to the states. The term horizontal federalisation has been used in the sense of the demands of these regional identities for equal participation in the federal power structure. The emergence of the coalition politics at the union level is in fact the federalisation of the union executive. The coalitional cabinet as such resembles a federation of social groups and regional identities. The diversity of India has discarded the umbrella of hegemony in the name of unity and moved into a federation of equal identities. Therefore, the process itself reaffirms something very positive that is the democratisation of the national social order.

If there is nothing new or anything actually bad about

coalition politics and if it is essentially a reflection of the democratisation of the polity, why is there a concern over coalition politics among a large section of Indian intelligentsia? Reasons are obvious :

(1) The era of stability ensured uninterrupted appropriation of national resources by the incumbents of governance for their personal gains and their unquestioned mastery over people. The confusion regarding a political power in a coalition government and frequent changes in the government do not allow them to build up sure and stable arrangements for themselves.

(2) The other reason is related to factors like caste and class or simply the status. The erstwhile dominant status groups are not comfortable with the rise of the underprivileged class, particularly of the lowest categories to the political power. Scheduled castes and lower castes people have risen from their ascriptive status of servitude to political prominence.

(3) The members of the middle class feel morally deprived with the entry of the underclass in the power circles and are harassed by these Lowly Upstarts.

Nonetheless there is darker side of coalition politics. However, this remains a positive phenomenon as it is the extension of the democratisation of society but it has its negative side because it's an outgrowth of the distorted democratisation. The most obvious distortion is the decline of the party system in India. Coalition politics in a way is based on the decline of a role of the parties. In India the emergence of the coalition is the result of the fragmentation of the party system, which started with the end of the predominance of the Indian National Congress. This decline of the party can be attributed to a number of factors:

(1) The parties now appear more as political arms of various ethnic or economic groups rather than championing national cause. More accurately many of these smaller parties hardly champion the cause of any group. Their leaders mobilise the vote banks by exhorting

the parochial identities of the voters for personal gains, any public good if that is at all served by their actions is by and large incidental. The parties thus decline in organisation, function and their social base and above all in political role.

(2) The party earlier could sustain its mega presence by using things like charisma, tradition, parochialism or utopianism. The charisma and the system of personal patronage and loyalties were good for the bygone time but are no longer viable these days. People are now more informed, more politicised and more exposed. They cannot be mesmerised by charisma or bullied by local bigwigs, swayed by parochial and utopian appeals.

As the national parties on their own are not in a position to get 30-35 per cent votes to win a Lok Sabha seat, they have to enter into some kind of an electoral alliance with small players at their terms and conditions. No section is too small to be overlooked in the present scenario.

However, cohabitation with the enemy is uncomfortable and at times embarrassing, but our politicians have now willy-nilly accepted the idea of coalitions.[10] They are, however, choosing their partners not on the basis of an identity of views but purely out of a desire to acquire power.[11] Ideally, the three major contenders for power should have worked out coalitional arrangements before the polls and presented clear choices to the voter, but the disinclination to do so shows that they wanted to be guided by post-poll arithmetic which, incidentally, has not turned out to be helpful to any major player. The fall of one coalition can lead to that of another and with the attendant risk of horse-trading, the situation can become messier and precipitate an early dissolution of the new Lok Sabha and fresh elections. A search for new ways might help to end the impasse. One such idea is to induct a wider coalition — a national government-consisting of all-important national and regional parties. A national government would require a new mindset, the taming of conflicting ambitions and the replacement of competitive politics with a collaborative, consensual approach for steering the nation say, during the next five years.[12] However, the formation of a national government is not going to be easy. Beside, favoring the presidential form of government some have tempered their case by suggesting a remarkable variation: Let Parliament elect the Prime Minister; in other words if not a national government, let us have a "national" Prime Minister! If no party has a majority, a PM elected by a majority in Parliament, obviously with the help of MPs from other parties, will not be troubled by the specter of instability and will therefore concentrate on governing rather than on horse-trading.[13] A little reflection will show the vacuity in this reasoning. If MPs from some other parties support the leader of a particular party, presumably for good reasons, then why not take this to its logical end and form an open and honest coalition?[14] While the common feature of various experiments at coalition at the power center is that they have been forged without reference to the electorate in other words, the political parties have not faced the voter on the strength of their combined election commitments. Rather, they reflect only the fractured nature of party-system in India today.[15]

POLITICAL PROCESS, ROLE OF ELITES AND PARTY-SYSTEM

The political set up of India is undergoing rapid transition where the old power centers are collapsing and the new alignments are emerging. Near disappearance of public priority, growing coercive power of the state over the citizens, corruption, debasement and criminalisation of political process have characterised the political system.

Over the decades, there has been some significant change in the voting pattern for the electorate, while all the elections held between 1971 and 1984 were 'plebiscitary', marked by overriding national issues, to which the electorate responded in a broadly uniform pattern, either almost all over the country or at least in the Sutlej-Ganga-Brahmaputra valleys, the elections since 1989 have become much more regionalised. Since the 1989 polls, the electoral map has become dotted with an ever-increasing number of political parties resulting from the fragmentation of existing national and regional parties as well as formation of myriad new regional parties.[16] During the

1990s, beginning with the Ninth Lok Sabha elections of 1989 to the Fourteenth Lok Sabha elections of April/May 2004, the Indian voters have not decisively voted for any one party to rule over the country. Its consequence has been, that the Central Government of India has become weak, unstable and fragmented. Contrary to shibboleths, India is not evolving towards a two-party system, but towards a more complex structure to which regional parties are crucial. The BJP-Congress collective vote is just about half the total — and not rising. Indeed, their political strength has decreased. BJP remains estranged from and irrelevant to the concerns of the under-privileged. It has not reached out to the poor. The verdict confirms many trends in Indian politics. Among these are growing regionalism, declining importance of charisma-based politics, identity-related issues and rising demand for accountability. The results reinforce long-term tendencies of self-assertion of Dalits and OBCs and increasing tendency of Muslims to vote secular-political candidates.

Political process of the 1990s has many specificities, but one fact which deserves mentioning is that the role of money power is increasing because of frequent elections and the emergence of more than 50 parties and groups which are competing for the Lok Sabha elections. Every political party and group has a fund-collector for fighting an election.[17] The fund-givers play critical role in political process before and after the elections. During the 1990s, four Lok Sabha elections have been held and the new economic policy, which is a break with the past, has never been brought before the voters. Political parties opposed to the new economic policy have contested the elections by criticizing the NEP, but while in power, every political party has implemented very enthusiastically the NEP. The new economic policy does not enjoy the voter's verdict. The NEP is based on a very narrow political consensus among political classes, bureaucrats, upwardly mobile parasitical middle classes, big industrialists and capitalist farmers. Thus the foreign policy of India in the 1990s, irrespective of party/parties in power in the Central Government, has been pursuing the goals of new economic policy which does not have democratic approval but which has support of powerful sections of the ruling classes, urban and agrarian and functionaries of the Indian state.[18]

C. Wright Mills had stated that the 'ruling elite' rule on the basis of elections. Hence it is absolutely wrong to maintain that India has evolved a national consensus in the 1990s on foreign policy irrespective of serious differences among political parties. On the contrary, political process has been hijacked by a very powerful and narrow-based social elite, which is promoting its own interests through foreign policy of India. Thus the foreign policy of India has become a tool in the hands of a very limited powerful elite, who are using electoral and political democracy for their own group benefits.[19]

In concise, if on the one hand political class is involved in serious internal conflict, competition and politics of confrontation, on the other domestic powerful groups are able to determine national priorities in their own interest and collaborate with foreign centers of capital. The mediating role of the state *vis-à-vis* domestic powerful groups and external powerful nations has become weak because of the multiplicity of parties and the emergence of farcical coalitional governments at the centre.[20]

In the recent years, the party system in India has suffered severe setbacks. Some of these pertain to an overall sink of the social system, which is evident in almost every walk of life. Some of these ailments, which affect the party system include absence of inner party democracy, negligible number of female representatives, disappearance of ideology from politics, declining ethical values and prevalence of opportunism and expediency and lack of transparency in funding of party organisations, Casteism, Communalism, Regionalisation of parties.[21] The growing violence and criminalisation of politics, fractionalisation and coalitional tensions compound these problems in varied ways.

1. Lack of Ideology and Moral Values in Politics. There has been very sharp erosion in the ideological orientation of Indian political parties. The democratic norms and institutions and the inspirational values have been destroyed systematically over the last fifty years of the working of our constitution. There also is a crisis of character amongst the politicians, as the system does not encourage honest leaders. Due to these facts, there exists a drop of morals in public life. The criminalisation of politics and politicisation of criminals have become the norms. The major principle, which is conveniently followed and widely practiced by politicians, is opportunism and expediency often called as pragmatism. Besides, astronomical sums of tainted money have been poured to play a decisive role in pre-and post-election situations. These criminals rise to the positions of ministers in politics and political parties, which cover their misdeeds. In this way the lawbreakers transform themselves into the lawmakers.

2. Absence of Inner Party Democracy. The leadership in most political parties in India may be democratic in appearance but highly oligarchic in reality. Leaders refuse to understand that a political party is a public institution and cannot be treated like a personal fief. Without intra-party elections, without regional support and encouragement of a variety of opinions the ministers, the political parties are likely to wither away. It is obvious that parties based on oligarchic principles cannot play a positive role in a democratic country.

3. Party Funds. To perform its functions and contest elections every political party needs funds. But this financial aspect of party budgets is kept secret while other organisational details are kept open for public. The parties and candidates use dubious methods in raising funds like kickbacks, funds from foreign sources and even donations from Mafia gangs and other criminal elements. To let the parties get honest funding from legitimate sources for their political activities has emerged as one of the most crucial and contemporary concerns of the reform agenda of political parties in India.

4. Representation of Women. Representation constitutes a major issue of concern in the reform agenda regarding political parties in India. How can women who constitute half of the population be denied a legitimate share? All parties have attempted to create women wings in their organisations but no political party has exhibited courage of fielding a satisfactory number of women candidates in national and state elections. The parties do not even want to reserve thirty three per cent seats in the legislatures as provided in the amendment to the constitution, leave aside the fifty per cent share.

5. **Leadership Quality.** The older leadership in Indian political parties used to rise from the ranks. They respected party discipline. As a contrast, the present day political leadership seems to be in a tremendous hurry to reach up to the top and is not averse to use short cuts, dubious methods, money or muscle power to achieve their self seeking objective. The entry of criminals to responsible positions is a serious consequence of these trends. As a result important issues facing the nation do not get attention and policy-making and good governance suffers in the process.

6. **Campaign Methods.** The film and T.V. idols have taken away the element of serenity and the spirit of public service from political leadership. The election campaigns at the regional and national levels have become some kind of stage shows. The matinee idols are being paraded to attract voters in support of their candidates without seriously educating the electorates about the issues at stake in the elections.

7. **Casteism.** In place of ideological polarisation, the policies, programmes and electoral candidates are being finalised on the caste considerations. Castes also in turn influence the parties by voting en bloc for candidate of their castes without considering merits or demerits of the candidate.

8. **Regionalisation.** The regionalisation has compelled political parties to mould their policies to suit to interests of their regional units. They adopt different policies in different states according to the prevailing conditions there. Regionalism has made 'ethnicity' respectable. These regional parties form coalitions with national parties and pressurise the Central Government to make more allocation of funds and grants to their states. This implies their regional aspirations. Moreover, the Central Government, which is a coalition government, has to cope with these pulls and pressures of plurality of regimes in the states.

9. Communalism. Communal polarisation posed a threat to political ethos of pluralism, parliamentarianism and federalism in India. Despite the adoption of the principle of "secularism" as a constitutional creed, the trend towards communalism has grown day by day. The spirit of tolerance, which is essential for a secular society, seems to be vanishing from the country. The covert communalism practiced by political parties, in pursuit of electoral gains through vote banks has earned the epitaphs of "psedo-secularism" and "minorityism". The dynamics of politics of the last decade is a mute witness of the clashes and conflicts between the so called "secularist" and "communalist", more particularly in Kashmir, Uttar Pradesh and Gujarat. Further, caste and religion have recently gained much momentum as formulas or equations that give parties a winning edge over their counterparts.

10. Criminalisation. The persons in politics today are not only helped by the criminals but also by the professional outlaws have discovered a new and safe heaven in politics. Formerly they had to plead and take help from the politician for saving them from the clutches of law but today they are discovering themselves in a new role of the members of legislatures and even ministers (lawmakers), to cover their misdeed. Earlier the criminals were playing the role of a second fiddle to help the politician win elections but now the roles stand reversed and politicians are seeking protection from these criminals. The Election Commission and the People's Representation Act are toothless in preventing criminals from contesting elections.

11. Fractionalisation and Coalitions. Efforts were made by the coalition partners to set up institutional mechanisms to evolve consensus on the common minimum programmes for action and coordination vertically and horizontally. They tried to institute multi-layered coalitional structures and created steering and coordination committees for inner-party and party-government consultations to resolve differences through emissaries of the Prime Minister. But then all these efforts remained ad hoc in nature and could not institutionalise devices for effective action.

12. **Political Parties and Governance.** Four major factors have influenced the nature of political change in India: (1) the de-institutionalizing role of national and regional leaders, (2) the impact of weak political parties, (3) the undisciplined political mobilisation of various caste, ethnic, religious and other types of groups and (4) the increasing conflicts between the haves and have-nots in the civil society. If these trends continue unchecked, India's political crisis is likely to become worse.

13. **Jumbo Council of Ministers.** The experience of minority and coalition governments resulted in the practice of creating abnormally large or what is known as jumbo size council of ministers to accommodate the coalition partners in government. It has given rise to serious impediments in the process of governance. Besides the inherent problem of conflicting jurisdictions of the various ministers, personality clashes and egos and the woefully inadequate physical facilities and assistance for their effective and efficient functioning. Inefficiency, delays and slackness increased because of the inflated governmental machinery, which caused malpractices ad corruption. The recent amendment limiting this size to fifteen per cent of the strength of the legislature is a welcome change that promises discipline and stability.

Conclusively it can be said that although political parties in India suffer with many problems, these must be remedied either through legislations or by making the people aware, including the politicians.

Rising Communalism and Regionalism

The most vital role which independence of India played is the construction of a modern national identity and a new civilisation around the values of liberty, equality, justice, dignity of the individual and unity of the nation and within the framework of a political system committed to a union-type of federal democracy, secularism, rule of law, open society and an egalitarian polity. In this gigantic endeavor, two sets of factors — one of diversity and the other of dissension — impede the process of preferred and intended change. The factors of dissension congregate around plurality of regions and sub-regions marked by distinct languages/dialects, social transformations and culture-forms, set patterns of economy and level of material development, a specific background of local history, particular psychological make-up and over all impress of sub-national identity and homogeneity. The factors of diversity manifest in an undue attachment to one's own religious community, caste, *jati* or tribe, that tends to weaken national solidarity and disrupt the process of national integration, so essential for the unity of any plural society and federal system.[22] Therefore the terms regionalism and communalism should be treated differently. The real task is to reconcile legitimate regionalism with valid nationalism.

As far as communalism is concerned, as a political phenomenon, it seeks to destroy the four pillars of India's modern identity, namely, nationalism, secularism, democracy and fraternal unity. In this sense communalism is the most disastrous factor of national dissension and decay. Adherence to religion and religious system is not communalism. Exploitation of religion is communalism. Attachment to a religious community or religiosity is not communalism. Using a religious community against other communities and against the nation is communalism. Communalism is perversion of religion from a moral order to a temporal arrangement of contemporary convenience, from a faith into an electoral constituency, from a strategy of living into a tactics of politics; in brief, from an end into a means. Communalism exploits both religion and politics. It is promoted by a real or an imaginary fear of other communities and of the process of modernised transformation and secular change, which is wrongly perceived as detrimental to religious community's welfare. It is conversion of religiosity into political bellicosity. Communalism is the enemy of progress, revolution, democracy and of federal nation-state building on rational scientific lines. In this sense, communalism is not a phenomenon of conservative reaction, but of modernised reaction and therefore more subtle and complex. It is a sectarian, restrictive and negative response to the process of modernisation and modern nation building.

Ruling classes and strata have used communalism and communal cleavages to remain in power, by obtaining electoral support, by creating electoral pockets and vote-banks. Of the eight religious communities, the main problem of reconciliation and accommodation in India arises mainly in the case of the Hindus, the Muslims, the Christians and the Sikhs. Likewise politicians misused casteism in their own benefit — to get electoral support and divided Indian society. Politicians instigated the sentiments of Hindu and Muslim communities, when demolished the *Babri mosque* and tried to construct the *Ram temple* in Ayodhya. Likewise, Gujarat carnage is a burning instance of political selfishness, inhumanity, immorality and cruelty. Even within one community, there are several rival groups on the basis of caste. In the name of social justice, each group wants to make its own political identity. By unjust means, they are hoping to get so-called justice — the credit goes to the politicians, who interpolated the mind of masses. By and large, the whole society gets divided along caste lines and political parties are using one caste against other.

DECLINE IN PARLIAMENTARY CULTURE

In place of the intellectuals, it is the professional politician that is firmly rooted in Parliament. The most animated discussions that have taken place in Parliament in recent years concern granting of privileges to the MPs, during which the vote is unanimous and boisterous. No national issues ever attract either that level of debate or interest. Also the educated people of India and the industrialists, on whom the country depends for development, have been delivered into the hands of the professional politician.

Unfortunately, most politicians of today are more concerned with sharing the spoils of power than doing anything for the country. This is evident from their day-to-day antics, which show a callous disregard for national concerns. There may be some truth in Mani Shankar Aiyar's view, that there has been deterioration in public life as those who are unemployable are now in politics. The major difference appears to be that while earlier, serving the nation was seen as a privilege and attracted many well-meaning people, now it is the privilege that attract the politician.

The politician had subverted all systems. The scandals just grew in size. As scandals broke out with alarming regularity, it seemed that nothing was spared: whether it was buying stamp papers, medicines or even fodder for animals, leaders were making money. The people of India slowly tired of the party, which had no morals left. Since the fifties, the Congress commanded an absolute majority in Parliament; the number of seats it won has declined. It was not just the Congress, which has lost the faith of the people. No other political party has been able to fill the gap, and all over the country, electorates are delivering hung verdicts. The politician is not trusted anymore. Today party leaders face serious charges of cheating, corruption, communalism and terrorism. The people today are fed up of corrupt politicians. They want morality in public life. If the Congress — or for that matter any other party — can offer this, the confidence of the people can be won. For that, three things are required: honesty, morals and concern for the common man. Unfortunately, these are the three things that are almost extinct in India's public life.

SECESSIONIST INSURGENCIES

The roots of insurgencies in India lie in the post-independence process of nation-building and uneven economic development of the economy. These two processes were not independent, but converged and their effects led to the marginalisation and alienation of certain ethnic groups. Fallout of this process has been the increasing use of violence in the articulation of demands of the deprived sections and where the conflicts have become protracted, they have transformed into insurgencies.

The political arrangement envisaged in the Indian Union constituted several provincial states organised on the principle of quasi-federalism. Subsequently, the reorganisation of states in on the basis of language accommodated the ethno-linguistic aspirations of a number of groups.

The demands for autonomy or a separate sovereign state

do not only arise out of ethnic consciousness, but are also linked to the process of economic development. In developing societies, the economic disparities often coincide with the ethnic divisions and ethnic groups have assumed political identities to seek redressal. The demands for political autonomy to fulfill developmental aspirations are, therefore, being articulated in the language of ethnicity.[24]

The roots of most insurgencies, with the exception of Kashmir and Punjab, therefore, may be traced to socio-economic factors. The basic causes of separatist movements may be located in deprivation and discrimination *vis-à-vis* an equal share of political, administrative and economic power. Most ethnic conflicts have originated with a demand by minority ethnic groups to be accommodated and given a share in the power structure. Mobilisation is on the basis of various demands like "affirmative discrimination, autonomy and secession."[25] Since the 1970s most of these groups have developed separatist tendencies, which earlier used to be mainly autonomist.[26] These conflicts have taken a violent turn as the majority group shows no willingness to concede to the demands of the minorities and insurgency has become the basic mode of confrontation. A major factor that has given sustenance to these conflicts is the involvement of external powers, which exploits these situations either for strategic or economic reasons.[27]

Thus secessionist or separatist movements also known as extra-systemic movements are by ethnic, religious or ethno-religious minorities, which question the sovereignty and territorial integrity of the state and affirm their right of self-determination.

Most secessionist insurgencies in India rely predominantly on guerilla warfare and use this method both in jungles and urban areas depending upon the terrain they are operating from. The hilly terrain in Kashmir and the jungles in north-eastern India provide ideal conditions for waging guerilla warfare. However, the Kashmiri militants predominantly use urban guerilla warfare because of the support they enjoy among the local population. Generally, their strategy includes hit and run tactics with the intention of weakening the resolve of the administration.[28] This is carried out by attacking security personnel and assassinating political leaders and high level government officials opposed to the movement. The Sikh insurgency has been the weakest in terms of strategy. All insurrectionary movements seek external support whether it is moral support, material aid or sanctuary for their effectiveness and sustenance. This may be covert or overt in its nature and also varies in intensity, particularly over period of time.

Apart from seeking support from sympathetic neighboring states, insurgent groups in India have also tried to forge links with each other and with groups in the neighboring countries, irrespective of their ideology and goals. Perhaps the necessity for these linkages arises from their difficulties in procuring weapons to sustain the insurgency. In some cases, these linkages could be due to purely mercenary reasons. For instance, some reports indicate that Afghans and Tamils have been involved in training Kashmiri militants in camps located in the PoK.[29] Besides, the JKLF is believed to have established links with the Sikh militants[30] and the Hizbul Mujahideen has been more successful in establishing contacts with the Khalistan Commando Force (KCF), the ULFA and the People's War Group (PWG).[31] Other reports point to links between the LTTE and the ULFA militants. Earlier ULFA had established contacts with the KIA in Burma in 1986, which agreed to train ULFA militants in the Burmese jungle hideouts, but at a very high price.[32] In 1988, Munim Nobis, an ULFA leader had gone to Pakistan via Bangladesh to ask the ISI to facilitate a meeting with the Afghan Mujahideen. Apparently, the ISI arranged a meeting of five ULFA leaders with Gulbuddin Hekmatyar, the chief of the Hizb-e-Islami in Peshawar in 1990. The Hizb started training them, but the ULFA leaders felt that it was too elementary as they had already mastered the same and thus left after a week or so.[33]

The geographical location of the north-east helped the insurgents find a safe haven in the unadministered regions of Myanmar and Chittagong Hill tracts in Bangladesh. In the 1960s, it was much easier for them to operate from the then East Pakistan due to adversarial relations between India and

Pakistan. But the emergence of Bangladesh in 1971 adversely affected the strategy of the insurgents. However, reports point to the possible involvement of the Bangladesh government in training the National Socialist Council of Nagaland (NSCN).[34]

The north-eastern region of India has been plagued by insurgencies since the early years of independence. Various factors such as ethnic heterogeneity, linguistic diversity, demographic changes, historical and geo-political developments, lack of economic growth and infrastructural development, gave sustenance to insurgencies in this region.

The Nagas were the first to initiate an armed insurgency in 1956 to be followed by the Mizos in 1966, the Tripuris in 1978, and in Assam in 1979. The Naga insurgency is the oldest in India. The Nagas, led by the Naga Nationalist Council (NNC), had declared independence a day before India got its independence.[35] They boycotted the general elections in 1952 and the NNC, under the leadership of A.Z. Phizo, started a violent and organised insurgency in 1956. Laldenga formed the Mizo National Front (MNF) out of the Mizo Famine Front (MFF) in 1959 with independence as its goal. The MNF formed a Mizo National Army (MNA) to fight the Indian forces. In 1966, Laldenga launched "Operation Jericho". The 20 year long insurgency in Mizoram ended as a result of Rajiv Gandhi's accord with the MNF leader, Laldenga. Laldenga agreed to the conditions of recognizing the Indian constitution, laying down arms and joining the main stream. Elections were held on February 16, 1987. He became the Chief Minister of Mizoram. On February 21, Mizoram became a full-fledged state of the Indian Union.

The genesis of insurgency in Tripura lies in the massive influx of settlers from Bangladesh and other parts of India, thus, upsetting the socio-economic pattern in the state and increasing pressure on land. The insurgency in Tripura has been primarily led by the Tripura National Volunteers (TNV) formed in December 1978 to fight for an independent tribal Tripura state.

The United Liberation Front of Assam (ULFA), formed in

April 1970, has led the violent insurgency in Assam. It was essentially an offshoot of the Assam agitation led by the All Assam Students Union (AASU), and was against migrants and Indian rule. Till 1985, ULFA was dormant. By 1990, the ULFA was at the peak of its power and had a highly effective system of levying taxes, and also organised community work, at times by coercing people.[36] The Indian government's military action was able to immobilise ULFA by early 1992. Simultaneously, a section of the leadership decided to hold talks with the government. This resulted in a split in the organisation and while some of its cadres have been rehabilitated, its hardcore members have managed to take shelter in Bangladesh.

The Akali Dal has spearheaded a movement for more autonomy under the Anandpur Sahib resolution of 1973. Violence against Hindus on a large scale had started around September-October 1983. The Dal Khalsa along with the All India Sikh Students Federation (AISSF), was believed to be behind this violence. By this time, the Sikh's demand for autonomy had taken separatist overtones and a violent form. Due to antagonistic relations between India and Pakistan, the latter readily provided armed support to the Sikh militants for destabilizing India. Jagjit Singh Chohan, leader of the National Council of Khalistan, had claimed that Z.A. Bhutto whom he met in 1972 (before the signing of the Simla Accord) in New York had offered to help to start a movement for Khalistan from Pakistan's territory.

Finally, in June 1984, the Central Government launched an assault on the Golden Temple where Sikh extremists had sought sanctuary. Anti-Sikh riots in different parts of the country following Indira Gandhi's revenge killing by her Sikh bodyguards in October 1984, further fuelled violence in Punjab. Prime Minister Rajiv Gandhi signed an accord with Sant Longowal in 1985 to resolve some of the outstanding issues, but it failed to end violence in the state. The government managed to restore the political process in March 1992 and thereafter by strong counter-insurgency measures was able to contain violence by early 1993. During the course of Operation

Rakshak-II in December 1991, the Army only played a supportive role in cordoning areas while the police and para-military forces carried out search and sanitizing operations to flush out the insurgents.[37] But before this operation, K.P.S. Gill, the Director-General of Police in Punjab, had already weakened the Sikh insurgents considerably by using very unconventional methods, at times, exceeding the limits of law.[38]

Pakistan's support for the subversive activities in Kashmir may be traced even to the period before its accession to India in 1948. However, it is important to note that both in 1947 and 1965, the local Kashmiri population did not respond to Pakistan's support to the tribal incursions and infiltration. But by late 1980s, the situation had reversed and now various militant groups sought support from across the border.

At the time of independence, Kashmir had been given a special status under Article 370 of the Indian constitution. Over the past five decades, New Delhi has progressively curtailed the powers and scope of Article 370 by extending most of the provisions of the Indian constitution to that state. Often the center adopted both fair and foul methods, including the rigging of elections, dismissal of duly elected governments and appointing state Governors of its own choice, even against the wishes of the state government. These lapses on the part of the central leadership, along with corruption and dismal employment prospects for the Kashmiri youth, led to their growing alienation and disenchantment with the policies of New Delhi. It was against this background, that Rajiv Gandhi and Farooq Abdullah had arrived at an electoral agreement in 1986, whereby an alliance of the National conference and Congress-I was formed to fight the 1987 elections. Having lost faith in the democratic political process, the disgruntled elements soon took to the path of militancy. Following the installation of the National conference government, violent protests over the issue of unemployment and power shortages took place throughout 1988-1989. The state bureaucrats and political leaders had misappropriated central government assistance for the development of the state. Due to lack of satisfactory life chances and political opportunities to express them dissatisfactions, coupled with the corrupt behavior of the state politician the Kashmiri youth took up arms.[39] There is little doubt that Pakistan has sponsored the insurgency in the Valley by exploiting the alienation of the people.[40] Apparently, the JKLF was approached by the ISI in 1984 for initiating an insurgency in Kashmir, and after 1988, a significant spurt in their activities was discernible. While Pakistan has been covertly providing arms and military training to the Kashmiri militants,[41] in some instances, they have also provided covering artillery fire to help them cross into the Indian Kashmir. This strategy was adopted after intensive deployment of Indian security forces on the Line of Control had made the task of infiltration much more difficult and at times even hasardous.[42] By the end of 1989 and early 1990, the militants were holding sway in the Valley and the politicians were getting marginalised.

There have been reports of mercenaries, especially Afghan Mujahideen joining hands with the Kashmiris to fight a *jihad* in the Valley.[43] The last decade has witnessed the resurgence of Islamic fundamentalism and Muslims from various countries have been to Bosnia, Central Asia, Kashmir and other Muslim trouble spots to fight a *jihad*.[44] Besides, some fundamentalist Muslims from Sudan are also believed to have infiltrated into Kashmir.[45] While for many Muslims, it is *jihad*, for Pakistan it is a proxy war against India.

State responses to insurgencies in India have been varied. The first approach is cooption or accommodation. This approach is applicable mostly in the case of insurgencies based on ethno-nationalism. For instance, it was used against MNF and TNV, whereby they were weaned back to the parliamentary process by giving substantial concessions in terms of political power. The dialogue between government and NSCN is on the progress. Both NSCN and government are trying hard to get some permanent solution of the problem. Central Government's mediator K. Padmanabhaiya told that Naga leaders are now ready for decisive talks. In fact UPA government indicated that State Reconstruction Commission may consider the merger of Naga speaking areas of Manipur, Assam and Arunachal Pradesh into Nagaland. But, its decision will not be obligatory for Central Government to accept the demand of NSCN for Greater Nagaland. The Commission will also give importance to the views of other states in this regard, which are going to be affected. There is demand for social, religious and traditional unification of Naga speaking areas. However, NSCN is itself aware of the complexities and reality that political merger of Naga speaking areas is barely possible. In fact, there are severe contradictions not only in the neighboring states, but also among the Nagas about the construction of 'Nagalim'. With these contradictions in hand it is impossible to touch political boundaries of the states.

Indo-Bangladesh talk over the problem of insurgents has been on the cards in recent years. All these developments are significant. The other approach is coercive by adopting strong counter-insurgency measures. This is the approach to most insurgencies inspired by revolutionary ideologies. Thus, the Naxalite insurgency came under severe repression. In the case of separatist insurgencies, a dual process of captive and coercive methods is used. Such coercive methods used by the two Army operations — Operation Bajrang, and Operation Rhino were instrumental in immobilizing the ULFA insurgents.

The failure to accommodate ethnic minorities in the process of nation-building has been the basic cause of insurgencies in India. The uneven process of development, which has economically marginalised some ethnic minorities, has further compounded this. Swarna Rajagopalan in his book "State and Nation in South Asia", talked about the incompatible visions and has beautifully summarised the contradiction between the vision of state (about itself and its constituent units) and vision of its constituent units (about itself and the state). He has insisted upon building political communities out of states through twin principles of reconciliation and accommodation.

The ethno-nationalist insurgencies are continuing due to popular as well as external support. In north-east India, the change in the Chinese attitude towards the insurgent groups has helped the government in controlling the situation to some extent. In contrast, Pakistan's moral and material support to Kashmiri insurgents has intensified the level of conflict there.

LACK OF A COHERENT POLICY

In India, the compartmentalisation in the planning of defense and development exists. This is because it does not have an integrated national security policy-making process that seeks to harmonise defense policy, economic policy, foreign policy and internal security policy with one another and with an overall national strategy. Indeed, an integrated approach is essential, for, no matter how potent the military or economic power of a country might be, it will remain inchoate and diffused unless it is welded together through coherent policy formulation.

Like NSC (National Security Council) in the United States, where it composed of a dedicated group of professionals, which are often drawn from outside with a life time of specialisation in their subjects, as for instance even an intellectual giant like Dr. Samuel P. Huntington found it attractive to serve in a middle-level capacity in the Carter NSC. In India, too we can have an efficient NSC, provided it is empowered by law and not by an executive order and which can, outside the routine bureaucracy, attract the best talent available in the country.

CRISIS OF GOVERNANCE

With the passage of time, the people are protesting sometimes violently and more often by keeping away from electoral processes. It may be worth asking as to why the incumbency factor has acquired importance during the elections. Why is the electorate expressing anger by voting out the incumbent governments whom they had favored earlier? Is it not time that the polity moves from governing to governance that assigns primacy to the people's participation? To a system that enables the people to govern themselves?[46] In the prevailing milieu it is difficult to offer good governance and engineer relevant people-oriented social change in the absence of an active participation by the civil society.[47]

The 1999 Human Development Report on South Asia, authored by the late Mahbub-ul-Haq, points out that

"South Asia (including India) is facing a crisis of governance, which, if left unchecked, could undermine the region's democratic progress, and the economic and social well being of its teeming masses. Home to nearly one-fourth of humanity, the region is characterised by government that represents the poor, but aids the rich; taxation that is insufficient and regressive; and expenditures that are misdirected, and ineffective. The report provides an in-depth analysis of the phenomenon of corruption and advocates a concrete and realistic reform agenda for promoting 'humane governance'. The concept of humane governance puts people at the center of all governance policies, strategies and actions. The basic precepts of the human development model are to improve the capabilities and expand the opportunities of all people, irrespective of class, caste, gender and ethnicity. The concept of humane governance takes this model forward by asserting that governance, if it is to promote human development, has to be not just pro-people or people centered, it has to be owned by people.... Humane governance has three inter-linked dimensions: economic, political and civic. Economic governance consists of those factors required to sustain economic development. Political governance is defined as the use of institutions by the government to govern and civic governance as the right and responsibility of the governed to participate in, and promote good governance. It is to be expected that a country with high economic, political and civic governance would also have high human development. Humane governance can only be achieved through a combination of all the three dimensions of economic, political and civic governance. One dimension does not come before another. They must occur in unison for the concept of humane governance to be realised."[48]

The Human Development Report may be viewed as a part of the worldwide debate on the needed modifications in styles and expanse of governance. The Japanese believe that for "deciding the public good" radical changes are called for. Such changes should accord centrality to the civic society.

Liberalisation demands changes. Since India is now soaked in the process of globalisation, we have to take notice of the worldwide trend that is seeking to ensure that the changes would place the people at the center and enthrone the civil societies.[49]

Governments alone cannot and need not run human societies nor build nations without a great deal of active and conscious help from the citizens. There are some basic requirements for the creation of the civil society.[50]

(a) To build a legal foundation of the state from the top to the bottom and to ensure that the laws of the land are universally and impartially enforced.

(b) An independent, efficient judiciary, that speedily hands out justice.

(c) The government has to be vastly decentralised, with the people given opportunities to govern themselves and take charge of their own affairs.

(d) The concept that the government is the giver of everything and the sole provider, is inimical to the building of such a society. The citizen must be empowered and enabled to appreciate that in many ways he or she is, his or her own master and responsible for the sustenance of a peaceful social order based on co-operative co-existence of different interests in society.

An enlightened civil society alone can assist in ensuring that every child goes to school, that teachers actually teach and doctors attend regularly on patients at rural health centers. The importance of Directive Principles of State Policy — Part (iv) of the constitution from Articles 38 onwards are fundamental for the welfare of Indian Republic. But unlike Fundamental Rights, the Directive Principles of State, though equally important — did not get similar treatment for their judicial enforcement. The Directive Principles provide the fundamentals of good governance, and for this the state is duty bound to implement them by legislation. Unless the Directive Principles are accorded the needed legal resonance, the roadway to people's participation will continue to be full of potholes and speed-breakers; and without making governance people-centric, the promise of the constitution that was framed by "We, the people", gets fossilised.

ECONOMIC REINTEGRATION

The main threat to India's future is not political, but economic.[51] The Indian economy has been semi-closed for most of the post-World War II period. Since independence in 1947, the Indian government has pursued a strategy of self-reliance with autonomous industrialisation at its core. The state has attempted to transform the material basis of Indian society through detailed intervention in the economy.

But, beginning in the 1980s and more recently in 1991, the government decisively moved away from an interventionist posture by drastically altering its industrial and trade policies in favor of an 'open' economy. To understand the shift in economic policies India's post-independent capitalist development trajectory is divided into two phases. The first phase (roughly from 1950 to 1980) is called the phase of resistance, a process by which the Indian state along with the Indian bourgeoisie attempted to resist the forces of global capitalism and foster self-reliance. The second phase (1980 onward) is called the process of reintegration with the world economy, whereby previous attempts to fend off external economic forces are substituted by a desire to participate in the world economy.[52] Resistance denotes a national response to colonial experience, while reintegration indicates an ongoing accommodation of global economic and other forces. With the emergence of the middle class, global reintegration is perceived as an economic necessity, but the process is mediated by the structures and politics of Indian society. The process of resistance sowed the seeds of reintegration. The self-reliant model, in the Indian socio-institutional context, cultivated an economy of shortages, lethargic technological development, inefficiency and corruption and 'rising expectations' of the middle class. Over the time, it became difficult for the national productive structure to meet the changing demands of an increasingly differentiated Indian society. Moreover, international pressures to liberalise the Indian economy and the collapse of the Soviet

Union have called for a thorough re-evaluation of the model of Indian resistance to global capitalism.[53]

Globalisation

Between 1980 and 1990 the amount of capital directly invested in foreign lands nearly tripled. It is needless to underline that capital has assumed global character and its upsurge and diversification has been leading to changes in economies and polities of all countries of the world. Thus, globalisation, though not a novel concept, has assumed new significance since the turn of the 1990s mainly because of the changed international balance of forces resulting from the collapse of the Soviet Union, the disintegration of the world socialist system and the end of the Cold War.[54] Globalisation means the attempt to bring the world under single domination and one system.[55]

Marx and Engels in The Communist Manifesto[56] had clearly presented their "vision of capitalism's triumphant globalisation".[57] They had written:

"Modern industry has established the world market, for which the discovery of America paved the way...the bourgeoisie has through its exploitation of the world market given a cosmopolitan character to production and consumption in every country.... In place of the old local and national seclusion and self-sufficiency, we have...universal interdependence of nations. And as in material, so also in intellectual production."

Further, in the course of his unique address to the nation on the eve of Republic Day 2000, K.R. Narayanan, the then President of India, came forward with a scathing analysis of the goings-on in the country particularly on the economic front. It is simply unprecedented. On the issue of globalisation and excessive focus on advertisement-driven consumerism he said:[58]

"The unabashed vulgar indulgence in conspicuous consumption by the *nouveau*-rich society has left the underclass seething in frustration. One half of our society guzzles aerated beverages while the other has to make do with palmful of muddied water. Our three way fast-lane of liberalisation, privatisation, globalisation must provide self-pedestrian crossing for the underpowered India also so that it too can move towards equality of status and opportunity."

Another most severe indictment on the issue of globalisation has emanated from no less a person than the Director General of the International Labor Organisation (ILO), Juan Somavia. He has characterised the process of globalisation as the glorification of "casino capitalism."[59]

Globalisation and India

The origin of the process of globalisation in India can be traced, when, during Indira Gandhi's Prime Ministership she organised the Asian Games in New Delhi. She indulged in this extravagansa and spent crores of rupees to project her son, Rajiv Gandhi, as her future successor. She for the first time decided to import luxury goods like color TVs etc. to cater to conspicuous consumption of the upper middle class section of our country at the expense of the common tax payer. As a matter of fact these color TVs had no takers then, as those were very much expensive. Gandhi's government had to give subsidy so as to enable the affluent section of Indian society to purchase these American goods. Rajiv Gandhi tried to pursue these policies once he assumed the office of the Prime Minister after the cruel assassination of Mrs. Gandhi.[60] He initiated a process of liberalisation and decided to integrate the Indian economy with the global economy.[61]

But it was Narasimha Rao, who became the chief architect of the process of globalisation after he assumed the office of the Prime Minister in 1991 in the Tenth Lok Sabha. He appointed Dr. Manmohan Singh as his Finance Minister. It was left to him to usher in fundamental changes in the Indian economic structure at the instance of the International Monetary Fund and the World Bank. The IMF/WB Group suggested that India should adopt a programme of structural adjustment, which they had recommended to other countries, particularly those in Latin America, in similar situations. They promised India that if their conditionalities are strictly observed, India could get adequate financial support in the form of structural adjustment loans (SAL) to implement the structural adjustment programme (SAP). India seems to have agreed to all the conditionalities.[62] This was revealed in the letters Union Finance Minister Dr. Manmohan Singh wrote to the President of the WB on 11 November 1991 and to the Managing Director of the IMF on 2 June 1992, besides the Union Budget for 1992-93 and the Memorandum for Economic Policies for 1992-93 covering the Performance Criteria for Domestic and Financial Policies in 1992-93. The World Bank Confidential Report No. 8998 of 30 November 1991, considered as the "Mother Document" on the SAP relating to India, reviewed how much India had done since July 1991, and spelt out how much more India should do in 1992-93, 1993-94 and 1994-95.[63]

Dr. Manmohan Singh repeatedly asserted that his government inherited an economy on the verge of collapse. He also pointed out that lenders always imposed conditionalities and India in the present context of its history had no other alternative.[64] Dr. Manmohan Singh has taken a U-turn in his approach when he straightway went against all those principal recommendations contained in South-South Report, at the South commission in Geneva, of which he was the Secretary. This South-South Report was prepared under the chairmanship of the late lamented Julius Nyerere, the former President of Tanzania and a senior world statesman. The report categorically and forcefully recommended that the economics of the Third World countries would be devastated in case those countries take recourse to structural adjustments in their economies as a sequel to the globalisation of the economy.[65] In the report, he stated:

"Developed Countries were able to use the international financial institutions to impose their view on Third World countries and at the same time demand that the latter should adjust their economies through contradictory polities. This was a form of neo-colonialism. The debt crisis was used by the North as an opportunity to influence their domestic choices and to impose on them externally determined values, policies, concessions and patterns of development. The social and political costs of inappropriate measures were then paid by the victim countries and their people...and any resulting instability was used by the North as a further opportunity for external intervention.... The establishment of a system of international and economic relations in which the South's second class status would be institutionalised is an imminent danger."[66]

Furthermore, it is one of the greatest tragedies of our times that neither the Parliament of India was taken into confidence nor the then ruling Congress party under the leadership of Narasimha Rao debated the issues of globalisation prior to its announcement in the Lok Sabha as a *"fait accomplice"*. The country's economic sovereignty was bartered away without the consent of the people and Parliament.[67] Many State Governments like those of Bihar, West Bengal, Tamil Nadu, and Orissa approached the Supreme Court in 1993 and complained that they had not been consulted before the Government of India committed the country to the concept of structural adjustment, particularly in the context of agriculture being a state subject as per the provisions of the constitution. But the Supreme Court is yet to hear these petitions. Beside, a people's commission was constituted under the chairmanship of the former Supreme Court Justice, V.R. Krishna Iyer, the other members were the former Supreme Court Justice Chennappa Reddy and a former Chief Justice of the Delhi High Court, Justice Rajindar Sachar. They submitted a unanimous report and recommended that globalisation is completely antithetical to the Preamble of the Constitution of India and it is also ultra vires of the Fundamental Principles of the constitution. Another people's commission was constituted under the chairmanship of Justice Krishna Iyer with members like noted economist Dr. Prabhat Patnaik and famous scientist and former UGC Chairman Dr. Yashpal to report to the nation as to whether the 1970 Patent Act should be changed or not. The nation is grateful to the members of this commission for their unequivocal declaration, that the 1970 Patent Act has not only served the best interests of the nation, but has helped the growth of indigenous pharmaceutical industries in a big way. The modern medicines (allopathic medicines) are sold to consumers in India at the cheapest rate, which is unique in the world due to the provisions of the 1970 Patent Act. They have also specifically recommended that any dilution in the 1970 Patent Act would impinge on the right to life enshrined in the Fundamental Rights of our constitution.[68]

During Narasimha Rao's regime, the mainstream political parties, up to the dictates of the IMF, WB and World Trade Organisation, okayed the provisions of the Marrakkesh agreement, and got a resolution passed in this regard in 1994 in Parliament. All the provisions of this agreement militate against our national interest. It is on record that the BJP, which was then functioning as an opposition party, opposed this on the floor of Parliament. But when Atal Behari Vajpayee became the Prime Minister of the country in the thirteenth Lok Sabha he okayed this infamous Patent Bill thereby abrogating the 1970 Patent Act.[69]

Reforms and the New Economic Policy

In a review of India's New Economic Policy (NEP), the IMF/World Bank have expressed happiness though they are not satisfied with the pace of reforms. India's economy, which had lumbered along at 3.5 per cent growth per year from 1950 to 1980, picked up to 5.5 per cent in the 1980s and averaged 7 per cent growth in fiscal years 1995 to 1997. Some claimed that India had joined the ranks of Asia's tiger economies. However, India looked more like an elephant again, as the industrial growth in the first three quarters of fiscal year 1998 was half that of the same period the previous year and a third of its peak between 1994 and 1996.[70]

A slower pace of reform and lower growth rates will not only cause economic pain but will also endanger India's social and political progress. One reason for the slow progress of reforms is the fear of the Indian government on the possible risks involved. Mainly three risk factors are identified:[71]

(a) The failure of the government to implement the package of structural adjustment programme due to social and political reaction to cuts in subsidies, retrenchment of labor on account of exit policy and high inflation.

(b) The failure to generate strong supply response from the domestic private sector, NRIs, and foreign investors.

(c) Related to the external sector developments and political developments unfavorable to India.

The experiences of countries, which have already implemented SAP, have suggested that structural reforms do not automatically lead to high growth. Like Mexico and others, India faces the quandary of a half completed reform process. Even so, further reform is critical for several reasons:[72]

(1) India's financial sector still cannot effectively mobilise and mediate capital to respond to economic changes. The resulting high cost of capital makes Indian industry and exports less competitive.

(2) India's abysmal infrastructure is a major constraint on growth.

(3) Indian trade has been opened enough to expose many companies to greater competition, but not enough to provide a strong, sustained impetus for growth.

(4) Uncertainty about Indian macro-economic policy worries investors and managers.

(5) India needs greater labor market flexibility to make its companies more competitive and its economy more productive.

(6) Foreign investment in India, while much increased in recent years, remains far too low.

(7) Political instability and gridlock in Delhi may frustrate restructuring, as they have in Japan. A government dependent on many parties for its political survival will find it hard to enact even those reforms it favors.

(8) The political base for reform remains narrow. The only significant constituency for reform is the urban middle class, which is at most a quarter of the electorate.

The international environment for reform may be worsening. True, India has been spared the worst of the East Asian troubles, because of its lower dependence on exports, healthier current account balance, modest short-term debt and the limited convertibility of the rupee.[73] Beside, India has a powerful and experienced regulator in the form of the Reserve Bank of India. It keeps a watchful eye on commercial banks and other financial institutions and has prescribed guidelines and framed rules and regulations, which they have to follow, and they have to report their dealings to the RBI. There is a system of disclosure whereby the banks have to make public their assets, liabilities and lendings and it is not easy for them to fudge their operations and conceal bad debts. Further, India has a vibrant parliamentary democracy. The government is responsible and answerable to Parliament. The media world too is vibrant and never hesitates from bringing to light suspected shady deals. In this situation, it is not easy for the Indian financial and banking sector to behave as its counterpart did in East Asian countries. But, nobody can say the same thing about the years to come if the government goes in for full-scale liberalisation in order to become a part of the globalised world economy because it will lead to three things, namely, freeing the prices including the exchange rate of the rupee, *i.e.*, making the rupee fully convertible; retreat of the state, *i.e.*, state giving up most of its role including that as a regulator of in the economy; and selling public enterprises to the private sector to bring in a greater measure of competition.[74] All these steps are fraught with dangerous implications. In the present age of revolution in the sphere of information technology and electronic banking, financial capital can take flight from one economy to the other without much difficulty. In this situation, it will be difficult for a nation-state to regulate its activities, not to speak of controlling it.[75]

Globalisation—Dangerous Implications

Obviously, India has to be very cautious in deciding to globalise its economy. MNCs have been eyeing India's vast market and resources for a long time and they will not like India to have its own independent economy. We do not totally oppose the idea of India becoming internationally competitive.[76] But what India should do first is to open up the domestic economy to domestic competition and thereby improve efficiency of Indian economy and its producers to prepare for facing global competition. If this is not done and instead if India just jump for globalisation on a full scale, it might result in the collapse of domestic industry, which was surviving under the insulated/protected environment for the four decades since Independence.

Furthermore, the other factors, related to the very survival of India, should be seriously taken into account.

The national movement and the governments after independence have been committed to the removal of regional disparities in economic development. To recall, the policy of the British government as well as its discriminatory attitudes to various regions and their inhabitants led to the rise and growth in regional economic disparities. Bihar and most parts of UP after 1857 and Bengal after 1905 were knowingly neglected while Punjab was favored in various ways. In order to reduce regional disparities, governments prior to 1991 gave special attention to hitherto backward areas and formulated special packages. Backward area development schemes were incorporated in almost every plan. Now, with focus shifting from state directed to market-propelled economic development and the reliance being placed on private, both Indian and foreign, investments, only those areas will be receiving investments which are already ahead in development and have infrastructural facilities besides no worry on account of law and order situation. This means, the regions east of Delhi will be neglected and further go down the ladder of development. If this happens, it will have serious political repercussions for the survival of India as one nation.[77]

Add to this is the formulation of the World Bank,[78] which talks of localisation and globalisation. In other words, a unified national market is thought to be irrelevant. It means that no region or part of India needs the unified national market. It can develop its own local market and link it with the global market to reap all the benefits and with the revolution in the field of information technology, it will not be in any disadvantageous position. One may recall that the entire struggle against imperialism before and after independence, has been for building and protecting our national market and reserving it for our goods.[79] Now with this formulation being nullified by the World Bank thesis, the very basis of India as one nation will disappear and the way will be paved for disintegration. "Politically, globalisation is helping to spawn the atomisation of countries. When international barriers to trade and financial flows crumble, nations lose one of their main weapons against separatist sentiment. If the world market is open, the threat of being cut-off from the national market isn't much of a threat at all."[80]

"Yet another idiosyncrasy of contemporary globalisation is that it goes hand in hand with degeneration. Even as economies integrate, entire companies and industries are disintegrating. It is possible that one day soon a major manufacturer will own no factories of its own. In fact, some technology companies are already at this stage."[81]

With globalisation, unemployment is bound to increase. "We have already lost two crore jobs when almost thirty five crores of our people are below the poverty line. Lakhs of our indigenous and small scale industries have been closed down as a result of such government policies that categorically and specifically favour importing such consumer goods like women's *bindi* which were exclusively reserved for the small and tiny sector industries in our country. This import policy of the Government of India runs counter to the basic philosophy of *swadeshi* and self-reliance as propounded by Mahatma Gandhi."[82] The American multinational companies like Coca Cola and Pepsi have the dubious record to destabilise national governments in many countries[83], which refuse to serve their commercial interests.

Further, new industries and activities will require new kinds of skills. Mostly the upper segments of the society, which can afford to pay for them, can acquire new kinds of skills. Obviously, inequalities in the society will increase and this coupled with demonstration effect and consumerism, fueled by the modern electronic media will lead to crimes, anarchy and chaos. With the governmental activities and public sector shrinking, the total number of jobs there is getting fast reduced and in this situation reservation for SC, ST, and OBCs has lost all significance. Thus globalisation is going to nullify another national objective, namely, socio-economic homogenisation.[84]

Moreover, it is worth recalling the fact that the first Finance Minister of the Indian Republic, the illustrious and late lamented C.D. Deshmukh, did a yeoman service to India's financial sector when he in 1950 nationalised the insurance sector, which was in the private sector at that time. On the other hand, Yashwant Sinha, would share the ignominy of handing over a portion of Indian nationalised insurance industry to the private and multinational companies, when Indian insurance companies are making profits and America's are on the decline. Hence, it is bound to result in the outflow of India's capital to America and other countries rather than the inflow of their capital to India. In this regard, who loses? America or we? It is we who are bound to lose in this unequal bargain.

Opportunities and Challenges

Despite these severe implications of globalisation, what is important, now, is to take urgent and effective steps to explore, harness and use available resources and opportunities for the furtherance of national economy and development.

It is estimated that there are approximately 15 million Persons of Indian Origin (PIOs) and Non-Resident Indians (NRIs) outside India. When one considers the growing strength and potential of overseas Indians, it is evident that they can be a formidable asset to India, both in political and economic terms. While in countries like Mauritius, Surinam, Fiji and Trinidad and Tobago, they enjoy power and influence, in countries like South Africa, the U.S., Canada, the U.K., Singapore and Malaysia, they occupy an important position in the power structure of these countries because of their relative economic strength.[85] It took Indian government an unduly long time to understand, appreciate and use this enormous asset India has. Even now very little organised efforts are there to inform and involve the Indian communities in overall national efforts — potential, economic or even cultural. For most of these overseas Indians, their links with their motherland continue to remain strong, abiding and deep and many of them would not only be prepared but would consider it a privilege to remain associated with India and be of assistance to the country of their origin. The growing financial strength and success of NRIs and PIOs now, more than ever before, is available for furthering India's national interest and developmental needs. Apart from financial resources which could be tapped, the considerable technological and scientific skills and talents of Indians are recognised and acknowledged the world over and can under certain conditions become a major impulse for India's own scientific and technological advancement.[86]

Unfortunately, so far India paid very little focused attention to this aspect. Apart from the need to have a full-fledged and separate department or ministry to handle this, Indian diplomatic missions must now play a more proactive and meaningful role in mobilizing and harnessing this resource for India's national advantage, be it in science and technology, culture, investments, tourism or for using their growing and now considerable political clout and influence to further national objectives. For this to happen, overseas Indians should be looked at as an extension and an inseparable part of India and given national treatment in all matters thus involving them fully and incrementally in India's national efforts. Overseas Indians are now poised to play a significant role in India's economic development and in creating a more propitious international environment conducive to India's national interest. This is a major opportunity and a challenge to India's diplomacy and missions abroad. While the conduct of India's external economic diplomacy should primarily be the responsibility of the Ministry of External Affairs (MEA) and its diplomatic missions abroad, that in practice is simply not the case. The direction of India's external economic diplomacy is neither coherent nor the overall responsibility of any one single government Ministry or Department. Economic work, broadly speaking, is currently distributed between the ministries of Finance, Commerce, Industry, Agriculture, Petroleum, and External Affairs. However, international and multilateral economic diplomacy in the coming century is likely to be a serious and specialised job profoundly affecting the vital national interests of countries. In the changed and emerging situation, it cannot be the responsibility of five or six Ministries/ Departments who at times do not even keep each other informed, much less involved, while taking decisions affecting overall economic interests.[87]

Development and Human Freedom

Another area, which requires an immediate attention, is to tackle the basic problems of the people. The reforms must be seen to benefit India's huge rural population. Without their support, agricultural subsidies cannot be reduced or eventually eliminated. In the end, the most important constituency for the reforms is the rural poor, whose increasing political participation and rising economic expectations must be accommodated to maintain political stability.[88] In this regard Robert A. Dahl (1971-74) suggests 'a very general hypothesis' that:

"The chances that a country will develop and maintain a competitive political regime (and, even more so, a polyarchy) depend upon the extent to which the country's society and economy: (a) provide literacy, education and communication, (b) create a pluralistic rather than a centrally dominated social order, and (c) prevent extreme inequalities among the politically relevant strata of the country."[89]

In a similar vein John D. Aram (1997) also finds 'strong evidence' supportive of the hypothesis that 'growth leads to democracy' and that increasing affluence and democratisation go together.[90] Likewise, going a step further Dr. Amartya Sen, in his book *Development as Freedom* (1999) argues that growth is not enough. While not denying the importance of raising output and per capita income, especially in very poor countries, he argues for a broader goal for development: increasing the capability of all human beings to achieve those things that they most value. Higher income, of course, increases such capabilities in important ways, so it is a significant component of development. But it is not the only part. It does not assure good health, adequate education, greater longevity, the ability to influence the political decisions that affect one's life, or the freedom to choose alternative lifestyles — or even goods and services beyond those that are immediately on offer. Therefore, higher income is not sufficient to assure development — only necessary. Development is not merely an economic process but a political one as well. It therefore ultimately requires a "democratisation" of political communities to give citizens a voice in important decisions made for the community. To fail in this regard, Sen argues, is to limit human freedom and, by extension, the possibility for full human development.[91]

NUCLEARISATION

Investments in defence, however affordable, but which do not establish a credible capability in relation to the likely challenges and tasks, become totally infructuous and, because they might provide a false sense of security, counterproductive. The reverse can be to allocate so much in defence in order to make it highly credible and capable, but development would suffer heavily.[92] The full story of India's path to nuclear capability acquisition is bumpy but absolutely absorbing and spread over fifty years.

Indian scientists, particularly Dr. Homi J. Bhabha, foresaw the coming in of the atomic age even before the Americans conducted their first nuclear test at Alamogordo in New Mexico on July 16, 1945. In 1944, Dr. Bhabha wrote to the Tata Trust urging them to establish a training and research institution for fundamental research in nuclear physics so that when the nuclear era was ushered in, India would have trained people already in place.[93] Dr. Bhabha was able to enlist the support of Pt. Jawaharlal Nehru from the beginning. An Atomic Energy Commission was established in the forties through a Government resolution with Dr. Bhabha as the Chairman, and the Prime Minister always held the portfolio. Subsequently, the commission was made statutory through an enactment. Nehru's strong tilt towards science-technology development in India provided the sinews, and Bhabha transformed this dream into a glowing reality.[94]

The horrors of Hiroshima and Nagasaki were followed by a new vista of atoms for peace, of nuclear power generation, transformations in agriculture with nuclear technology and medical diagnostics and therapy using atomic science and technology. Dr. Bhabha was elected to preside over the first international conference on Atoms for Peace in 1956. He predicted that fusion energy was not far away and once energy at very cheap cost was available, countries like India should be able to advance rapidly.[95] But in the backdrop the ultimate horror of nuclear weapons still loomed large.

India's path to acquisition of nuclear capability has been distinct, with several features which mark it out from all other countries opting for nuclear technology — whether for weapons or power generation. India's was the middle path — prioritizing atomic power generation and other peaceful uses of nuclear technology, but at the same time keeping the weapon option open. In the early sixties, Dr. Bhabha told a special gathering of MPs in the central hall of Parliament: give me 18 month's notice and you can have the atom bomb. But focusing on weapons would be too costly for India; a country like ours should invest on nuclear science to combat poverty — for power generation, medicine, agriculture and other spin-off benefits.[96] However, many people, both in India and abroad, charge that Dr. Bhabha was intending to build a bomb from the beginning and he was misleading the Prime Minister. The real truth is that in the initial years Dr. Bhabha was opposed to India exercising nuclear option. According to Dr. Gopal, who is studying Dr. Bhabha's papers, at one time Dr. Bhabha even suggested to Pt. Nehru that India should unilaterally give up the nuclear option. Jawaharlal Nehru, who knew international relations better, told Dr. Bhabha that India should keep its nuclear capability as bargaining chip.[97]

Thus, for both areas — peaceful applications and the weapon option — Bhabha had a clear strategic vision and priorities. A poor country like India cannot afford to give priority to atomic weapons. And uranium enrichment based on the diffusion method, then the prevalent route to weapon making, was ruled out absolutely for the massive input of electricity and other resources that it involves. Bhabha's vision tied Indian weapon option to envisaged breakthrough in plutonium technology, the cheapest route and one most suited to Indian need of a nuclear watchdog. The Indian weapon option then was to be a byproduct of India's nuclear power generation development plans.[98] Bhabha was able to chart this path for India — realised after his sudden death — because of a breakthrough in the advanced technology of reprocessing spent fuel for extracting plutonium.

The path to nuclear capability charted out by Dr.Bhabha had two basic features. One, that Indian nuclear technology acquisition gives primacy to a long-term strategy for power generation, along with all round growth in allied scientific knowledge, a spin-off for industry in metallurgy, and nuclear applications for agriculture and medicine. Weaponisation takes a low priority in this scheme of things.[99]

The second basic feature of the Bhabha route to nuclear capability is stress on indigenous, self-reliant growth by laying a sound foundation. Which meant building an extensive infrastructure of research and development to achieve what in scientific jargon is called capability along the entire nuclear fuel cycle.[100] Build up of nuclear and related industrial capability all along the line — from uranium mining and refinement, fuel fabrication for diverse reactors, designing and construction of reactors, building heavy water plants and nuclear industrial units, and finally running atomic power stations. Safety and the problem of nuclear wastes management were of course given primacy right from the start.[101]

His fifty year plan for Indian Atomic Energy Development had three phases. In the first phase, India will construct natural-uranium-heavy-water reactor using indigenous uranium and heavy water. These reactors will produce plutonium. The plutonium will be separated and used as fuel for the fast-breeder reactor in the second phase. Fast-breeder reactors produce more fissile materials than they consume. By using India's abundant thorium in the fast-breeders as blankets, the thorium will be converted into Uranium 233, which is a fissile material. In turn, that will be used to fuel the enriched-uranium-light-water reactor in the third phase. With this long-term plan in view he contracted to set up the Canada-India experimental reactor at Trombay, which was a natural-uranium-heavy-water reactor. As this reactor was established, he also took steps to develop indigenously the technology to separate plutonium from the irradiated uranium rods of Canada-India reactor. No nation was prepared to transfer this technology and India developed this on its own.[102]

A landmark in the build up of infrastructure for India's nuclear capability was the construction in 1964-65 of a nuclear spent fuel reprocessing test plant at the Bhabha Atomic Research Center (BARC) by a team of scientists and engineers headed by Homi Sethna. It is this breakthrough that provided the link between nuclear power production and the weapon option based on the plutonium route. Over the years, as Indian scientists acquired a grip over spent fuel reprocessing, the plutonium route to atomic weapons opened up, by-passing the enormously costly uranium enrichment method. India now has four reprocessing plants — while the pioneering BARC unit has become a full-fledged plant, at Tarapur a spent fuel reprocessing plant was built and has been operating for a decade and a half, and the most modern and advanced reprocessing plant has come up at Kalpakkam. The fourth unit, a specialised reprocessing plant, has recently been commissioned at Kalpakkam itself. The acquisition and rapid development of spent fuel reprocessing technology justifies the Indian claim that this country's route to the nuclear weapon option is a spin-off from the power programme and the cheapest weapon programme anywhere in the world.[103]

However, Prime Minister Jawaharlal Nehru tirelessly denounced the trend towards nuclear arms race. It became a passion for him to plead for disarmament.[104] As early as 1940, Jawaharlal Nehru had said "we believe that complete disarmament by all nation states should be aimed at, as in fact an urgent necessity if the world is not to be reduced to barbarism." As early as 1948, at the time of consideration of the report of the newly created UN Atomic Energy Commission, India had proposed limiting the use of atomic energy to peaceful purposes and elimination of nuclear weapons from national arsenals.[105] It was on India's initiative that the UN undertook a study of the economic consequences of disarmament, which debunked the thesis, so fashionable those days, that propagated that disarmament would lead to large-scale unemployment and the disruption of the economy of the developed countries.[106]

Following the Chinese nuclear test on October 16, 1964, Dr. Bhabha became a fervent advocate of India exercising its nuclear option. However, there were strong West-oriented lobbies that had great faith in West supporting India against China. Under the influence of that lobby, Prime Minister Lal Bahadur Shastri approached Britain for a nuclear umbrella. Britain was not willing to provide any security guarantees. By 1965, it was also becoming clear that the West had no intention of assisting India in its defence preparedness programme against Pakistan-China and India had to rely increasingly on the USSR for its defence equipment and technology. Thus, as early as, in 1965, Dr. Bhabha was able to persuade the then Prime Minister to sanction the subterranean nuclear explosive project (SNEP). That would have made India a recognised nuclear power in the international community at that stage.[107] The work on the project unfortunately came to an end when Dr. Bhabha was killed in the Mont Blanc air crash on January 24, 1966 (the very day Smt. Indira Gandhi was sworn in as the Prime Minister). Dr. Bhabha's successor, Dr. Vikram Sarabhai, did not subscribe to the idea of India going nuclear. Indira Gandhi sent her envoys, Dr. Vikram Sarabhai and L.K. Jha, to Moscow, Paris, London and Washington to seek security guarantees from these four powers. Their quest for security guarantees failed and they came back empty-handed.[108] At that stage the two super powers came out with their draft Non-Proliferation Treaty and brought to bear on India an enormous amount of pressure to accede to it. India rejected the NPT and decided not to accede to it. Further, in 1971 India faced a Pakistan-China-US line-up when General Yahya Khan cracked down on the Awami League and population of East Bengal. Faced with this hostile combination of powers Mrs. Gandhi was compelled to sign a Peace and Friendship Treaty with the Soviet Union to generate adequate deterrence against Chinese adventurism. US President Nixon dispatched the nuclear-powered and nuclear-armed aircraft carrier US Enterprise into the Bay of Bengal on an intimidatory mission. The Soviet navy sent its task force behind it and the Soviet Naval Headquarters generated a lot of signals to their submarine fleet at sea in a deterrent exercise. Obviously, all these incidents (factors) persuaded Mrs. Gandhi to order the scientists to go ahead with the Pokhran-l test.[109] Thus India exploded her first nuclear device in Pokhran in 1974, within four years of the NPT coming into force. Dr. R. Venkatraman, former President of India, argued that in 1974 there was no threat perception to India's security, as, India's defence capabilities and reputation stood high after the 1971 Bangladesh war. According to him, the first Pokhran test was a protest against the arbitrary and inequal Non-Proliferation Treaty. It was undertaken to demonstrate India's nuclear capability to the rest of the world.[110] India has more convincingly broken China's nuclear monopoly in Asia.[111] No doubt Smt. Gandhi got cold feet after the tests and suspended further testing.

The UN charter recognises that a country can take measures for its own self-defence. India has experience of aggression from both Pakistan and China and has also suffered from the clandestine acquisition of nuclear weapon technology by Pakistan from the West and by Pakistan acquiring nuclear and missile technology from China[112], while the nuclear weapon states stood idly by. There is no evidence of India proliferating nuclear or missile technology to any third country. There is also no evidence of India obtaining any such technology clandestinely. However, the 'nuclear option', which had been implicit for Non-signatories to the NPT, had been repeatedly hinted at by successive Indian governments. India felt it had gained nothing by abstaining from further testing since 1974, while the nuclear weapon states continued to test after that time. The principles and objectives for Nuclear Non-Proliferation and Disarmament stated, "pending the entry into force of a Comprehensive Test Ban Treaty, the Nuclear Weapon States should exercise 'utmost restraint' (emphasis supplied) in carrying out further tests." Notwithstanding the solemn declaration, China conducted on 15 May, 1995, its 42nd test and on 17 August 1995, its 43rd nuclear test. France declared its intention to carry out a series of eight tests starting from September 1995 and ending with May 1996. These are two interesting examples of the "utmost restraint" that the nuclear powers had undertaken to observe before the CTBT came into force.[113] No wonder, India declined to join the Comprehensive Test Ban Treaty. In fact, the Nuclear Powers had no interest in genuine disarmament or elimination of nuclear weapons.

Despite India's efforts to this end during the negotiations of the NPT and CTBT and in bilateral discussions with the nuclear weapon states, there was no evidence of movement towards elimination of nuclear weapons within a certain time frame, although the USA and the former Soviet Union did move through the INF, START-I and START-II agreements towards elimination of intermediate range nuclear forces in Europe and deep cuts in tactical nuclear weapons and in the total number of nuclear warheads possessed by both sides.[114] Thus, the West, instead of marching towards the goal of elimination of nuclear weapons and general and complete disarmament, began to talk of arms control and arms control negotiations. Having irrationally built nuclear arsenals which are excessive and a significant portion of which is unusable, they are now rationalizing their arsenals and cutting them down to sizes which are still several times what is required to destroy human civilisation. At the same time they are doing research in new generation weapons. They insist on sustaining the legality of the use of nuclear weapons.[115]

About a decade later, in 1983, India made preparations for a second nuclear test at Pokhran. It was undertaken to demonstrate again India's nuclear capability to the rest of the world. "The preparations for the test", said former President of India, "were completed and as Defence Minister, I had gone down the shaft and seen all the arrangements. We did not, however, conduct the test at that time for several reasons including pressures from international sources".[116] Again, in 1988, faced with the challenge of China-Pakistan nuclear collaboration Prime Minister Rajiv Gandhi ordered a programme of Indian nuclear weaponisation. As V.P. Singh disclosed in the BBC "Hard Talk" interview, India was ready for testing during his tenure of office and he did not do it because India was economically weak and would not have been able to withstand sanctions.[117] However, the programme has been sustained and developed by his successors Chandrashekhar, Narasimha Rao, Deve Gowda and I.K. Gujral. Further, following the legitimisation of the nuclear weapons by the international community through the unconditional and indefinite extension of the NPT in 1995, Narasimha Rao ordered testing of the weapons. Again they were called off because of US pressure. But the shafts made were available for fresh tests at short notice, as most of the preparations for the tests were completed.[118]

Furthermore, in 1996 the CTBT was adopted and the Chinese acted in an unfriendly manner by bringing in at the last moment the entry into force clause. China persuaded other permanent members of the Security Council to introduce article XIV in the CTBT which insisted that India should sign the treaty to bring it into force, after India had declared that it would not sign the treaty, since it would be against its national security interests, it was a clear attempt by China to curb India's independence and assign India's security a standard lower than China's. That made India's nuclear tests inevitable. Moreover, the kind of pressure built against India following the Shakti tests would have been built to compel India to sign the CTBT. It was better for India to face the sanctions after conducting the tests and declaring itself a nuclear weapon state instead of facing them without having conducting the tests.[119]

On May 11 and 13, 1998 India detonated five nuclear devices at Pokhran, with yields ranging from 15 KT — 45 KT, one device with a yield of 45 KT was a hydrogen or H-bomb. Between Pokhran-I and Pokhran-II a vast scientific and nuclear technology acquisition by Indian scientific institutions is revealed; a striking advance on all sectors of nuclear capability made possible by the linkage between Indian nuclear capability for peaceful applications and the weapon option.[120] Simultaneous testing of a weaponised fission device, a low yield fission device and a thermonuclear device is an unprecedented event in nuclear history. The two subsequent sub-kiloton tests have yielded additional data; and our capability in computer simulation of new designs has been enhanced. Atomic Energy Commission, Chairman R. Chidambaram and Director of the Bhabha Atomic Research Center Anil Kakodkar played crucial role in this effort; they also provided a link with Pokhran-I. Defense Research and Development Organisation gave necessary support to BARC in fabricating and testing the nuclear explosives. Indian scientists and engineers can now fabricate nuclear weapons of different configurations and for various delivery systems. Bharat Ratna Abdul Kalam, therefore, announced: "Nuclear weaponisation is now complete." He added, that the Agni and Prithvi missiles could now be armed with nuclear warheads. A new vision of Agni being developed with a range much higher than 2500 kilometers would be able to carry nuclear warheads weighing 1000 kilograms. The data generated by the tests should be used for developing a modest missile-borne nuclear deterrent capability. We should not repeat the nuclear follies of others by stockpiling redundant nuclear weapons.[121] Those protesting against Indian tests are themselves beneficiaries of nuclear peace. Their urgent pleas to adhere to 'nonproliferation norms' are designed to deny the status India deserves as happened after Pokhran-I. Derogatory remarks of Madeleine Albright, notwithstanding, India is a nuclear weapon state. Prime Minister Vajpayee has rightly observed "It is not a conferment that we seek; nor is it a status for others to grant. It is an endowment to the nation by our scientists and engineers. It is India's due, the right of one-sixth of humankind."[122] He emphasised that "I would, therefore, say that the greatest meaning of the tests is that they have given India Shakti, they have given strength, they have given India self-confidence."[123]

However Richard Grenier, a columnist for *The Washington Times*, analysed that the nuclear tests have given India what its Prime Minister calls 'Shakti' a kind of power possessed by Hinduism's Gods. And the vegetarian Hindus have also begun to eat meat.[124]

Implications of Pokhran-II

India has broken the monopoly of the Nuclear Five. The question is asked whether India should join the Nuclear Club and enjoy its privileges. Having pleaded for a total elimination of nuclear weapons, it would be immoral for India to join any group, which would have the privilege of increasing the nuclear arsenal. On the contrary, India should strive through the United Nations to bring about a Treaty on "No First Use" of nuclear weapons by any of the Member-States.[125]

After a gap of twenty four years, India has demonstrated its scientific and technological prowess to test a variety of warheads ranging from thermo-nuclear to sub-kiloton devices.

The tests conducted on 11th and 13th May 1998 proved beyond any shadow of doubt, India's superiority over Pakistan in nuclear capability. In contrast, Pakistan's nuclear and missile capabilities are limited by what China can provide for Pakistan. While China has decided to arm Pakistan with nuclear weapons and missiles, to countervail India it cannot be in its own interest to permit Pakistan to become an autonomous nuclear weapon power.

Now India (and Pakistan) have forced their way into the nuclear club. The tests have increased tension, made nuclear war very likely in the subcontinent and have unleashed an arms race. While India was aware of Pakistani nuclear weapon capability and Pakistani nuclear weapons have been there since 1987. Pakistan has behaved with restraint in spite of losing the fourth war in Kashmir — the covert war. The tests have brought only one new element to the India-Pakistan equation. Pakistan can now feel more secure *vis-a-vis* the larger India. That in fact is a contribution to stability.[126] Thus, the emerging symmetry with declared capability by both countries is less dangerous than an undeclared 'covert' nuclear situation, which lent to greater insecurity, unpredictability and furtive acts.[127]

India's claim to the status of a nuclear weapon state has been vehemently opposed by the United States. Thus the chances of India getting a Security Council membership has also been ruined by her nuclear tests. The United States and China will veto, if necessary to prevent India's membership in the Security Council. However, a large number of countries are supporting India's candidature for permanent membership of Security Council. These countries include Russia, France, Germany, Sweden, Australia, New Zealand, Poland, Japan, Singapore, Thailand, Malaysia, South Africa, Egypt etc., which cover all the regions of the world.

Challenges After Pokhran-II

Nuclear weapons are destructive, they degenerate security and create more insecurity. Henry Kissinger in 1957 reminded the Americans in his book 'Nuclear Weapons and Foreign Policy' that if the enormous US nuclear weapon capability was not related to a doctrine framework, it could lead to a nuclear disaster. The same is true of India as well. A nuclear doctrine is necessary that could define the role of nuclear weapons and their use or nonuse in a crisis situation as nuclear strategy aims at escalation and can lead to a nuclear war.[128]

Among the eight nuclear and undeclared nuclear weapon powers India stands alone in agonizing over its nuclearisation and confounded by its ignorance. There is no attempt among political parties, many of whose leaders nurtured the nuclear weapons programme to come together to evolve a consensus. In almost all nuclear weapon powers, when the weapons were acquired most of the population were not adequately informed about them. The depth of ignorance can be gauged from the fact that it took forty years from the dawn of the nuclear era for the strategists and political-military leaderships of the nuclear weapon powers to develop some understanding about the fightability of nuclear war. Even now if the people of those countries understood the true nature of nuclear weapons and their limitations they would not be paying their taxes to maintain such monstrous stockpiles. In that sense the inadequacy of knowledge in India is not worse than what it is in the US, UK, France, Russia and China. However, in those countries there is a consensus, however, misguided it may have been, to support the nuclear weapon policy of their respective governments. In India in spite of India's policy being more rational there is no consensus and not even a concerted attempt at building a consensus. The initiative to build the consensus must come from the government since it took this historic decision to make India a declared nuclear weapon state. The government needs to organise discussions and seminars for the parliamentarians, including ministers. It will be very helpful if politicians of the ruling party discipline themselves not to talk about the nuclear issue and leave it to one or two better equipped leaders alone to deal with.[129]

In democracies, government white papers are pre-eminent. The absence of any white paper on foreign and defence policies in India over fifty years is a shameful record and an indication of the clandestine and furtive manner in which both the defence and external affairs ministries function. Economic liberalisation is not the only liberalisation we need. If defence and foreign policy is to be receptive to world changes, they must be made more in the open.[130]

Indian Nuclear Doctrine

A draft nuclear doctrine of the national security advisory board (NSAB) headed by the eminent K. Subrahmanyam was released on August 17, 1999. It provides a broad framework for the development, deployment and employment of India's nuclear forces. It has proposed a credible, minimum nuclear deterrent-retaliatory capability, consisting of sufficient, survivable and operationally prepared nuclear forces with the necessary support of an effective intelligence and early warning system.[131]

It has called for a triad — bombers, land-based ballistic missiles and ballistic missiles launched from submarines. Such a triad is expected to constitute a "minimum and credible" deterrence against nuclear attack on Indian cities by the two main adversaries — Pakistan and China. But, since the present Indian capabilities are limited, the triad will take many years to materialise.[132] Inherent in the doctrine is the advocacy of a 'no first use' policy. This suggests that retaliation against a nuclear attack will be the preferred policy and not an offensive posture of the kind presently favored by the US, Russia, France and the UK as also Pakistan.

Since 1964 when China detonated its first atomic bomb, it has declared a 'no first use' policy. It has reiterated, however, that such a declaration does not apply to territories that are its own. This suggests that in so far as Taiwan and Arunachal Pradesh are concerned, China could contemplate first use of nuclear weapons of low yield (sub-kilotons) tactical weapons. The Indian doctrine of a 'no first use' rejects the development of tactical weapons. Hence in a second strike retaliatory mode the use of the weapons would be against cities and population centres. This is classified as a "counter value" as against a "counterforce" doctrine. Counterforce pertains to nuclear attacks against military targets.[133]

What distinguishes the proposed doctrine from all other nuclear doctrines is that it is anchored in India's continued commitment to global, verifiable and non-discriminating nuclear disarmament, describing it as India's national security objective. The Preamble categorically states that any use of nuclear weapons would constitute "the gravest threat to humanity and to peace and stability in the international system."[134]

Another distinctive feature of the proposed nuclear doctrine is the rejection of war fighting. Although often presented as complementary, there is a fundamental difference between strategies of nuclear deterrence and nuclear war fighting. For nuclear deterrence, it is not necessary that warheads should be matched with warheads and missiles with missiles. A modest sufficiency is enough. For nuclear war fighting, however, there is always a quest for nuclear superiority: more accurate delivery systems are also needed to destroy a large number of military targets. Nuclear deterrence threatens only punishment while the objective of nuclear war fighting is victory.[135]

Both the United States and the former Soviet Union invested billions of dollars and rubles in early warning installations, blast-proof bunkers, redundant communication networks, and airborne command posts like the so-called Looking Glass aircraft and Take Charge And Move Out (TACAMO) planes. The proposed doctrine rejects such nuclear follies. Operational Indian nuclear forces are going to be very modest.

The Chairman of the Atomic Energy Commission (AEC), Dr. R. Chidambaram, has claimed that the five nuclear weapons tests at Pokhran in May 1998 have provided enough data to his scientists and engineers to be able to conduct computer simulated sub-critical experiments (SCEs) at the laboratory not in the field.[136] Such a view has not been shared by many of his own former compatriots, such as Dr. P.K. Iyengar who has favored conducting further nuclear tests. Addressing a group of scientists, including those who participated in Pokhran-I and II. Dr. Iyengar said that from the scientific point of view "a survivable nuclear deterrent" envisaged in the proposed nuclear doctrine could not be achieved without further testing. He said that Indian nuclear weaponisation should include the development and testing of a neutron bomb because it is "more efficient in weight and total energy produce." In any case, it has taken the United States and Russia thousands of nuclear tests to arrive at SCEs. In any case, laboratory tests and computer simulations cannot provide complete reliability. India has to conduct many more tests to improve the warhead designs and maximise the yield to weight (Y/W) ratio as to reduce the payload on the missile.[137]

Further, commitment to no first use necessitated a robust command and control system that can survive a nuclear first strike and then deliver a devastating blow. "If command and control fails, nothing else matters".[138] However, an 'elaborate' command and control apparatus is not necessary.[139] It is implied, that the present system of the higher direction of war would fulfill the requirements with minimum modifications. The aim appears to be to find a low cost solution to an obviously complex challenge.

Beside, what is needed after Pokhran-II is a clear go-ahead irrespective of the costs involved to develop 10-15 Agni long range missiles and the same number of Prithvi missiles and emplace on them plutonium and hydrogen bombs. Only then can there be credibility to the Indian "minimum" nuclear deterrence.[140]

India's Missile Programme

Indira Gandhi took the first step in the development of indigenous missile capability and for this, she instituted the Integrated Guided Missiles Development Programme (IGMDP) in 1983. This was accelerated during the Rajiv Gandhi administration. India's 'Missile Man' Dr. Abdul Kalam provided dynamic leadership to this programme. The IGMDP draws its physical, technical and human resources from a wide range of DRDO agencies and beyond. Beside IGMDP, as the country's chief technology generator, the DRDO is the overarching agency tasked to develop the Indian missile programme. As a result, India has one of the most advanced and ambitious space programs among the developing countries:[141]

Prithvi

Prithvi is a single-stage, short-range, surface-to-surface missile (SSM). Transportable by road and equipped with two liquid-fuel engines, the Prithvi is reported to have the highest ratio of warhead-weight to overall-weight of any missile in its class.[142] The Prithvi comes in three variants. The SS-150 is a battlefield support system for the army (range 150 Km., 1000 kg. payload) and the SS-250 is dedicated to the Indian Air Force (range-250 Km., 500-750 Kg. payload). Between 1988-98, 18 field trials of the SS-150 and SS-250 designs were conducted. In 1994, the SS-150 version was inducted into the army and 20 SS-150s now form the 333rd Missile Regiment of the Xl corps based in Hyderabad. The SS-250 is expected to enter service soon. The third variant is the naval version. The SS-350 (range-350 Km., 500 Kg. payload). Currently in the advanced stages of testing and field trials, the SS-350 is designed to be launched from both the ocean's surface, as well as underwater.

Agni

Agni is a two-stage intermediate range ballistic missile (IRBM) fitted with a reentry vehicle that employs a carbon-composite ablative shield that heats up to 3500 degrees Celsius during flight while keeping the interior cooled to 40 degrees. Agni-1 (1500 Km./1000Kg. or 2500 Km./500 Kg. combination), employing liquid/solid fuel combination, was derived from India's first civilian satellite launch vehicle (SLV-3). It was tested thrice during 1989-94 and then recalled in December 1996 with the government classifying it as a "technology demonstrator" (TD). The Agni TD was revived following the 1998 nuclear tests and an extended-range Agni (ER-Agni or Agni-II, 3700 Km. 1000 Kg.) was successfully flight-tested on April 11, 1999.[143] This missile used solid fuel in both stages and was tested up to a range of 2000 plus Km.

Surya

Although the government will not confirm the status or even the existence of this intercontinental ballistic missile (ICBM) believed to have a 8000-12000 Km. range and 1000 plus Kg. payload, it is thought to be in advanced stages of design and undergoing simulated testing of components.

Sagarika

The Sagarika (Oceanic) is a single-stage, solid-fueled system being developed as a cruise as well as a sea-launched ballistic missile (330 Km., 500-750 Kg.). Configured to carry nuclear warheads, the ballistic missile variant (and perhaps also the cruise missile version) is designed to be launched from either the surface of the sea or from a submarine. The naval version of Prithvi is the same as Sagarika. The cruise missile variant of Sagarika was tested under the name Dhanush Bow.

In addition to the above nuclear-capable missiles, DRDO has produced a number of other units that strengthen Indian combat capability. A few prominent systems are:

Nag

Nag (Cobra) is a third-generation antitank guided missile that is hardened against electronic counter measures (ECMs) and employs an advanced tiny seeker head that can identify and lock onto targets (range 4 Km.). Two types of guidance systems are being developed for Nag: one based on an imaging infrared seeker (successively tested on January 22, 2000) and another on a millimetric wave seeker.[144] Its tandem warhead can defeat explosive reactor armor. The land version of Nag has been tested from a tracked vehicle commonly known as the MICA (missile carrier). It is also configured for use aboard the indigenous advanced light helicopter (ALH). Nag is in advanced stages of user trials.

Pinaka

Pinaka (range 38 Km.), a 214-mm. multi-barrel rocket launcher, has been inducted into the army.[145]

Remotely Piloted Vehicles (RPVs)

Two RPVs called Nishant (end of darkness) and Lakshya (target) are notable here. Nishant is undergoing field tests while Lakshya performed crucial surveillance functions for India during the later stages of the Kargil conflict in July 1999.

Hyperplane

The most ambitious project of DRDO is the hypersonic platform for Air-Breathing Ascent to Near Earth Orbit project, or Hyper plane. Still in its conceptual stages and likely to cost at least US $ 2 billion, this hybrid between jet aircraft and rocket will be a hydrogen-fueled, fully reusable (over 20 times) single-stage hypersonic (Mach 5-7) vehicle that can take off from a conventional airfield. Its unique feature will be its abilities to use high specific impulse air-breathing propulsion in the atmospheric phase of the trajectory and collect, liquely and store atmospheric oxygen in the cruise phase for fueling the rocket engine during the terminal phase.

Hypersonic Test Vehicle (HTV)

Although the Government of India has not yet approved the Hyper plane project, a miniature reusable version called the HTV is likely to be approved shortly. Costing only about $ 9.6 million, the 3-metric ton HTV will carry out surveillance, reconnaissance and intelligence functions but, unlike the rocket-powered Hyper plane, will not launch satellites. According to one of the designers of HTV, Air Commodore (Retd.) R. Gopalaswami: "cruising at a speed of Mach 7 at a height of 30 kilometers gives the hypersonic test vehicle a surveillance, reconnaissance and intelligence capability unmatched by satellites."[146] Also capable of dropping a 500 kg. Warhead up to 2000 Kms. away, the HTV can be built in three to five years, according to the project proposal.

In addition to missile development, Indian security planners are also engaged in developing significant antimissile capabilities as well as a rudimentary defensive shield:

Akash

Akash is a multitarget, command-guided, medium-range surface-to-air missile (SAM). Akash has a range of 25 Km. but can also detect and destroy aircraft at treetop height. It has a quick reaction time (from detection to launch) of fifteen seconds. Its fire control radar is a multitarget, multifunction phased array system called 'Rajendra'.

S-300 Defense Systems

DRDO is working to extend the range of Akash to 40-60 Km. and plans to modify it to also engage ballistic missiles.[147] In this context, the DRDO negotiated with Russia for the purchase of S-300 PMU-1 systems for the Indian army and S-300V for the air force.[148] In June 1998, India agreed to purchase six batteries of S-300 anti-tactical ballistic missile systems from Russia at a cost of about US$ 1 billion.[149] In addition, Indian scientists might be involved in testing and evaluation of the design parameters before receiving delivery of the system.

The modified Akash, a medium-range theater defense SAM, is expected to be integrated with the S-300 V to provide an effective air defense against incoming short-range ballistic missile (SRBM) or IRBM threats, and is to be deployed along the Pakistani and Chinese borders.[150] The army version of Akash is to be integrated with the S-300 PMU-1.

Trishul

Trishul (Trident), a short-range all weather SAM with an effective range of nine kilometers, is fitted with a high explosive fragmented warhead. Highly maneuverable, this missile is powered by a two-stage solid propellant system akin to the one used by the US Patriot antimissile array. The Trishul's detection-of-target to missile launch time is six seconds, making it a quick-reaction system. Trishul is available in army, air force and navy versions. The army and air force versions fly between 300-500 meters per second and can engage aircraft and helicopters using their radar command-to-line-of-sight guidance. The naval version will give the Indian navy its first antimissile missile capability.

Astra

Astra (weapon) is described as a beyond-visual-range air-to-air missile with a 100 Km. head-on range and a tail range of 15 Km. With a maximum speed of Mach 4 plus and altitude of 20 Km., it can also undertake 40-g turns close to sea level when attacking a maneuvering target. It is widely believed that Astra will be mounted on the indigenous Light Combat Aircraft (LCA).

WOMEN'S POLITICAL EMPOWERMENT

Introduction

In the contemporary feminist literature, the word 'women' has been replaced with the term 'gender' as a new category of analysis to assert that much of sexual differentiation is a social and political construct, related to but not determined by biological sex difference. It is seen as the process by which individuals who are born into biological categories of male and female become the social categories of men and women through the acquisition of locally defined attributes of masculinity and femininity. It has been a long battle to show that a woman is not a mere composite of female anatomy and physiology, sex and gender are not identical. In fact the invention of this word 'gender' is the result of two decades of intensive thought and research. In its most recent usage, gender seems to have first appeared among American feminists. It is through the application of the concept of gender that the feminist scholars challenged the structure of current socio-economic, political and cultural processes.

The concept of gender explains the division of spheres of action into private and public. The private sphere belongs to women while the male is assigned the public spheres. It is argued that the public-private divide has been used to legitimise women's exclusion from public politics (J.B. Elshtain: Public Man, Private Woman). Firestone argues against this separation of spheres of activity. However the public-private dichotomy has resulted in women being marginalised in all spheres of activity—social, economic and more specifically, political. Joan W. Scott, therefore, emphasises the need to expose the social construction of gender by deconstructing it.

In concise the socio-political environment determines the participation and involvement of women in politics. Right from the Mexico conference in 1975 through Copenhagen, Nairobi and Beijing, there has been a global awareness and realisation that political participation does not only mean the right to vote, yet women's presence in legislative bodies is scarce despite the absence of legal constraints. Thus, women have been accepted as voters but not as policy formulators and decision-makers. Anne Philips is in favor of politics of presence. She in her book, *The Politics of Presence* (1995) speaks about gender parity and accounts that a significant number of political parties (in South Africa and European countries like U.K., Germany, the Nordic countries) have adopted the measures to raise the proportion of women elected. It can ensure that there is a possibility of gender parity, as politics of presence can provide separate recommendation for the excluded group.

Women in Pre-independence Politics

In 19th century, for the first time, women's question came to the forefront, when the women's issues (such as *Sati*, child marriage, female infanticide, widowhood, *purdah*, polygamy, *devdasi* and education) were raised. It was mainly because of the efforts of social reformers and the cooperation of some of the colonial rulers that some progressive legislations such as banning *Sati* (1829), permitting widow remarriage (1856), and determining age of consent (1891) were passed. Gradually, women realised they needed their own forum, and some organisations came into existence. From the first two decades of the 20th century, the articulation of women's issues was based on liberal principles of equality. In this context, three major women's organisations, the Women's Indian Association (WIA-1917), the National Council for Women in India (NCWI-1925) and the All India Women's Conference (AIWC- 1927) played a major role in articulating women's issues. WIA was one of the earliest women's organisations to ask for women's right to vote.

Demand for franchise was made as early as in 1917 by the elite women, but ignored by the British government. The Government of India Act 1919, however, laid down that the provinces could settle the question of franchise. And thus, Bombay and Madras were the first provinces to grant franchise to women in 1921, the United Provinces followed in 1923, Punjab and Bengal in 1926 and Assam, Bihar, Orissa in 1930. Yet the number of enfranchised women remained very small. Women were also voicing their demand to be elected to the legislatures. Dr. Muthulakshmi Reddi became the first women legislator when she was appointed to the Madras Legislative Council in 1927. With the continuous efforts of Women's organisations for women's rights, two important acts: the Child Marriage Restraint Act (1929), the Hindu Women's Right to Property Act (1937) were passed.

Most of the women who attended the sessions of the Indian National Congress, worked mostly as volunteers, very few participated in the deliberations or rose to high positions, like Annie Besant, who became the first Woman President of the Congress in 1917, followed by Sarojini Naidu in 1925 and Nellie Sengupta in 1933. This, however, does not mean that women had no political sensitivity. Women's participation in the nationalist struggle was intense and they actively took part in the Civil Disobedience movement of 1930-32 and the Quit India movement of 1942. While the nationalist struggle provided women with an opportunity to enter the public sphere and bring about changes in their lives, it could not totally transform the reality. The basic issue of women's inequality and the traditional role of woman were not challenged. Women's issues and movement were submerged in the tidal wave of the nationalist struggle.

Women in Post-independence Politics

Planning was high on the agenda of independent India. J.L. Nehru emphasised the need for a special policy towards women. The Planning Commission of India defined three areas of women's development: education, social welfare and health. The period from the seventies onwards witnessed new awareness and sensitivity towards women's issues. In 1971, the Government of India appointed the Committee on the Status of Women in India. The committee submitted its historic report entitled 'Towards Equality', which proved to be an eye-opener for the government and concerned citizens. The women's movement, which was very visible during the seventies and mid-eighties, was confronted by certain serious challenges in the late eighties and thereafter. The major controversial issues during this phase were the Shah Bano case, the Roop Kunwar Sati incident, the reservation policy and the growing phenomena of communalism and fundamentalism.

Women and the Constitution

The Fundamental rights as guaranteed by the constitution tries to remove the inequalities, which Indian women had suffered. It seemed in 1950, that India had ushered in a new era of liberty and equality where women were equal to men. Some of the provisions in the constitution are incorporated in Article 14 (equality before the law and equal protection by the law), Article 15 (prohibition of discrimination on grounds of religion, race, caste, sex or place of birth), Article 16 (equality of opportunity in employment) and Article 23 under Fundamental Rights. Besides, some provisions are under the heading Directive Principle of State Policy, such as Article 39 (equal pay for equal work for both men and women), Article 42 (just and humane conditions of work and maternity relief), Article 44 (uniform civil code) and Article 51 (imposes fundamental duty on every citizen to renounce practices derogatory to the dignity of women), which provide equality, safety and dignity to women.

The Constitution has accepted the principle of affirmative action favouring women and children. Such principle has activated the state to make provisions for reservation for women in elected bodies of local government and other selected bodies. The 73rd and 74th Constitutional Amendments have provided for reservation of seats for women at the local level in the elected bodies in rural and urban areas. The sad reality remains that such provisions have not laid solid foundations for legal equality between men and women.

Women and the Law

The discrimination felt by the women in India is sanctified by tradition and seldom challenged by the law. In fact, women have a very feeble voice in the formation, implementation and interpretation of laws. The Fundamental Rights as guaranteed by the Constitution have not been able to ensure equality for women in all spheres and the Directive Principles of State Policy have remained mere pious words. Personal laws based on religion and at present continuing under the cover of freedom of religion hold women's lives in their octopus like grip, controlling issues of marriage, divorce, guardianship, adoption, maintenance and property. In spite of the shortcomings of the legal system in India, it is the law, which has been and is still expected to be effective as an instrument of social change, a strategy to free women from shackles of inequality and subjugation.

Secularisation of law has always been a formidable struggle in India because of the pluralities and diversities found among various communities and the ineffectiveness of the rulers in dealing with them. Most of the laws enacted before independence indicate this reality (the situation after independence has its own problems). The Hindu Women's Right to Property Act of 1937, the Muslim Personal Law (Shariat) Application Act 1937 and the Dissolution of Muslim Marriages Act 1939 granted limited rights to women but did not question the fundamental gender inequality experienced by both Hindu and Muslim women. Unfortunately, the two important legislations (The Special Marriage Act of 1872 and 1923 and the Indian Succession Act of 1925) could not be further developed to evolve into a uniform civil code.

The Hindu Code Bill created a furore in Indian society to such an extent that it had to be taken up later by piecemeal legislations: the Hindu Marriage Act 1955, the Hindu Adoption and Maintenance Act 1956, the Hindu Minority and Guardianship Act 1956 and Hindu Succession Act 1956. But the provision for maintenace to the Muslim divorced women has been a concern for progressive elements not only among Muslims but also among all segments of society. Provisions of maintenance to the divorced wife are limited to the period of *iddat*, which is usually three months and if the wife is pregnant it continues until delivery. The Shah Bano case, in this context, deserves a mention. The judgement in Mohd. Ahmed Khan *vs.* Shah Bano and others attracted the attention of the nation and had an impact on national politics. It was held here that a divorced Muslim woman, so long as she has not remarried, could claim maintenance under Section 125 of the Criminal Procedure Code. There have been previous judgements along this line, still this judgement is a landmark. The judgement recognised the right of the divorced woman for maintenance and pointed out the need for a common civil code. This stirred the conservative elements among the Muslim society. And the then government bowed down to the pressure and the Muslim women (Protection of Rights of Divorce) Act was passed in 1986. This law has provided for maintenance of the wife during the *iddat* period. This legislation was a rude shock to the progressive elements. The courts have, however, taken a progressive stand in a few cases pertaining to maintenance even after this Act was passed.

The situation today is that personal laws of the minorities continue to be operative and the state does not want to touch them lest such efforts invoke unrest and upset the political balance. In the case of Hindu women, the state has managed to get increased rights for Hindu women, but in the case of personal laws of Muslim, Parsi and Christian women, the state has not intervened. This issue demands attention. However, the dynamics of personal laws and the Constitution have been complex. All personal laws are discriminatory against women. They have been challenged time and again on the contention that they amount to discrimination on grounds of sex. The courts have generally adopted a hands-off attitude regarding personal laws. On the one hand they have been exhorting the state to enact a uniform civil code, and on the other hand they persistently refuse to apply the Constitutional mandate of non-discrimination in matters pertaining to personal laws.

Women and Political Parties

The Women's Movement and the declaration of 1975 as the women's year and later 1975-1985 as the women's decade brought some change in the perspective of political parties towards women. It is important to note that although all the parties give some place to women in their manifestos, the promises remain on paper. Most of them mobilise women for rallies and demonstrations. Women rarely find place in decision-making committees of political parties. So far, only a few women leaders have been able to reach the position of party president or leader in the legislative parties, as did Indira Gandhi and Sonia Gandhi (Congress), Mrinal Gore (Janata Party), Gita Mukherjee (CPI), Vijaya Raje Scindia and Sushama Swaraj (BJP), Mamata Banerjee (Trinmool Congress), Jaylalitha (AIADMK), Mayawati (Bahujan Samaj Party) and Jaya Jaitly (Samata Party).

In the 1999 election, it was observed that parties, which promised reservation of seats for women, did not encourage women to fight elections. There were only 277 women contestants for the thirteenth Lok Sabha, of whom only 47 won. Out of the 50 candidates fielded by the Cogress, only 14 won. The BJP fielded 54 women candidates, but only 15 won. The Telugu Desam Party sent three women to the Lok Sabha, and the Shiv Sena sent only one woman.

Political parties and leaders have not considered women's vote of much consequence. Beside, women also have not crystallised themselves into voter's bloc.

Women and the Legislature

The women members of Parliament perform a double role as representatives of the people and as representatives of the oppressed section of society, that is, women. Many important laws regarding women are a result of women's pressures and demands inside and outside the House.

However getting a ticket is in fact very difficult for women aspiring for political power. There are considerations of the strategies of the party leader, party politics, money power, caste affiliation, regional politics and individual capacity of the candidate. Parties are not willing to invest their energy in the election of women contestants, they are doubtful about their success. Often, women candidates are dropped to make political compromises, or are given tickets for constituencies where there is little chance of their winning.

So far, very few women have captured seats of power as ministers. Though the number of women elected is very small, the performance of elected women members in the deliberations of the legislature has been noteworthy. Women have been vocal on the floor of the house. They do not only concentrate their attention on 'womanly' and 'soft' subjects, but also express their views on sensitive political matters.

Despite, the statistics of the Lok Sabha reveals the fact that the percentage of women members in Lok Sabha never went beyond 8.8. It presents a zigzag trend. At the time of emergency in 1977, it touched upon the lowest 3.4 per cent. The pattern of representation of women in the Rajya Sabha is not very different from that in the Lok Sabha. The pattern of representation of women in the legislative assemblies of the states is puzzling. Kerala, with its high literacy rate and a matrilineal tradition, has only a few women legislators. Similarly, Manipur, where women play a dominant role in both the family and the community, did not produce a woman legislator until 1990. In contrast, Uttar Pradesh, Bihar and Madhya Pradesh, with their low education levels and repressive cultural norms for women, have sent a relatively larger proportion of women to the Lok Sabha and legislative assemblies.

There have been women Chief Ministers, too, such as Sucheta Kripalani (Uttar Pradesh), Nandini Satpathy (Orissa), Shashikala Kakodkar (Goa), Mayawati (Uttar Pradesh), Rabadi Devi (Bihar), Jayalalitha (Tamil Nadu), Sheila Dixit (Delhi) and Uma Bharti (Madhya Pradersh). It has to be noted that most of them were pushed to the top position by the forces of party politics and contemporary state politics.

Besides, there are multiple barriers to the participation and involvement of women in politics. These range from illiteracy, backwardness, caste, and culture to criminalisation of politics, communalism and corruption.

Women and the Reservation Policy

The 1995 UN Conference on Women in Beijing was a landmark, where the focus was on political empowerment of women and consequently, on the issue of women's reservation. This received an international recognition. The final consensus was that establishment of quota for women's political participation was legitimate and practical. In India, during Rajiv Gandhi's regime, efforts were made to amend the constitution so as to provide for 33 per cent reservation to women in local grassroots level Panchayat bodies. The amendments — 73rd and 74th were made in 1992 providing for one-third reservation to women in the Panchayats and quietly ratified in 1993. Between 1993 and 1996, women's organisations united for a joint demand for reservation in state assemblies and Parliament. The demand was accepted and featured in the manifestos of the major parties. The response to the demand was the bill for the 84th and 85th Amendment to the constitution, to allow one-third of the total number of seats in the Lok Sabha and State Assemblies to be reserved for women including for those from Scheduled Castes and Scheduled Tribes. The bill was tabled on September 12, 1996. It evoked spontaneous support as well as fierce opposition. Since then on number of occasions government tried to introduce the bill, but nothing could be achieved.

Political parties have no unanimous stand on the bill. Against all theoretical assurances, the major political parties are taking vogue positions on the issue of caste-based and religion-based women's reservation regarding four sub-categories within the women quota — backward caste, Muslims, Christians and Sikhs. In fact caste and communal card was used to confuse the whole issue and divide the women. Nevertheless, most women members of Parliament, cutting across party lines, have been vocal in their support for the bill.

The policy of reservation has certainly brought power within reach of rural women. Karnataka and West Bengal had already reserved seats for women in elected bodies in rural areas even before the 73rd Amendment. Their experiences and now those of other states have been largely positive. As women in rural India are getting absorbed into formal politics at the local level, they are shattering the myths regarding their inefficiency and inability to govern. Developmental activities are high on their agenda. There are many instances in Karnataka, Rajasthan, Haryana, Madhya Pradesh and other states where women have fought bravely against corruption, alcohalism and other social evils and have worked for the development of the community.

The reservation policy is not an end in itself, it is a means to achieve gender equality. It is important that women enter in decision-making bodies in sizeable numbers, this 'critical mass' is important if women's voices are to be heard in politics. The task is uphill, not impossible. Women's empowerment has to be seen in the larger context of the democratic system. It demands the percolation of the values of equality and justice in daily life, the support of citizen's groups in protest against oppression and acceptance of the feminist perspective in the public sphere. Women have to recognise, collectively and critically, the forces that limit them and to work collectively and continuously to change the unequal power structure. In other words they have to experience the process of empowerment.

Notes

1. Rekha Saxena, *Indian Politics in Transition*, Deep & Deep Publications, New Delhi, 1994.
2. *Ibid.*
3. Rekha Saxena, *Indian Politics in Transition*, Deep & Deep Publications, New Delhi, 1994.
4. *Ibid.*
5. *Ibid.*
6. In 1977-79 and almost all governments of 1990s.
7. Dipankar Gupta, 'Coalition Politics Making a Virtue of Necessity,' *Times of India*, 26 June 1998.
8. *Ibid.*
9. *Ibid.*
10. H.K. Dua, 'Hung Parliament', May 27, 1998. *Times of India.*
11. *Ibid.*
12. *Ibid.*
13. Sumer Kaul, 'Stability and the Poll', *The Hindustan Times*, January 10, 1997.
14. *Ibid.*
15. M.P. Singh and R. Saxena (Ed.), *Ideologies and Institutions in Indian Politics*, Deep & Deep Publications Pvt. Ltd., 1998.
16. *Ibid.*
17. C.P. Bhambhri, 'Political Process and Foreign Policy', *World Focus*, Oct.-Nov.-Dec., 1999.
18. *Ibid.*
19. *World Focus*, Oct.-Nov.-Dec., 1999.
20. *Ibid.*
21. The well-known idioms used by Morris Jones in his study of *Indian Politics.*
22. Rasheeduddin Khan, 'Challenges of Communalism in India', *World Focus*, August, 1988.
23. *Strategic Analysis*, January, 1996.
24. D.L. Sheth, 'State, Nation and Ethnicity', *Economic and Political Weekly*, Vol. 25, No. 12, March 25, 1989, p. 624.
25. See, Urmila Phadnis: 'Ethnic Conflict in South Asian States', in Phadnis and Others, No. 5, pp. 100-07.
26. *Ibid.*, pp. 100-01.

27. S.D. Muni, 'Dimensions of Domestic Conflicts in South Asia', in Urmila Phadnis and others (Eds.): *Domestic Conflicts in South Asia*, Vol. 1, New Delhi, 1986, p. 61.
28. Ajay Darshan Bahera, 'An Analysis of Separatist Insurgencies in India', *Strategic Analysis*, January 1996.
29. Although it is not clear who these Tamils are, one can presume that they are from the LTTE and could be doing it for some favours in return. See Chris Smith, n. 25, p. 31.
30. See, "JKLF: Diminishing sway", *India Today*, October 31, 1991, p. 102.
31. See *Frontline*, October 12-25, 1991, p. 12.
32. *Hazarika*, No. 15, p. 179.
33. *Ibid.*, pp. 170-74.
34. According to intelligence reports, NSCN has a training camp in Tarishdaba where Bangladesh Rifles and ISI of Pakistan are providing training. See, Soutik Biswas: ' Living on the razor's edge', India Today, October 15, 1993, p. 85.
35. The Naga leadership has maintained that the Nagas were not an Indian or sub continental community.They were probably of Mongoloid origin and have been demanding self-determination. See N.K. Das: *Ethnic Identity, Ethnicity and Social Stratification in North-East India*, New Delhi, 1989, pp. 243-45.
36. The ULFA was successful in carrying out these activities because of its widespread support among villagers, the urban middle class and Assamese students. *Hazarika*, n. 15, p. 175.
37. K.P.S. Gill, "The Dangers within: Internal Security Threats", in Bharat Karnad (ed.): *Future Imperilled: India's Security in the* 1990*s and Beyond*', New Delhi, 1994, pp. 130-31.
38. Some of these methods included summary executions, arming of civilians by employing special police officers who were paid Rs. 35 per day and pitting Jat Sikhs against Jat Sikhs. For details see, Tarun Tejpal and Ramesh Vinayak: "Punjab: New signs of independence", *India Today*, September 15, 1992, pp. 56-59; Kanwar Sandhu: "Official excesse", *India Today*, October 15, 1992 and Shekhar Gupta and Kanwar Sandhu: "True Grit", *India Today*, April 15, 1993, p. 64.
39. The former Governor of Kashmir, Jagmohan believes that it was due to these factors that "fundamentalists, pro-Pakistan elements and terrorists", aided and abetted by Pakistan came to hold sway over the minds of Kashmiris. See Jagmohan: *My Frozen Turbulence in Kashmir*, New Delhi, 1991, pp. 13, 112.

40. According to Noorani, the present uprising is a result of carefully laid out plans. The foundations of the insurgency were laid by the late President Zia-ul-Haq and furthered by Nawaj Sharif. See A.G. Noorani : "*The Betrayal of Kashmir: Pakistan's Duplicity and India's Complicity*" in Raju G.C. Thomas, n. 21, pp. 257-62.

41. Media reports about the ISI-sponsored camps or private training camps in Pakistan are a fairly consistent feature in both Indian and Pakistani Media. See, "Kashmir: Training the fighters", *View point*, October 10, 1991, pp. 23-24; "Kashmiris urged to help liberate Valley", *The Pakistan Times*, October 31; " sponsoring terrorism", Sunday, August 21-27, 1994, pp. 26-27. "ISI training camps in Kashmir now" No. 94, *Asian Age*, September 26, 1994.

42. For instance, in May 1991, Assam Rifles personnel killed 73 militants trying to cross over to India. See Rajesh Kadian, n. 37, p. 32.

43. This Development is linked to the Afghan Mujahideen's liberation struggle against the erstwhile Soviet-backed Marxist government in Kabul. During that struggle, a lot of Kashmiris had joined the Afghan Mujahideen. Thus, linkages were established with groups like the Hizb-e-Islami led by Gulbudin Hikmatyar, which have been providing training and arms to the Kashmiris. See *Strategic Analysis*, Jan. 1996.

44. Shekhar Gupta and Rahul Pathak, 'Pan-Islamic Fundamentalism—Exporting Terror', *India Today*, May 15, 1994, pp. 31-32.

45. Chris Smith, 'The Diffusion of Small Arms and Light Weapons in Pakistan and Northern India', London, 1993, pp. 31-32.

46. Excerpts from the lecture delivered by I.K. Gujral, at the India International Center, New Delhi, Feb 16, 2000; *Mainstream*, April 22, 2000.

47. *Ibid.*

48. *Mainstream*, April 22, 2000.

49. Excerpts from the lecture delivered by I.K. Gujral, at the India International Centre, New Delhi, Feb. 16, 2000; *Mainstream*, April 22, 2000.

50. *Ibid.*

51. Marshall M. Bouton, 'India's Problem is not Politics', *Foreign Affairs*, May/June, 1998.

52. Anthony P. D'costa, 'The Long March to Capitalism: India's resistance to, and reintegration with the World Economy', *Contemporary South Asia*, 1995.

53. *Ibid.*

54. Girish Mishra, 'Globalisation and India', *World Focus*, Oct.-Nov.-Dec., 1999.

55. History tells of a number of attempts in this direction. From Alexander to Chenghis Khan and Napoleon Bonaparte, efforts were made to bring all the world under one supreme ruler and the center of decision making was to be located in the capital of the conqueror's country. It needs to be noted that none of these conquerors (with the exception of Napoleon Bonaparte) disturbed and altered the prevailing mode of production in the conquered countries or areas.
56. Termed by *New York Times* as "Masterpiece" on the occasion of its 150th anniversary.
57. *New York Times*, 26 April, 1998.
58. Rabi Ray, 'Quo Vadis Globalisation?', *Mainstream*, April 1, 2000.
59. *Ibid.*
60. *Ibid.*
61. K. Ramachandran Nair, 'India and the New Economic Policy', in K. Raman Pillai (Ed.): *Indian Foreign Policy in the 1990s*, Radiant Publishers, New Delhi, 1997.
62. *Ibid.*
63. *Ibid.*
64. *Ibid.*
65. Rabi Ray, 'Quo Vadis Globalisation?', *Mainstream*, April 1, 2000.
66. K. Ramachandran Nair, 'India and the New Economic Policy', in K. Raman Pillai (Ed.): *Indian Foreign Policy in the 1990s*; Radiant Publishers, New Delhi, 1997.
67. Rabi Ray, 'Quo Vadis Globalisation?', *Mainstream*, April 1, 2000.
68. *Ibid.*
69. *Ibid.*
70. Marshall M. Bouton, 'India's Problem is not politics', *Foreign Affairs*, May/June, 1998.
71. K. Ramachandran Nair, 'India and the New Economic Policy', in K. Raman Pillai (Ed.): *Indian Foreign Policy in the 1990s*, Radiant Publishers, New Delhi, 1997.
72. Marshall M. Bouton, 'India's Problem is not Politics', *Foreign Affairs*, Vol. 77, No. 3, May/June, 1998
73. *Ibid.*
74. Girish Mishra, 'East Asian Crisis and India', *World Focus*, September, 1998.
75. *Ibid.*
76. K. Ramachandran Nair, 'India and the New Economic Policy', in

K. Raman Pillai (Ed.): *Indian Foreign Policy in the 1990s*, Radiant Publishers, New Delhi, 1997.

77. Girish Mishra, 'Globalisation and India', *World Focus*, Oct.-Nov.-Dec., 1999.
78. Given in the *World Development Report*, 1999/2000.
79. Girish Mishra, 'Globalisation and India', *World Focus* (Indian Foreign Policy), Oct.-Nov.- Dec., 1999.
80. Far Eastern Economic Review, while reviewing the *World Bank Formulation* , 14 October, 1999.
81. *Ibid.*
82. Rabi Ray, 'Quo Vadis Globalisation'?, *Mainstream*, April-1, 2000.
83. Like the democratically elected Marxist Government under the leadership of Salvador Allende in Chile in the seventies. When American companies engineered a general strike in Chile and indulged in large scale violence throughout Chile.
84. Girish Mishra, 'Globalisation and India', *World Focus* (Indian Foreign Policy), Oct.-Nov.-Dec., 1999
85. A.N. Ram, 'India's Economic Diplomacy', *World Focus*, Oct.-Nov.-Dec., 1999.
86. *Ibid.*
87. *Ibid.*
88. Marshall M. Bouton, 'India's Problem is not Politics', *Foreign Affairs*, May-June 1998.
89. See Rekha Saxena, 'Democracy-Development Interface', in M.P. Singh & Rekha Saxena (Ed.): *Ideologies and Institutions in Indian Politics*, Deep & Deep Publication Pvt. Ltd., 1998.
90. *Ibid.*
91. Richard N. Cooper, 'The Road From Serfdom', while reviewing *Development as Freedom* by Amartya Sen, *Foreign Affairs*, Jan./Feb. 2000.
92. Jasjit Singh, 'Indian Defence Planning', *World Focus*, Oct.-Nov.-Dec. 1996.
93. K. Subrahmanyam, 'Indian Nuclear Policy Perspective', *World Focus*, August, 1988.
94. O.P. Sabharwal, 'Nehru-Bhabha Legacy', *World Focus*, June-July 1998.
95. K. Subrahmanyam, 'Indian Nuclear Policy', *World Focus*, August, 1988.

96. O.P. Sabharwal, 'Nehru — Bhabha Legacy', *World Focus*, June-July 1998.
97. 'It is only after the Chinese attack and Chinese nuclear test that Dr. Bhabha became an advocate of Indian nuclear option', *World Focus*, August, 1988.
98. O.P. Sabharwal, 'India's Nuclear Strategy', *World Focus*, April, 2000.
99. 'Had this priority for weapon-making not been low, India's first Pokhran test might will have taken place in 1966 or 1967 rather than in 1974. India could then have been within the NPT's burra sahib's club. The terse reality is that the Indian breakthrough in spent fuel reprocessing in 1965 hastened the advent of the NPT, aimed specifically to keep India debarred from weapon status under the non-proliferation treaty's rules', *World Focus*, June-July 1998.
100. *Ibid.*
101. O.P. Sabharwal, 'India's Nuclear Strategy', *World Focus*, April, 2000.
102. K. Subrahmanyam, 'Indian Nuclear Policy Perspective', *World Focus*, August,1988.
103. *Ibid.*
104. Nikhil Chakravarty, 'Evolution of Foreign Policy', *World Focus*, Nov.-Dec., 1987.
105. Savita Pande, 'India and disarmament', *World Focus*, April, 2000.
106. Nikhil Chakravarty, 'Evolution of Foreign Policy', *World Focus*, Nov.-Dec., 1987.
107. K. Subrahmanyam, 'Indian Nuclear Policy', *World Focus*, August, 1988.
108. *Ibid.*
109. K. Subrahmanyam, 'Nuclear India', *Indian Defence Review*, April-June 1998.
110. R. Venkatraman, 'Nuclear Explosion and its aftermath', *U.S.I. Journal*, July-September, 1998.
111. T.T. Poulose, 'The Bomb and National Security', *Journal of Peace Studies*, Vol. 6, Issue 4, July-August, 1998.
112. By 1987 Pakistan achieved nuclear weaponisation with Chinese help. The weapon was of Chinese design tested in 1967 as a missile warhead.
113. R. Venkatraman, 'Nuclear Explosion and its aftermath', *U.S.I. Journal*, July-September, 1998.

114. Ashok Chakrapani, 'Plain Speaking About Indian Nuclear Testing', *The Round Table*, 1998.
115. K. Subrahmanyam, 'Nuclear India', *Indian Defence Review*, April-June, 1998.
116. R. Venkatraman, 'Nuclear Explosion and its Aftermath', *U.S.I. Journal*, July-September 1998.
117. K. Subrahmanyam, 'Nuclear India', *Indian Defence Review*, April-June, 1998.
118. *Ibid.*
119. *Ibid.*
120. Indian Nuclear Doctrine, *World Focus*, April 2000.
121. Matin Zuberi, 'Pokharan-II and Chagni', *World Focus*, June-July, 1998.
122. *Ibid.*
123. *Sunday Times*, 24.05.1998.
124. *Ibid.*
125. R. Venkataraman, 'Nuclear Explosion and its Aftermath', *U.S.I. Journal*, July-September, 1998.
126. K. Subrahmanyam, 'Nuclear India', *Indian Defence Review*, April-June, 1998.
127. Lt. Gen R. Sharma, 'The National Security Environment and Nuclearisation', *U.S.I. Journal*, July-September, 1998.
128. T.T. Poulose, 'The Bomb and National Security', *Journal of Peace Studies*, July-August, 1998.
129. K. Subrahmnayam, 'Nuclear India', *Indian Defence Review*. April-June, 1998.
130. *Ibid.*
131. Matn Zuberi, 'The Proposed Nuclear Doctrine', April, 2000, *World Focus*.
132. To develop such a triad would require 10-15 years with an expenditure of the 15000 crore annually. The most comprehensive study, on the costing of an Indian nuclear deterrence, was performed by the former MP and Economist Subramanian Swamy for the Bhartiya Jan Sangh in 1969. At that time his system analysis envisioned an expenditure of Rs. 500 crore annually for 100 nuclear tipped ballistic missiles. In the 21st century, that figure has to be inflated at least by a figure of 10-20 times to provide a mere 10 missiles on land and at sea.
133. R.R. Subramanian, 'A Minimum and Credible Deterrence for India', *World Focus*, April 2000.

134. *World Focus: Indian Nuclear Doctrine*, April, 2000.
135. *Ibid.*
136. *Ibid.*
137. *Ibid.*
138. Bruce Blair, *Strategic Command and Control*, Washington D.C., Brookings, 1985.
139. K. Subrahmanyam, 'Nuclear Force design and Minimum Deterrence Strategy', in Bharat Karmad (Ed.) *Future Imperilled: Indian Security in* 1990*s and Beyond*, New Delhi, Viking Penguin India, 1994, pp. 191-92.
140. R.R. Subramanian, 'A Minimum and Credible deterrence for India', *World Focus*, April, 2000.
141. Anupam Srivastava, 'India's Growing Missile Ambitions', *Asian Survey*, Vol. XL, No. 2, March-April, 2000.
142. The DRDO has decided to increase the payload of SS-250 to 1000 Kg. by using boosted liquid propellant to generate higher thrust-to-weight ratio.
143. "Agni-II Successfully Test Fired", *Hindu*, April 11, 1999.
144. "Fire-and-Forget System for Nag Tested", *Times of India*, Feb. 22, 2000.
145. Pravin Sawhney, "A Force in Waiting : India's Defense Organisation Sets Its Sights on the Future." *Jane's International Defence Review*, May 21, 1998.
146. "Next Indian Satellite Will Have Surveillance Capability", *Deccan Herald*, August 2, 1999.
147. Pravin Sawhney, "Anti-missile Role Planned for Akash," *Jane's International Defence Review*, January 1, 1997.
148. Vivek Raghuvanshi, "India Mulls Russian Air Defence dial," *Defence News*, February 24, 1997.
149. Vivek Raghuvanshi, "India Plans to Acquire Russian S-300 System, Pair Renew Trade Pact," *Ibid.*, June 29, 1998; and Dadan Upadhyay: "Indo-Russian Deal on Air Defence System," *Indian Express*, June 19, 1998.
150. "India Should Develop Anti-ballistic Missile System, Say Experts," *Times of India*, June 30, 1998.

4

The Indian Subcontinent and India

India had won its freedom in 1947 after the partition of the sub-continent, which, in Indian consciousness, was the outcome of British machinations. One country had become two independent countries. The cry for Pakistan in 1939-46 was a war cry against India's National Movement. Pakistan was, therefore, conceived and born in hatred, supported by the British intrigue. Since its birth in August 1947, it has been locked in a military conflict with India on the Kashmir question. The most outstanding question of internal politics in the sub-continent, before 1947, for the Congress, had been to agree or not to agree to the making of Pakistan and after it was conceded, the most important problem of India's foreign policy was how to deal with this freak. India's relations with every country in the world were conditioned largely by its response to the Indo-Pakistan conflict. Thus, the first and the most persistent problem of Indian foreign policy has been that of Pakistan. While Pakistan continues to be the most "potent security threat", the next most important source of threat to India, is China, both in terms of its power potential and its strategic ties with Pakistan. Besides, the post-Cold War geopolitics has offered enormous opportunities to the countries of this region to fashion and articulate their policies in tune with hardboiled realities of the emerging global political order.

THE PAKISTAN FACTOR

The partition of India, as was to be expected, did not resolve the problems of the two communities. Instead of ending the Hindu-Muslim conflict, the division of the country merely elevated the inter-community blood bath into inter-state rivalry. Michael Brecher observed: "India and Pakistan have been in a state of undeclared war, with varying degree of intensity, throughout there brief history as independent states."[1] Thus Indo-Pakistan relationship came to be viewed as a zero-sum game where the gain of one was seen as the loss of the other.

Power Structure of Pakistan

To this day the nature of the Pakistani power structure has remained elitist, feudal, militaristic and unrepresentative of the Pakistani masses.[2] If one undertakes an analysis of the socio-economic background of the leadership, one finds the validity of this observation. Nobody of the category of a Lal Bahadur Shastri[3], or a Laloo Prasad Yadav,[4] or a Mayawati[5] has figured or can ever figure in the centers of power in Pakistan. Further the extremist theocracy and militarism dominating the political processes in Pakistan, whatever the government in power. The nub of the matter is that no Government in Pakistan reflects the normal desire for peace and stability and for a secure political environment among the common people of Pakistan.

Identity Crisis and Hostile Policies

It is believed that India still does not accept the partition of the sub-continent and wants to undo it in line with the concept of *akhand Bharat* ("Indivisible India"). Another belief is that the validity of the two-nation theory can be reasserted and reaffirmed only if the Muslim-majority Indian state of Jammu and Kashmir secedes from India and joins Pakistan.[6] Yet another belief is that not only should Pakistani society be put into a straitjacket of Islamic doctrine fashioned by the Pakistani power structure but that Pakistani should also assume the role of protecting and talking about the safety and future of the Muslim minority in India. An attempt is also being made to subvert the Muslim citisens of India in the hope that it would confirm the validity of the two-nation theory.[7]

Furthermore, Zulfiquar Ali Bhutto kept writing secret memoranda to President Mohammad Ayub Khan asking him to initiate military action to separate Assam and the north-eastern parts of India from the rest of India by using East Pakistani territory as a spring board for the military operation involved. Ayub Khan was a professional military man. Perhaps he had better political sense as well than Bhutto. He, therefore, did not act fully on Bhutto's recommendation although he was not averse to the idea in general.[8]

Moreover, the entire educational and cultural orientation of Pakistani society is directed and nurtured in line with an anti-Indian stance. The process starts generally at the level of primary school itself. Pakistani books on history which young people read in their formative years are written so as to give them the impression that the history of the subcontinent commenced only some time in the second half of the seventh century A.D. with the Arab invasion of Sind. Little attention is paid to the earlier period. It is as though the events of those days belonged more to myth and legend than to history and were irrelevant. The emphasis is on the inculcation of an anti-Indian attitude of mind as an essential component of Pakistani patriotism. The inescapable conclusion, that one reaches is that the whole internal dynamics of the Pakistani polity is designed to protect the vested interests of a narrow political spectrum of people who constitute the Establishment in Pakistan. The armed forces of Pakistan would lose their justification to go on acquiring more arms and increasing their coercive clout within Pakistani society if the bugbear of Indian hegemony and hostility is replaced by a rational, co-operative approach towards India.[9] The same is true of political parties, religious parties and the Islamic leaders of Pakistan, which cannot afford to let the ordinary people of Pakistan come into contact with the people of India for fear that it would give the lie to the arguments of antagonism propagated by these power elite and would expose Pakistani public opinion to the vigour and vibrancy of India's pluralistic democracy in spite of all its shortcomings.

Even the big gestures displayed by Indian, over the years, towards Pakistan, did not help abate the Pakistani antipathy to India — and Hindus. Pakistan did not pay their share of the Public Debt of United India — and India let it go. In 1965, Indian forces captured the strategic Haji Pir Pass in Pak-occupied-Kashmir and politicians presented it on a platter to Pakistan. After the 1971 war India returned 93,000 prisoners of war to Pakistan against an oral — and therefore, worthless — promise of no more agitating of the Kashmir issue.[10]

When I.K. Gujral placed the Gujral Doctrine — which is a doctrine of making goodwill gestures towards neighbours, in the hope, that before long they will respond positively, it was seen with suspicion in Pakistan. Altaf Gauhar, a leading Pakistani columnist argues that the Gujral Doctrine is in fact "a three-phase operation"—

(1) To grant economic benefits to smaller neighbours and bring them under Indian domination.

(2) To exert immense pressure on Pakistan for regional economic co-operation, while putting the existing differences on the backburner and

(3) To integrate the contiguous areas of the Pakistan like west Punjab and Sindh, with neighbouring states in India.

Thus Gauhar writes: "The Gujral Doctrine is not a doctrine of good neighbourly relations but a '*Bharati-Plan*' to seize the neighbour peacefully."[11] Likewise, 'Hillal', the joint weekly publication of the three Armed Services of Pakistan and the ISI, carried a blood-curdling editorial, which said, "Islam bars the Muslims from extending a hand of friendship to the Hindus unless the latter change there thinking and nature."[12]

Kashmir—the Core issue

India's experience with Pakistan had convinced that the dispute in Kashmir was a symptom rather than the cause of the Indo-Pakistan rivalry; the real problem was Pakistan's paranoia about India which would not be swept away by merely resolving the conflict in Kashmir and that disputes were bound to manifest themselves in other arenas.[13]

The princely state of Jammu and Kashmir was under the rule of the Maharaja Hari Singh. While the ruler was a Hindu, the population of Kashmir was predominantly Muslim. The Indian Independence Act of 1947 had, in theory, left the states legally independent when 'the sovereignty of His Majesty over the Indian states lapses.'[14] But in reality the states had to seek accession to one or other Dominion in accordance with the broad principles of the partition's itself. In the event five hundred odd states[15] were integrated with India or Pakistan without any major difficulty. Maharaja Hari Singh was in a state of confusion. During that stage a strong-armed group from North-Western Frontier Provinces of Pakistan attacked Kashmir and occupied several towns. They were receiving assistance from their Government. Before the fall of Srinagar the ruler after a thorough negotiation decided the Accession of Kashmir to India on 26th October 1947. As soon as India received the Instrument of Accession it dispatched airborne troops and reinforcements to Srinagar. The rebellion was quelled and the Pakistani tribesmen were pushed out of Srinagar. India was in control of over two-thirds of Jammu and Kashmir, the rest remained in Pakistan's hands. The Government of India was convinced of the legality of its position. In those circumstances, on 1st January 1948 India lodged a complaint under Article 35 of the UN charter to persuade Pakistan to stop the aggression by withdrawing its regular troops and denying the 'invaders' the access to and use of, its territory for operation against Kashmir[16]. In taking the Kashmir dispute to the UN Nehru was convinced, that India's case was so clear-cut that the Security Council could not fail to condemn Pakistan's aggression.

The Government of Pakistan grabbed this opportunity to broaden the debate to discuss the entire gamut of Indo-Pakistan problems. Sir Muhammad Zafrullah Khan, the Foreign Minister of Pakistan and a former Judge of the Indian Supreme Court, used all his skills as a lawyer both to obfuscate the immediate issue and turn the table on India. In a speech, which lasted over five hours, Sir Zafrullah not only rejected India's charge of Pakistani aggression, but instead attempted to portray India as an expansionist power determined to swallow a small neighbour. India, he argued, was not reconciled to the existence of Pakistan and was carrying out extensive 'genocide' both in India and Kashmir to frighten the Muslims into submission; and it was also claimed that, India had not only secured the accession of Jammu and Kashmir by 'fraud and violence' but had earlier 'forcibly occupied' Junagarh, Manvadar and Kathiawar which had 'lawfully acceded' to Pakistan[17]. By selective use of evidence and combining the Kashmir dispute with the larger and more complicated issue of Indo-Pakistan relations, Zafrullah Khan won the sympathy of many of the members of the Security Council, who were unaware of the complexities and saw it as harassment by a larger state of its smaller neighbour[18].

Though the Indian troops had pushed back the tribesmen and a government under the Prime Ministership of Sheikh Abdullah was formed, the valley remained under tension. Pakistan refused to recognise the accession. The assistance to the so-called government of Azad Kashmir formed in the forcibly occupied area of Kashmir, by the government of Pakistan continued. The Security Council resolution, which caused the formation of United Nations Commission for India and Pakistan and Admiral Nimitz, Owen Dixon and Frank Graham, were appointed as mediators subsequently to look into the arrangements. The Commission in its proposal on 11th December 1948 included a free and impartial plebiscite to be conducted after ceasefire and fulfillment of truce arrangements and restoration of peace. Officially India and Pakistan accepted the proposals of the Commission and a ceasefire agreement was signed which became effective from 1st January 1949.[19]

However, the differences between India and Pakistan proved unbridgeable. The issue of the withdrawal of forces created many problems. Pakistan, it was argued, had no *locus standi* in Kashmir and therefore India and Pakistan could not be treated at par in Kashmir. The accession of Kashmir to India was complete and could only be reversed if the people of Kashmir voted against India. But until then it was India's duty to defend Kashmir against internal and external aggression and therefore the Indian army could not be withdrawn.[20] Pakistan simply rejected the validity of India's claim to Kashmir as an integral part of India and continued to insist on a plebiscite under UN supervision for the entire territory.[21] India has clearly misjudged the politics of the UN. On 18th March 1948, at the behest of the British, the Chinese delegate presented a draft resolution.[22] Nehru accepted the resolution but was appalled by the various amendments brought in during the discussion, which virtually ignored Kashmir's accession to India and consequently India's sovereignty over the state. The resolution not only failed to censure Pakistan's 'aggression' but also toned down Pakistan's responsibility for withdrawing its forces and nationals and insisted on the formation of a coalition government, which India regarded as interference in its internal affairs.[23] Nehru was understandably angered and despite his genuine commitment to the UN he was prepared to defy it rather than 'surrender' to the gangster tactics of Pakistan and the raiders or to the attempts at bullying by Britain and the US.[24]

Thus the plebiscite Administrators Admiral Nimitz and Sir Owen Dixon, as a mediator negotiated with both the governments, but could not reach positive stage. Finally a joint US-UK draft resolution was moved in February 1951 and Dr. Frank Graham was appointed as the new mediator who tirelessly negotiated from June 1951 to February 1953 for a meaningful demilitarisation, so that plebiscite could be conducted. But Graham's efforts were foiled and could not bring a desirable result and with this all the three UN's mediatory missions failed[25].

At the other hand Nehru was aware of the dangers of the subcontinent being dragged into the cold war and was anxious to avoid it. Therefore, when the Soviet Union, for the first time in 1952, criticised the Anglo-American stand over Kashmir, Nehru was quite worried and privately explained to the British and the Americans, that India had not sought Soviet assistance.[26]

Nehru's disappointment with the UN was intense. Although Nehru was convinced of the right of the people of Jammu and

Kashmir to self-determination but could not agree to their incorporation into Pakistan simply on grounds that the majority of the people were Muslims. Nehru was confident that in a fair and free plebiscite the people would choose to remain in India. There were a number of reasons for his optimism[27]:

(1) The people of Kashmir had developed a distinct Kashmiri nationalism.

(2) In the long history of peaceful co-existence the two communities had evolved common political associations.

(3) The popularity and landslide victory of Sheikh Abdullah's secular National Conference Party in the election to the Constituent Assembly was sufficient evidence of the people's attachment both to secularism and to India.

However, there were certain underlying tensions[28]:

(a) The problem arose over Kashmir's relations with the government of India.

(b) Kashmir's privileged status aroused resentment in the other states of the union.

(c) The sectarian political parties[29] joined hands with the Kashmiri communalist group, the Jammu Praja Parishad, to bring pressure on Delhi to reverse Kashmir's autonomous status.

(d) Kashmir raised the Hindu-Muslim tensions throughout the country.

(e) The real motive of the agitators, especially the communalists, was to oust Nehru from power by embarrassing him for his supposedly pro-Muslim bias.[30]

In this tension-ridden atmosphere, in January 1948, Abdullah had toyed with the idea of an independent Kashmir.[31] The idea of a small independent state on the border of China and the Soviet Union, dependent upon the West, could not have been unwelcome to the West.[32] In 1953 Abdullah publicly advocated an independent Kashmir as one of the possible solutions to the problem. Further, popular passion was aroused when S.P. Mookerjee died. Abdullah's anti-Indian tirades and the severe handling of the agitation in Jammu had alienated the support of many of his National Conference Party members and thus, he was dismissed by the government in August 1953.[33]

Trapped between Abdullah and Mookerjee, writes Professor Gopal, for the first time since 1948 Nehru began to feel despondent about the future of Kashmir. He could face Pakistan and the United Nations and even the prospect of war; but with Abdullah and Mookerjee working in tacit concert to divide the state on Hindu-Muslim lines, the problem became almost insuperably complex.[34]

J.F. Dulles recognised Indian's reluctance to hold a plebiscite and suggested the partition of Kashmir as a way out.[35]

When Dr. Frank Graham failed, he left the problem to direct negotiation between the two disputants. Accordingly, both the Prime Ministers met at New Delhi from 17 to 20 August 1953. While the dismissal and arrest of Abdullah was constitutionally correct, India's moral claim to Kashmir had been weakened and Nehru could no longer be sure of the support of the people of Kashmir for India in view of the communal violence. Nehru asserted that he would rather lose Kashmir in a plebiscite than hang on to it against the popular will. When Bakshi Ghulam Mohamed, Kashmir's new Prime Minister, threatened to resign, Nehru was sympathetic, but firm: 'we have to consider the various forces at work and...try to fashion our policy so as to get the best advantages out of it...we have to think of the future...(and) chose a path which not only promises the greatest advantage but is dignified and in keeping with our general policy.'[36]

The earlier insistence that any settlement of the Kashmir dispute must recognise the accession of that state to India was dropped. Indeed Nehru had offered virtually everything that Pakistan had been seeking since 1947. What is also significant is the fact that Nehru's offer was not made under any external or internal pressure but from a genuine conviction that India must not hold Kashmir against the wishes of its people. He was prepared to risk a plebiscite even though it might mean the loss of Kashmir.

Pakistani Premier Mohammad Ali returned home triumphant with the end of the conflict in sight. But once in Pakistan he began to waver. He raised a whole array of trivial objections, which were clearly intended to delay a settlement. Indeed the continuation of the conflict in Kashmir had emerged as an important factor in the struggle for power that was going on in Pakistan. General Ayub Khan, backed by the civil-military bureaucracy, was at that time involved in his elaborate scheme to seize power by subverting parliamentary democracy; and hostility with India was needed to legitimise the role of the military and give him time to implement his scheme. Mohammad Ali, a mere puppet whose overriding concern was to remain in office obliged his puppeteers by duly dragging his feet. Thus it is one of the ironies of history that just when India appeared to be willing to settle the Kashmir dispute, the Prime Minister of Pakistan allowed the opportunity to be frittered away.[37]

In addition, USA and Pakistan entered into an agreement by which the former agreed to provide all military assistance to Pakistan. This was an event of serious concern to India. Nehru wrote to his Pak counterpart: "A great accession of military strength to Pakistan has, therefore, a very direct and material bearing on the Kashmir issue, more particularly, on the question of demilitarisation in Kashmir."[38] After this agreement the growing dialogue between India and Pakistan ended and the New Delhi-Washington link found scope for further worsening. Despite the assurances of the US Administration that the military help was meant to contain the growing menace of communism and were not directed against non-communist countries. India as a neighbour of Pakistan was sure that Pakistan could not be trusted when conflict arose between India and Pakistan.

Further, the year 1954 was a crucial time for India and also for the sub-continent. "For it was then, that America's PACTOMANIA, ostensibly against international communism and Pakistan's search for external military props to achieve an artificial parity of power with India meshed together."[39] The man behind this was General Ayub Khan, the ambitious

Commander-In-Chief of the Pakistan army who had risen from a Lieutenant Colonel in 1947 to become a General four years later. Ayub was a clever manipulator, who has emerged as a kingmaker during this period and had quite early on hatched his plot to capture political power. Before he could stage his coup *d'etat* he needed to strengthen and modernise the armed forces to establish his hold over it.[40] He sought to achieve his objective by manipulating Pakistan's foreign policy to suit his designs. At a time when the US was looking for allies in the cold war and India would not play ball[41], Ayub's offer to ally[42] Pakistan with the US fell on receptive ears.[43]

In these circumstances, there were certain political developments in Kashmir. The Constituent Assembly of Jammu and Kashmir ratified the accession of Jammu and Kashmir to India. It was done on 6th February 1954. A constitution for J&K was adopted on 19 November 1956. The Constitution made the J&K an integral part of India. On 26 January 1957 India formalised the accession of the state and made it irrevocable.

In March 1957 the Security Council again considered the Kashmir issue and Gunnar Jarring, the Swedish President of the Security Council, was appointed to negotiate. His mission also failed. The Jarring Report on Kashmir implicitly admitted the new problems that a plebiscite would create and also lend support, to the fact that Kashmiri people's progress and Pakistan's adherence to military pacts had in a way changed the context of the Kashmir question. By then Pakistan was a full-fledged member of the CENTO and SEATO and was in receipt of adequate military assistance.

The western support to Pakistan, both moral and military found the growth of intimate relationship between India and the Soviet Union and India could get a positive Soviet help on the floor of the UN over the Kashmir issue. Whenever an anti-Indian Western-piloted proposal was tabled in the Security Council a quick Soviet veto was available to nullify the designs.

In October 1958 General Mohammad Ayub Khan, the

man who had sabotaged the Nehru-Mohammad Ali formula for resolving the Kashmir dispute by engineering the US-Pakistan agreement, achieved his objective by capturing political power. A ruthless schemer, Ayub, was however aware that despite the massive military build-up, Pakistan was scarcely in a position to challenge India Militarily.

On 27 April, 1962 the Kashmir issue was again brought before the Security Council by Pakistan. But India affirmed that Kashmir's accession was 'full, complete and final'. As neither side was willing to budge from its staunchly held position the stalemate continued. It is only after the outbreak of the Sino-Indian border conflict in October 1962, that the Kashmir dispute returned to the forefront. The border conflict with China had led to what was believed to be loss of Indian Territory; and it was inconceivable that Indian public opinion would tolerate the voluntary surrender of territory to Pakistan in Kashmir. What made compromise at this juncture even more difficult were military considerations.[44]

At this moment of time Averil Harriman, the US Assistant Secretary of State for Far Eastern Affairs and Duncan Sandy's, the British Secretary of State for Commonwealth Affairs, shuttled between Delhi and Rawalpindi and persuaded Nehru and Ayub to start negotiations for an equitable solution to the problem. There was anxiety in the minds of both Harriman and Sandy's. Ayub Khan with his long track of record of anti-communism was trusted both in London and Washington and there was an apprehension that unless the Kashmir problem was resolved urgently, Ayub might be overthrown and replaced by 'wilder men.'[45] They were probably thinking of Zulfiquar Ali Bhutto, Pakistan's vitriolic anti-Indian foreign minister, who was also the architect of Pakistan-China rapprochement and might lead Pakistan away from the western alliance. Lord Mountbatten (then the chief of the UK General staff) and Dean Rusk, the US Secretary of State, also brought gentle pressure on Nehru to accept a 'Low key mediation' or 'good offices' by an American or a Briton in the Kashmir dispute.[46]

Nehru was in no position to resist the reopening of discussion and announced that the foreign ministers of the two countries would discuss bilateral relations with 'no restrictions or preconditions'. Between December 1962 and May 1963, Sardar Swaran Singh and Zulfiquar Ali Bhutto met no fewer than six times. Some progress was discernible. Neither side was any longer claiming the whole of Jammu and Kashmir. Pakistan was willing to give up the Hindu-majority Jammu, but remained adamant, that the fate of Kashmir could only be decided by a plebiscite.

In 1964, shortly before Nehru's death, the Chinese Prime Minister and Foreign Minister paid official visit to Pakistan. They expressed the hope that the Kashmir dispute would be resolved in accordance with the wishes of the people of Kashmir in terms of the pledge given to them by India and Pakistan. At the conclusion of President Ayub's return visit to China in April 1965, the two powers celebrated their growing friendship by making further veiled charges against India. Also, with the aim of building up a bridge to the Soviet Union, President Ayub Khan payed a trip to the Soviet Union in April 1965.[47]

In April 1965, before Lal Bahadur Shastri had completed one year in the high office, serious trouble broke out between India and Pakistan in the Rann of Kutch. The armed clashes assumed quite menacing proportion. "The outcome of the Rann of Kutch episode made Pakistan dangerously over confident and India dangerously frustrated."[48] According to India's General J.N. Chaudhuri, in the Kutch episode Pakistan's strategy in April 1965 was to induce India to move down heavy re-enforcements from the main Punjab theatre to the Rann of Kutch area. Having got India to divert its strength from the Northwestern theatre, Pakistan had planned to capture with the help of its regular army the key point of Akhnur. This would have cut off Kashmir from the rest of India. Thus the Indian army's main concentration was in the strategically important Northwestern area.

Bhutto, the Foreign Minister of Pakistan said: this dispute has arisen not because the boundary is undemarcated (as was the Indian stand), but because the disputed territory is in India's adverse possession.[49] The Pakistani leadership, with its armed forces greatly strengthened by the arms and the equipment imported from the United States, took full advantage of India's military unpreparedness, tactical weakness, lay of the ground and the confusion caused by leadership change.

With the mediation of the British Prime Minister Harold Wilson, the cease-fire agreement was signed on June 30, 1965, in New Delhi in the presence of the British High Commissioner. The agreement provided for the restoration of the status quo as on January 1, 1965 and withdrawal of forces. Also the agreement acknowledged the existence of a territorial dispute in the Rann of Kutch area and provided for bilateral negotiations for the settlement of the dispute. On the negotiations not resulting in an agreement, the two Governments committed themselves to the reference of the dispute to an International Tribunal. The perceived weakness of India's new government tempted Wilson to play an imperial role and Shastri, the Indian Prime Minister, had succumbed to Mr. Wilson's diplomatic pressure. The mediation skill of Harold Wilson (or Shastri's diffidence) was so overwhelming that, Shastri agreed to extend the scope of the dispute from a mere demarcation of the border on the ground to adjudication of Pakistan's substantive territorial claims in the Rann of Kutch area.[50] This was certainly a feather in the cap of Wilson and a victory for President Ayub. For Shastri and India, it was a tactical defeat. India lost the strategic territory in the Rann of Kutch area as a result of the Tribunal's verdict.

Besides the uncertainties of transition from one era to another and the new Prime Minister's lack of experience and stature, much of the weakness of India's position in the world was due to its lack of material strength. In modern times what must prevail is the economic, industrial, scientific and technological power and India was backward in all these areas. Throughout the fifties and sixties, India not only had to import modern military equipment and industrial machinery, it was also heavily dependent on North America for large quantities of food grains imports. The decline of Indian prestige had started in the last days of Jawaharlal Nehru when India's military inferiority was demonstrated on the battlefield in 1962. The leadership change was only an additional factor in the aggravation of India's international position.[51]

The Rann of Kutch episode had, as has been noted, increased the self-confidence of Pakistani army. The frustration caused by the deadlock on the Kashmir issue and the boundless confidence created by recent skirmishes in the Pakistan's defence forces led to President Ayub's "fateful decision to play for larger stakes by sending Pakistan trained guerillas into Kashmir".[52] As the American writer has observed the cautious Ayub for the first time in his career "Overreached himself."[53]

In fact Ayub Khan miscalculated the whole situation. He believed that Pakistan's incursion into Kashmir would not provoke the Indians into extending the area of hostilities along the Indo-Pakistan international border.[54] Ayub Khan had an increased faith in the military superiority of the Pakistani forces[55]. Further, President Ayub Khan, relying on his intelligence sources, overestimated the goodwill and support Pakistan enjoyed among the people of Kashmir. He expected a people's revolt in support of the guerillas.

The Indo-Pakistan war started in September 1965. Soon after the hostilities started, President Ayub sent the former Air Chief abroad to canvass material support for Pakistan. Turkey and Iran advised a speedy termination of the conflict while China's response was positive. The Chinese accused India of border violations and issued an ultimatum of sorts. The Chinese statement expressed firm support for Pakistan in its "just" struggle.[56] It was to serve the double purpose of restraining Indian action and encouraging Pakistani resistance.

General Chaudhuri has admitted, that the Indian armed forces were not in state of total preparedness in 1965. Although the size of India's armed forces was much larger than that of Pakistan, it had to make dispositions keeping in view the possible threat from China.[57]

When the fighting in Kashmir became serious, the Security Council took note of the situation and called upon Pakistan and India to cease-fire and withdraw their armed personnel to their side of the old cease-fire line. This resolution was reiterated two days later on September 6, when Indian forces crossed the Punjab border to relieve pressure on the troops desperately trying to preserve the land communications between Jammu and Kashmir and the Indian Punjab. After a lot of back stage discussions among big powers and twisting of arms, the Security Council changed its tone, made it more strident and demanded that the cease-fire take effect of September 22, 1965.[58]

After the cease-fire the Soviet Union, which had supported the Security Council resolution, offered its good offices and invited India and Pakistan to come to Tashkent to discuss their differences. The soviet initiative was an earnest effort of their new even-handed policy towards the two South Asian states. The Russian leaders exerted considerable pressure on India and Pakistan and persuaded them to sign the declaration. The Tashkent declaration affirmed the resolve of the two countries "not to have recourse to force and to settle their disputes through peaceful means."[59] Shastri not only agreed to mutual withdrawal across the Punjab and Sind-Rajasthan frontier, he also agreed to vacate the strategic points captured by India in Kashmir during the recent fighting.

The Tashkent declaration would have drawn fire in India and Shastri would have been criticised for his violation of his solemn assurances to Parliament on Haji Pir etc. But Shasrti suddenly died in Tashkent. The outcome of the contest on the battlefield in 1965 was far from decisive it was a stalemate.

Unlike the 1965 Indo-Pakistan war, the 1971 Bangladesh war[60] did not end in a stalemate. With ten million refugees on hand, an indecisive contest would have been a complete disaster. Gandhi had two clear objectives and she was determined to achieve them. One was the destruction of the Pakistani Army in Bangladesh. The other was the establishment of a sovereign and an independent Bangladesh, which alone would make the return of refugees possible.

Pakistan had sustained a terrible defeat in the war; Gandhi was conscious that India now was in a strong position. India held ninety thousand Pakistani soldiers captive. Gandhi firmly ruled out, third party mediation or interference in settling the outstanding problems. This marked a fundamental departure from the unhappy legacy. Her father had permitted outside interference in Kashmir affairs for a long time. Her immediate predecessor had made third party mediation and international arbitration a habit, almost the basis of Indian foreign policy. Gandhi broke with this unsavoury past. Henceforth nobody would be allowed to meddle in Indo-Pakistan relations. It would be a purely bilateral affair. The representatives of Pakistan and India met at Simla in June-July 1972, to discuss the problems, which had arisen out of the Bangladesh War and open a new page in the Indo-Pakistan relations. Bhutto himself led the Pakistan delegation and Gandhi headed the Indian team. India offered to return to Pakistan a little over 5100 square miles of territory captured by the Indian army in exchange for nearly 70 square miles in the possession of the Pakistan forces. Both counties decided to withdraw to their side of the international border. In Kashmir the two parties settled on the line of actual control as the effective dividing line as between their zones in Kashmir. They further resolved to settle all disputes through bilateral negotiations.[61] Bhutto realised that having fought three wars within a space of 25 years India was not likely to hand over Kashmir to Pakistan. Undoubtedly, Mrs. Gandhi's skillful handling of the Bangladesh war and its aftermath enhanced India's prestige.[62]

The Kashmir issue, remained in cold storage from 1972 to 1989, has been revived by Pakistan in a new international, regional and domestic setting.[63] When the JKLF (Jammu Kashmir Liberation Front) declared the beginning of its armed struggle on 1 August 1989, it marked the opening of a new strategy.[64] The chairman of the JKLF Amanullah Khan claimed that by the early 1980s the JKLF realised that it must cultivate young men in the valley if it was ever to succeed in bringing about an independent Kashmir. Thus during 1987-88 four promising young Kashmiri men[65] were recruited and slipped into so-called Azad Kashmir for training. Called the Haji Group, they become the core of the organisation that declared war in 1989. Until January 1990, the JKLF, the principal guerrilla organization, was not a very effective force. On 8th December 1989, the JKLF unwittingly unleashed a chain of events that changed all that. JKLF guerrillas kidnapped Dr. Rubia Sayeed, daughter of the then Federal Home Minister Mufti Muhammed Sayeed and demanded the release of five of their jailed colleagues in exchange for her release. The government capitulated after five days and released the JKLF men. JKLF supporters took to the streets in celebration, which sparked a police shooting that left several dead. A career civil servant named Jagmohan arrived in Srinagar to take over as Governor. The January massacres, Jagmohan's hard-nosed attitude and the strict regime of constant, round-the-clock curfews, search operations and severe harassment (illegal detentions, torture, random killings) as well as Jagmohan's 19 February dissolution of the state assembly, all contributed to a massive surge of support for the JKLF. In his memoirs *My Frozen Turbulence in Kashmir*, Jagmohan vehemently denies any role in the killings.[66] Jagmohan was finally dismissed in may 1990, after the CRP opened fire on the funeral procession of Maulvi Farooq, the most important religious leader in Srinagar and killed 55 mourners. The Governor's heavy hand had done considerable damage to India's cause, converting relatively minor insurgency into a full-blown popular revolt. As Ashok Jaitley, a highly respected senior officer of the Indian Administrative Service, who worked under Mr. Jagmohan in 1990 and became one of the Governors's most severe critics, said, "what Jagmohan did in five months they (the militants) could not have achieved in five years."[67]

Once the insurrection began to feed on the abuses of the Indian security forces, the number of guerrilla recruits and insurgent groups began to multiply rapidly. Sheikh Abdul Hamid, then one of the principal leaders of the JKLF, in an interview in April 1990, admitted that the JKLF did not have a long-term military strategy because the leadership believed that they would triumph by arousing international pressure against India. The Sheikh said his aim was 'to create the problem and our biggest success has been to put it before the world.'[68]

New Delhi was quite capable of deploying brute force in

the interests of national integrity. As many as 200,000 men from the army, the CRP and the Border Security Force were deployed in the valley. By mid-1991, the Indian forces, though still facing frequent attacks, had contained the insurgency. Unlike 1990, when there was near panic in the ranks of the security forces, which had little intelligence on the insurrection and were operating blindly, there was a new confidence. Girish Saxena, who replaced Jagmohan as the governor was able to declare, 'we can keep this up for years, the way we did in Nagaland (a long-running tribal rebellion in the northeast).'[69] Thus the Indian forces gradually improved their counter-insurgency efforts. The keystone of the effort was repeated 'Cordon-and-search' operations, which involved sealing off areas of a city or a town, then systematically searching every house and structure within the area for weapons. Suspicious young men were taken in for questioning and often faced severe torture. Those Kashmiris who break under torture sometimes agree to act as 'cats'[70], a Kashmiri term for collaborators. Police authorities also claim that in 1991, as some Kashmiris lost their enthusiasm for the secessionist movement, they were able to buy information with bribes or even have it proffered in the public interest, though this was almost certainly a small part of the overall intelligence effort.

Amanullah Khan, in an interview, claims that from spring 1990, the ISI mounted pressure on the JKLF, harassing its leadership, hijacking recruits and inducing or coercing JKLF members to join Hezbul Mujahedin.[71] Today the JKLF is almost defunct as a fighting force, though it is still very popular, while Hezb was clearly the most important fighting force in the valley at the end of 1991.

Thus, since 1989, Pakistan has been waging a 'proxy war' against India by aiding and abetting Kashmiri militants to rise against the Indian state. Although in the first few years of militancy in the Kashmir valley, up to 1992-93, the militants had received local sympathy due to the Kashmiri people's perceived grievances against the Indian state. However, it was never a grassroots movements and the Kashmiri people were soon disillusioned by the brutal un-Islamic terror tactics of the militants whose leadership had passed into the hands of mercenary Mujahedin, inducted by Pakistan[72] in large numbers to wage a *Jehad*. These mercenaries were from Pakistan, Afghanistan, Iran, Saudi Arabia, Iraq, Libya, Sudan, Turkey and even Bosnia. The militants exploited the power of the Kalashnikov.[73] The systematic ethnic cleansing carried out at the behest of the ISI resulted in the forced migration of almost the entire Hindu population out of the Kashmir Valley into the Jammu region and other parts of India. This was contrary to Kashmir's sufi culture.

Frustrated in their efforts to create a popular uprising in Kashmir, the Pak Army-ISI[74]-Jamate Islami combine then evolved a plan to spread the area of militancy to other parts of J&K and to the neighbouring states. From the summer months of 1996, a new phase of state-sponsored terrorism from across India's western border commenced in the Jammu Division of J&K. The aim was clearly to create an ethnic divide so as to trigger an exodus of the Hindu population from these areas too. However this diabolical attempt to change the demographic pattern of J&K through terror tactics was quickly thwarted by the Indian Army and other security forces. Pak-sponsored terrorism has claimed the lives of over 29,000 innocent civilians and rendered about 2,80,000 persons homeless. The loss to public and private property has been estimated at Rs. 2,000 crore. Throughout this prolonged period of proxy war, India has shown tremendous restraint and immense tolerance in the face of grave provocation to its security. It is inconceivable, that any other nation would have acted with the sense of responsibility that India has, in not launching trans-Line of Control (LoC) operations to eliminate militant training camps and interdict known routes of infiltration[75].

But, behind the scene there is another story, the Jamiat-e-Ulema-e Islam (JUI) was the Taliban's closest link in Pakistan. The Taliban were to bank upon the JUI's 'madarsas' in Pakistan as an important level of support. In 1996, the Taliban handed over Camp Badr near Khost on the Pakistan-Afghanistan border to the Harkat-ul-Ansar, a splinter group of the JUI known for its extreme militancy in Kashmir. The

Harkat-ul-Ansar changed its name to Harkat-ul-Mujahideen (HuM) after it was declared a terrorist organisation by the United States in 1997. Together with Lashkar-e-Taiba (LeT) another group dominated by Afghans and supported by the Taliban, the HuM was to join hands with the Pakistani army to launch Operation Badr, the 1999 Kargil war with India. This operation was the first joint operation in Kashmir by the Pakistani army and Taliban-supported extreme militants trained in Afghanistan. Thus, by sending heavily armed foreign mercenaries and army soldiers in civilian clothes across the LOC into the Kargil district of J&K to physically occupy territory on the Indian side (Pak-occupied-Kashmir-II), Pakistan has added a new dimension to its ten year old 'proxy war' against India. Pakistan's provocative action has compelled India to launch a firm but measured and restrained military operation to clear the intruders. 'Operation-Vijay', finely calibrated to limit military action to the Indian side of the LoC.

The "Operation-Vijay" enhanced the prestige of India. The credit undoubtedly goes to the Indian armed forces whose efforts were behind the grand victory of India at both diplomatic and strategic level. Eventually, India has got success in getting support from all over the world including all time allies of Pakistan, USA and China (in a sense these nations did not favour Pakistan, instead pressurised for the withdrawal of Pakistani troops from Kargil). Perhaps for the first time the USA accused Pakistan for its terrorist activities so explicitly and warned to stop all these immediately, certainly makes good sign for India. What India could not do in last fifty-two years (*viz.* to convince the only surviving Super Power that Kashmir is an inalienable part of India and if there is any dispute, that is the restoration of Pak-occupied-Kashmir-I (PoK-I) to India, if this is not acceptable to Pakistan, Simla agreement is there, but all disputes should be resolved bilaterally with Pakistan), Pakistan herself done by creating warlike conditions in Kargil.

In the post-Kargil era, the Talibanised Mujahid's number increased dramatically. The control over the Mujahids' was slowly but surely shifting from Islamabad to Kandhar with far-reaching consequences. Consequently, Musharrf was probably right when he said that he did not have any effective control over the post-Kargil Mujahids. (The full text of Musharraf's speech can be viewed at www.pak.gov.pk/ public/ president address.htm).

However, India-Pakistan relations improved significantly in the recent past. India's Prime Minister Atal Behari Vajpayee undertook a well-publicised bus ride across the India-Pakistan border to Lahore on February 19, 1999, hailed as a major breakthrough in their troubled bilateral relations. The Lahore Declaration issued at the conclusion of this visit affirmed the strong desire of the prime ministers of India and Pakistan to resolve their problems, including Kashmir, through negotiations. But the optimism generated by these developments nose-dived, with the conflict in Kargil.

Since September 11, Pakistan has been under intense interational pressure to discontinue the strategy of using terrorism as an instrument of State policy. But, it is very difficult for Pakistan to curb 'Kalashnikov culture' in the near future. President made a special point of Pakistan disassociating itself from terrorism in any of its manifestation. But, he has very little control over the Talibanised terrorist groups which are not only concentrated in and around Pak but also taking active part in terrorist activities in India especially after the defeat of Taliban government in Afghanistan. Their groups are creating problems for Musharraf also. In fact, Musharraf has embarked on an extraordinary bold and risky mission in which he will face the opposition not only of *jihadi* militants inflamed by the Taliban's defeat in Afghanistan but also some of his militant colleagues.

Fresh efforts are now being made by both the countries to minimise the security threat in the region. A step forward towards good relations lies in growing economic cooperation, beginning with major infrastructure projects in the energy sector such as gas pipelines and interlinking electricity grids. There are clear-cut incentives of cumulative economic gains for both the countries. Such common projects will create stakes in continuing cooperation and can catalyse trade and investment relationship overtime.

Both the governments are now agreed on a compact dialogue at different levels to resolve all the issues. Few successful rounds are over. Phase of hatred and animosity seems to be the thing of the past. Both the governments are behaving in a responsible manner.

Prime minister Manmohan Singh's invocation of the fall of the Berlin wall during his meeting with his Pakistani counterpart is significant. No one can deny the very real yearning of people on both sides of the border to get to know more about each other. India is right to ask for a bus from Srinagar to Muzaffarabad to increase people-to-people contact. From 30 visas in 2002, India now issued 10,000 visas for Pakistanis. There have been numerous reports of the Indian government offering medical assistance to Pakistanis, especially children. All this can only serve to build goodwill for India in Pakistan. Encouraging more Pakistanis to come here will also give them a chance to see India's free and open society at work. It will help remove many misgivings they have about India. In the end, a swell of public goodwill towards India will make it easier for any Pakistani government to move forward with the peace process. Hardliners may argue that when dealing with a military dictatorship, security and political issues must first be resolved. But as we have seen for decades, it is not likely that the dreaded K-word will be solved overnight nor indeed the issue of cross-border terrorism. So the next best thing is to work on less contentious issues like making it easier for ordinary citizens on both sides to meet each other. By keeping people apart, successive governments on both sides have been able to demonise the other. With the movement of people will come an understanding and appreciation of each other. This will help us put our bitter past behind us and move on. But an element of caution has to be taken in every such move, because Pakistan is still run by the same man who waged a treacherous war against India and scuttled the hope for peace that preceded it.[76]

THE CHINA FACTOR

"From friendship to confrontation, from confrontation to détente and then to normalisation, Sino-Indian relations have gone through a tortuous process". Both India and China have paid a price for past errors, from which both have many lessons to learn and many questions to reflect upon.[77] Pakistan and People's Republic of China are two prominent neighbours of India. Both of them had waged wars in the past. After detonating five nuclear devices in 1998 India categorically mentioned that it was designed only to give a clear signal to the rest of the world of India's intension to acquire a minimum nuclear deterrence. The main motive of this minimum nuclear deterrence will be to prevent Pakistan and China from a nuclear war against India. The Indian deterrence in that sense will be of a defensive character.

While justifying the tests, the government stated, "the nuclear environment in India's neighborhood had necessitated the tests to provide reassurance to the people of India that their national security interests are paramount." In a letter to the US President, Vajpayee stated, "we have an overt nuclear state on our borders...a state, which committed armed aggression against India in 1962."[78]

However, prior to the partition of the country, the mind-set of the rulers attuned to the British rule was to regard Russia as the threat. As far as India's security was concerned, it was from the North-West Frontier Province and Kashmir and the west of the Punjab, Sindh and Baluchistan, that the defence and security was maintained. The situation changed *vis-a-vis* China with the partition. The Chinese empire now emerged as a major power after the Communist take over in 1949, whereas earlier China was plunged in civil war and ravaged by foreign (Japanese) occupation before the departure of the British from India. Otherwise the scenario of defence from the north appeared not to have changed.[79]

India recognised China within two months of establishment of PRC. Among non-communist countries India was second to do that after Burma. Also, India fought for China's entry into the world body. The Sino-Indian relationship entered into a bright phase in 1955. India sincerely wanted China's participation in international affairs. In April 1955 an Afro-Asian conference was held in Bandung, China participated in the conference, which was possible because of the good offices of Nehru. China got an opportunity to enter into world diplomacy and at the first instance could succeed to woo the Afro-Asian nations away from India's leadership. China had the ambition to lead the uncommitted block and to become the spokesman of Asia. Nehru was the stumbling bloc to the Chinese designs. From 1954 to 1957 the Sino-Indian relations were very cordial and it was called as honeymoon days. "The foreign policy of China had a dual role to perform; on the one hand it had to show that good neighbourliness was its perennial concern and on the other that it had the most important military strength in Asia."[80]

The worsening of the relationship was unfortunate. The bitterness of relationship grew over the cartographic invasion of China. India was surprised to see an officially circulated Chinese map where incorrect boundary alignment between India and China was shown and that also incorporated 50,000 sq. miles of the Indian Territory in China.[81] For nearly a decade New Delhi sincerely wanted a peaceful and good neighbourly China. But the imperial image pursued by China could not provide friendly atmosphere. In July 1959 the Chinese forces entered into Ladakh and arrested the Indian patrol party in Aksai Chin. A similar action was observed in NEFA in August 1959. The intention was that both the regions fell in China. In September 1959 Chou Enlai, the Chinese Premier, demanded 50,000 sq. miles of the Indian territory and within a fortnight the Chinese forces entered into Ladakh and waged a limited war.

In April 1960, the two Premiers met but their talks did not result in resolution of differences. In 1961 under pressure from the opposition Nehru, adopted a forward policy the purpose of which was to establish some symbolic posts both in Ladakh and NEFA. The fortification of the Indian border with the creation of many outposts came as 'Irritants' to undeclared intentions. This provoked them to cross the McMahon Line on 8 September 1962 and initiated a large scale war on both Eastern and Western sectors, on 20 October 1962, The Chinese troops overwhelmed the Indian frontier posts. The Chinese proposal for ceasefire and disengagement after sufficient entry was turned down by India, which demanded a status quo on the border as on 8th September 1962. On 21st November 1962 China declared unilateral ceasefire and its decision to withdraw. This resulted in a stalemate.

Sino-Pak Alliance

The Sino-Pak closeness became clear after the Belgrade non-aligned summit, 1961. They could initiate cordial relationship, notwithstanding, both of them differ in their political systems and perceptions of several domestic and external issues. Both of them started an anti-Indian propaganda. Pakistan signed a border agreement with China, though it had no border with China. The agreement covered the illegally occupied Azad Kashmir. India lodged protests to both countries regarding the legitimacy of the agreement.[82]

China played a crucial role in the South Asian Power balance. China's role was not so much to actively support Pakistan — although it certainly did that in some respects — as to separate Indian forces and thus weaken India.[83] At times, such as during the 1965 Indo-Pakistani war, China maneuvered on the border and issued ultimatums against India in order to pin Indian troops down and assist Pakistan. In the lead-up to the 1971 Indo-Pakistani war, India was forced into closer alliance with the Soviet Union in order to neutralise China.

Pakistan's failure to achieve its objectives in the wars of 1947-48, 1965 and 1971, and the breaking away of its eastern half into Bangladesh, resulted in Pakistani leaders becoming paranoid about the threat from India. Further, Pakistani decision-makers were not unaware of the continued development by India of nuclear technology and China's nuclear test in 1964 (and first hydrogen bomb two-and-a-half years later) raised the fear in their minds that India, as a response to China's test, might emerge as the sixth nuclear weapons power.[84] Pakistan's President Z.A. Bhutto is reported to have said that Pakistanis would be prepared to eat grass if they had to, if this became necessary for Pakistan to build its own nuclear deterrent.[85]

Although the military dictator Ayub Khan had made some effort during the early 1960s to explore the possibilities of co-operation in nuclear technologies with China, nothing significant had transpired between Islamabad and Beijing. Bhutto, however, was determined to acquire nuclear weapons and with this end in mind, he pursued all options available to Pakistan, taking direct responsibility himself for the Atomic Energy Department between 1971-1977. He conceptualised Pakistan's weapon as an Islamic bomb and sold this notion to the radical Islamic leaders who were persuaded to provide cash. It is no exaggeration to describe Zulfiquar Ali Bhutto as the architect of Pakistan's nuclear programme. As regards China's help, Bhutto can similarly be credited with having laid the foundation of Sino-Pakistan nuclear co-operation, which he had worked out with relentless zeal during his three visits to Beijing in February 1972, September 1974 and April 1976.[86]

The Indian nuclear explosion had a catalytic impact in generating a strong drive in Pakistan for nuclear weapons technology. In the National Assembly of Pakistan the Prime Minister Bhutto while expressing his anguish said, "a more grave and serious event has not taken place in the history of Pakistan. The explosion has introduced a qualitative change in the situation between the two countries."[87] Further, India's test of a nuclear device also changed the context of the Sino-Pakistani ties and it was during Bhutto's third visit to China, that the first important Sino-Pakistani nuclear agreement was put into black and white. Towards the close of 1975, Dr. Abdul Qadeer Khan, a migrant from Bhopal, returned from the Netherlands to Pakistan to take up an ultra-centrifuge enrichment project known as Project 706. Since Dr. Khan had stolen important blueprints from the Dutch laboratories[88], and Chinese scientists working on centrifuge technology could have benefitted from useful information provided by the Pakistanis for the design and fabrication of the ultra-centrifuge technology based on manufacture of enriched Uranium, which the European nuclear consortium (URENCO) had developed. On January 29, 1977, Pakistan and China signed a protocol on scientific and technical co-operation. Chinese assistance for the development of nuclear energy was implicit in the protocol. Pakistan in fact, had begun playing the Chinese nuclear card when American military and economic aid was terminated in 1977 and in 1979 (on the basis of the 1977 Glenn-Symington Amendment[89]) by the Carter Administration in the hope that the Pakistani nuclear weapons programme could be brought to a halt. In 1981, in the wake of the Soviet occupation of Afghanistan, the United States, for six years, suspended the application of the Uranium enrichments sanctions provisions of the Glenn-Symington Amendment to Pakistan and provided greatly increased military and economic assistance to it. Reagon Administration officials also argued, that the restoration of aid would advance US non-proliferation objectives by enhancing Pakistan's overall security, thereby reducing Islamabad's motivation to acquire nuclear arms.[90]

Pakistan, however, continued its nuclear weapons programmme.[91] In the wake of the Soviet intervention in Afghanistan, Islamabad obtained special consideration from both the US and China in building up its nuclear facilities.[92] Reports of Chinese assistance to Pakistan 'for creation of atomic weapons' had begun to appear from early 1979. Encouraged by the Chinese response, President Zia-ul-Haq visited China in 1980 and 1982,[93] while Chinese Premier Zhao Ziyang went to Islamabad in June 1981. This was followed by a report in the New Scientist, that an agreement had been reached on exploding a Pakistani nuclear device on China's soil.[94] According to studies by scholars like Leonard Spector, Leslie Gelb, Simon Henderson and Hedrick Smith, China not only supplied Pakistan with a nuclear weapon design, but also supplied enough highly enriched uranium to build a modest arsenal in the early eighties. With the assistance of the Chinese nuclear scientists at Kahuta, Pakistan's nuclear weapon efforts picked up momentum.[95] The fact that the Americans knew of the Sino-Pakistani collaboration was later corroborated by

Paul Leventhal of the Nuclear control Institute of the US. He pointed out that the Chinese had conducted a nuclear test at Lop Nor in Xingjiang in May 1983, in the presence of the Pakistani Foreign Minister, Yakub Khan.[96]

Both the US administration and the Soviet officials have asserted more than once that China had a definite role in Pakistan's nuclear weapons programme. Leslie Gelb, who held an important position in the Carter Administration, as also in the US intelligence services, is on record saying that China had provided Pakistan with the design of its fourth nuclear weapon test. Similarly, in the Moscow World Services Report (English) of August 26, 1984, it was stated that China had "...made a direct contribution to the development of Pakistan's nuclear potential."[97] Other sources confirmed, that the Chinese had supplied to Pakistan the original design of their fourth nuclear bomb model in 1983, which was tested at Lop Nor in 1966. It was also reported, that Pakistan had later carried out 'one cold test in September 1986 in the hills west of Chagai in order to verify the Chinese design.'[98] According to a survey conducted by the International Herald Tribune during late 1991, US Officials described Pakistan as the largest importer of China's nuclear technologies. It concluded that by this time, China had supplied Pakistan with enough weapons grade Uranium to produce at least two nuclear devices and Islamabad was possibly in possession of at least one nuclear bomb weighing only 180 Kg.[99]

In the 1990s, despite West's increasing concern on nuclear non-proliferation, Beijing has continued to assist Pakistan develop its nuclear weapons programme. Reports surfaced during 1995 about China's supply of a 40 MW heavy water research reactor for Pakistan's secret enrichment facility at Khushab.[100] This new facility is expected to take Pakistan from the stage of conventional uranium bombs to the production of plutonium and tritium, which will make it possible for it to develop more advanced compact nuclear warheads for their missiles.[101] Early in February 1996, the US intelligence sources reported that China had supplied 5000 ring magnets to Pakistan, which were said to have been sold to the A.Q. Khan

Research Laboratories in Kahuta in 1995.[102] Since 1992, China has formally become a signatory to the nuclear Non-Proliferation Treaty (NPT) and has agreed, in writing, to adhere to the provision of the Missile Technology Control Regime (MTCR), which places severe restraints on its nuclear collaboration with Pakistan. However, China seems to be using these non-proliferation regimes as a cover while continuing its nuclear dealings with its strategic partners. China and Pakistan continue collaboration on civilian nuclear technologies is another dimension of their nuclear alliance. China has supplied to Pakistan a 300,000-KW stabiliser and 300,000-KW streamers, as also large quantities of heavy water, which have been suspected of being diverted to other, unsafeguarded facilities, like the Khushab Plutonium production reactor.[103] Similarly, China's official news agency, Xinhua, reported that China had exported to Pakistan a sophisticated simulated nuclear power plant control room, which it said was aimed at training Pakistani technicians.[104] China remains determined to supply nuclear power technologies to Pakistan. No other nuclear relationship between two countries has been of such a long duration.

Furthermore, Pakistan with the assistance of North Korea and China has developed a series of missiles. Some of these missiles have been named provocatively 'Ghauri'[105] and 'Ghaznavi.' Pakistan had developed enriched uranium weapons in 1987. The Ghauri, Ghaznavi and the follow up Shaheen are all derivatives of the North Korean Nodong missiles with ranges of 800 and 1200 Kms. respectively. Shaheen-2 according to some reports could have a range of 2400 Kms. China transferred to Pakistan in July 1991 the M-11 missile with a range of 300 Kms. That can carry nuclear or chemical warheads. Pakistan has in place a 'launch on warning' posture that could enable it to strike at targets within India.

The extent of Sino-Pakistani collaboration became clearer following Pakistan's nuclear tests. However, preparations for Pakistani nuclear tests did not start after Pokhran-II, as claimed by official spokesmen. A member of the Pakistani Atomic Energy Commission has revealed that work on digging tunnels at the Chagai Hills for testing purposes was actually started as early as 1978 and was completed in 1982.[106] Dr. A.Q. Khan says that Pakistan had attained the capability to explode a nuclear device in 1984 and he told Gen. Zia that "whenever you order, it will not take more than a week or two to do it."[107] In February 1992 the then Foreign Secretary Shaharyar Khan declared in Washington, that Pakistan had acquired the capability to fabricate at least one nuclear weapon. After Pakistan's nuclear tests on May 28 and 30, 1998 Prime Minister Nawaz Sharif announced that by conducting six nuclear tests Pakistan had "settled score" with India. Dr. A.Q. Khan says, "they were all boosted fission devices using U-235."[108] Some western analysts claim that only three Pakistani nuclear devices were actually tested. Jane's Intelligence Review estimates, that Pakistan has already exhausted a significant portion of its meagre resources in these tests. An interesting aspect of the tests is the emergence of the Pakistani Atomic Energy Commission as a major player.[109]

As expected, China's reaction to Pakistan's tests was muted in comparison to its reaction to India's tests. After May 1998 tests Nawaz Sharif lauded his country's 'time-tested' relations with Beijing and said that, "Our friendship has been further strengthened."[110] In June 1998, a month after India's detonation of nuclear devices, a committee of the five permanent members of the UN Security Council and headed by China passed resolution 1172 which asked India to sign the CTBT and revert immediately to non-zero nuclear weapons status. This suggests that China will act to maximise Pakistan's interests at the expense of Indian interests.[111]

In the mountainous caves and valleys of the Tibetan Autonomous Region, China has deployed medium and intermediate range ballistic missiles. These missiles are in the range of 800 and 2000 Kms. respectively and have the capability to target several centers (both population and industrial) in eastern India. In addition, China has developed ICBMs and SLBMs that can strike at the western US and Russia. It is presently developing multiple independently targetable re-entry vehicles (MIRVs) that enable it to deliver several warheads on a single target.[112] China has today in its arsenal some 400-600 nuclear weapons aboard the Dong Feng (East Wind) series of missiles on land and Julang (Giant Wave) submarine launched ballistic missiles (SLBMs). For Indian deterrence of Chinese missiles targeted on cities in India, it is necessary to have missiles of the range of Agni I, II and III that is of medium, intermediate and intercontinental range so as to destroy cities in China like Beijing, Xian and Shanghi.[113]

Future Prospects

Both India and China have struggled hard to find a place in the international community. Being neighbors, each is also unlikely to accept an inferior position *vis-à-vis* the other. The initial momentum to China's relations with South Asian countries came from its quarrel with India. But since eighties, when domestic reforms gathered momentum in China, its social, cultural and economic interlinkages with societies across its borders facilitated stability in relations. China has abandoned the overtly hostile anti-Indian slant to its policies, opening the prospects for a healthier and more balanced relationship. There is widespread realisation that economics can provide a stronger foundation for bilateral ties. It can prove to be a more effective security against incidental attempts at derailment of the relationship and should be given special attention and a higher priority. Clearly both need a peaceful environment in which faster economic growth can be achieved. Thus, there is a good case for separating politics from economics.[114]

There are many similarities in the challenges both countries face in modernizing their economies and in their participation in the process of globalisation. Given the prevailing flux in the international economic situation and evolving international trade regimes, there is ample room for exchanges of experience between Indian and Chinese socio-economic experts.

It is worth noting that officials and non-officials in China unanimously believe that the visit of the former Prime Minister Rajiv Gandhi to China in December 1988 contributed greatly to the establishment of a strategic frame for India-China relations. Also that his visit contributed to freeing the relationship from being hostage to adverse events of the past. Since the beginning of nineties, significant progress has been made in the field of economic and technological cooperation. The volume of trade between India and China rose from $0.2 billion in 1988 to $1.16 billion in 1995, an increase of more than four times in five years.

The key to China's growth is infrastructure. In China, Rationalisation was implemented with a sense of urgency. Once a nation of opium-eaters, it is now on a 'long rail march'. It has restructured and liberalised its railways. A comparison between the Chinese and Indian systems is instructive. Indian Railways (IR) had laid 53,596 route kilometers in 1950, against 22,161 in the case of Chinese Railways (CR). By 2003, CR had laid 73,002 route km against 63,122 in the case of IR. IR covered 63 billion passenger km in 1950, against CR's 21 billion, but by 2003 the later had reduced the gap, covering 479 billion passenger km against 515 in the case of the former. Recent developments in China would serve to explain these differences. CR is driven by a three-fold ambition: introducing market principles; spinning off non-core activities; and inducting new technologies.[115]

Moreover, from 1997 to 2002, the Chinese government invested $30 billion in building infrastructure. Before 1985, China didn't have a single highway. Now, it has over 20,000 km of highways. China is next only to the US. There is a need to build better infrastructure for rural China. Without infrastructure, one can neither have growth nor extend the benefits of growth to people. The GDP per capita in coastal areas has touched $4,000 compared to $400 in rural areas. China has problems in the countryside. Regional disparity is increasing and its big challenge is to bridge the gap. FDI has contributed in a big way to the economic development of China. Over $500 billion has been invested in China. Last year, FDI investment in China was $53 billion; the US received only $40 billion.

According to the Chinese experience, foreign investment contributed to the economic development of the country.

India is opening most of its sectors to the outside world. The new government has proposed FDI hike in insurance, civil aviation and telecom. This would bring in more investment. Developing countries like China and India need money for growth. That should be the target. This year, China expects FDI investment to surpass $60 billion. China has 600 million phones for a population of 1.3 billion. There is great potential for the telecom sector in China. There are 395 million TV sets. It is set to go up as people move from small TVs to the LCD models. All these are necessary if one has to develop like China.

India is 15 years behind China. China started reforms in 1978 and India in 1991. In China the GDP grew from $140 billion in 1978 to $1.4 trillion last year. The average growth rate is about 9.4%. China will continue to grow beyond 9%. China has specialised in manufacturing. China's strength is hardware and India's is software. China has infrastructure while India's advantage is human resources.

The ultimate winner won't be China or India. It will be China and India. Let's do business together. It is destined that China will develop and so will India. China is keen to sign a free trade agreement (FTA) with India. There is a talk about cooperation between China and South Asia. Both are cooperating with ASEAN countries. India and China could be complementary destinations for global business houses and that would converge businesses of both the countries.[116]

SAARC

Regional cooperation in South Asia began in 1981 with a series of secretary level and minister level meetings that provided a unique opportunity to lay down the foundation of SAARC. The historic moment came in 1985, when all the seven nations of South Asia adopted the SAARC charter in Dhaka. The charter adopted at the Summit spelt out the objectives *inter alia*:

(1) to promote the welfare of the People of South Asia;

(2) to accelerate economic growth, social progress and cultural development in the region;

(3) to promote collective self-reliance;

(4) to contribute to mutual trust and understanding;

(5) to strengthen co-operation among themselves in international forum on matters of common interest.

Actually, the countries of South Asia have not only inherited a shared past but also have a common destiny. South Asian countries have been tied together with intricate bonds of culture, religion, tradition and ethnicity.[117] This is the fact of history, which needs to be precisely acknowledged at the earliest for the betterment of region. These countries must not be seen as rivals, but rather as partners, as constituent units, each contributing what it can to regional resilience. Just like different organs of the body, which are complementary to each other, constitute an organism and perform their specific functions. Countries of South Asia have to perform their complementary role to boost regional cooperation in order to form an organic South Asia.

Regionalism was confined to Europe till the 1980s[118]. Following the end of the Cold War, there was a dramatic spurt in the growth of regionalism. However, regionalism emerged in the aftermath of the Second World War as an important instrument for the attainment of two important objectives: (a) to achieve economic growth through efficient utilisation of resources and (b) to establish enduring peace in the world, especially in Western Europe, by bringing France and Germany together, which had historically been at war with each other. The signing of the Rome Treaty in 1957, which laid the foundations of the European Community, marked the beginning of a regional grouping for the achievements of these objectives.[119]

The late 1980s and the early 1990s witnessed the growth of regionalism[120] of a different nature — *i.e.*, transcontinental regionalism. In fact, economic compulsions are driving dynamic and resilient members of one regional grouping to have simultaneous membership of other regional groupings irrespective of the geographical logic of a 'region's' definition. The US membership of NAFTA and APEC illustrates this point clearly.[121]

Futher, consolidation into regional blocs could make it more likely that negotiated agreements can be reached simply because there are fewer players. A world trading system effectively run by a G-3 (Group of Three), or NAFTA (North Atlantic Free Tread Agreement), EC (European Community) and Japan pose fewer problems of free riding than one in which France or Italy are free to make independent demands and cheat on their own.[122]

Regionalism is thus found to be more efficient, more quick and more enduring.[123] Since the end of the Cold War, a number of regional groupings have emerged at various levels, *i.e.* US-Canadian Free Trade Area (1989), North American Free Trade Area (1993), Asia-Pacific Free Trade Area (1993-94), Pan-Americana Free Trade Area, Mercosur (1991). Co-operation and integration at the regional level is perhaps the single biggest change, that has taken place in the sovereign state system since its inception.[124]

All the developments the world over, where countries are regrouping themselves as megablocs, are bound to have long term implications for South Asia if it gets left behind. There is no doubt, that there is need for structuring a new paradigm on economic regionalism in South Asia based on co-operation in the wide ranging fields of human resource development, science and technology, infrastructure, telecommunication and energy which would optimise the full potential of the region. Greater economic co-operation would in time create its own momentum for moving beyond political obstacles to optimise economic opportunities.[125]

It need not to re-emphasise historical, cultural, religious linkages. In the current context too, an account of a number of common features can be placed. Besides being the country of the same region, they all lie in the southern belt of developing nations; have been suffering with the problems of ethnicity, insurgencies, terrorism and drug-trafficking. Due to liberalisation and globalisation their local interests seem to be afflicted severely. In the game of unequal (rich and poor nations), the rules are equal, that have been furthering even more inequalities in the world. The prevailing norms in the world are : openness, transparency, democracy and the representative institutions, but the functioning of international institutions doesn't seem to be following these norms. Be it UN Security Council, IMF, WB or WTO, everywhere, there is the salience of dual nature of policies.

What is needed on the part of South Asian nations is an identical perception and a just, genuine and organised feeling of sensitivity towards all these crucial issues which could alone generate a positive atmosphere and prepare a solid ground to address, articulate and project their common cause and concerns in an effective forceful manner before the international community. This has also been laid down as one of the important principles of the SAARC charter — to stregthen cooperation among themselves in international forums on matters of common interests.[126] There have been several occasions when the SAARC countries took a common position on the matters of mutual concern and the coordination of such position at the relevant international flora. Such as a SAARC Environment Ministers Conference was held in 1992 to evolve a joint position at the UN Conference on Environment and Development. Likewise, a SAARC collective position was formulated for the fourth World Conference on Women in 1995, as well as the World Food Summit in 1996.[127] These resolves should be kept going also with the cooperation of other like-minded countries.

The fifth WTO Conference (August 2003) held at Cancun, is a remarkable development in this regard. The developing countries firmly placed their views on the prevailing pattern of inequality in the economic sphere, put up their case for reduction in farm subsidies in US, European Union, free outsourcing, movement of workers, protection for the unorganised sector and resisted the discussion of Singapore issues related to investment, trade, competition.[128] For this purpose, two groupings of developing countries (G-16, G-21) emerged during the conference. Interestingly China also participated and emphatically supported the demands put forward by southern nations. The concept of Cancun trio evolved at the end of conference, that is: Haves, have-nots and have-somes, as a new global trade line up. India[129] belongs to third category and therefore its role is of a leading nature and important in getting the rich nations convinced about the desperate necessity to take some positive measures concerning alterations in the present international economic policies. Because simply rising of issues at the world conference is not sufficient but these would have to be made in such a manner that these could not only be better understood and acknowledged but also positively responded by the developed countries. This could be done only when the developed countries get convinced that in this inter-dependent world whatever afflicts one part has to afflict others. In this regard the views of the former chief economist of World Bank and the winner of the Nobel Prize for Economics in 2001, Joseph Stiglitz are significant and encouraging. He opines, "in the Cancun WTO Conference, there was discussion about openness and transparency. There is at the very least a beginning of an awreness of the problem which is a step in the right direction".[130] When asked about the IMF, which is perceived to be pushing a neo-imperial agenda, he said "there are many interests in the developed countries that coincide with the interests of the developing countries. When the developing countries do better. They do better. Unfortunately, those interests are not represented at the IMF. So, only one part of the developing countries interests gets represented. And since it is really a group of people in the developed world dictating IMF policies, I'm hopeful of reform being possible".[131]

Further, India is not a South Asian country, it is South Asia. The Indo-centric character of the cultural, religious and ethnic mosaic of South Asia is a fact of history, which India cannot avoid and its neighbours cannot ignore. In terms of the regional configuration of power, no single country dominates its region in the way India dominates South Asia. Geographically, India forms the core of South Asia and its neighbours the periphery. India shares borders with each of the other countries in the region, while none of its neighbours share borders with any South Asian country other than India. Indian power far outweighs the collective power of all its regional neighbours.[132] Thus it has a natural leadership role here. The benefits to New Delhi are not likely to be direct, but will be reflected in its larger international personality as the leader of the largest population group in the world. It is overwhelmingly in India's national interest to strengthen regional co-operation by harnessing the collective power of these countries. What is more important is an acceptance of the fact, that the Indian subcontinent is a single economy zone. Today India provides the second largest consumer market in the world. When South Asian Free Trade Area (SAFTA) is fully realised, the region will be the largest market in the world. This in turn, will enormously increase India's own importance and potential.[133]

Furthermore, given the logic of bilateral equations in the region, there is some advantage in consciously moving at a faster pace on the economic track, insulating it from the pressures of political volatility. Even if some South Asian countries find it politically expedient to keep contentious issues alive, a degree of political will can still be generated for widening the bases and sources of economic co-operation. This would in turn lead to mutually beneficial linkages triggering its own logic for political relations. Regional co-operation is no longer a matter of choice, but a vital necessity. India's credibility outside the region would depend not only on its power profile, but also on its ability to carry its South Asian neighbours with it in a co-operative framework.[134]

Given the geopolitical realities in the region, bilateralism is going to remain an enduring feature of inter-state relations in South Asia. SAARC can generate impulses for building new patterns of relationships but it cannot obviate the need for addressing bilateral problems in a bilateral framework.[135]

Already a new chapter in Indo-Bangladesh relations has been opened with the signing of the historic agreement on the sharing of the Ganga water. This augurs well for taking up other outstanding issues in a mutually trusting atmosphere. It was Bangladesh, who promoted the idea of an association among the states of South Asia for common development and gave practical shape to it. The main irritants in Indo-Bangla relations include the illegal infiltration, smuggling of goods across the frontiers, Chakma refugees in India, border enclaves[136] etc. Indo-Sri Lankan relations have shown an upward curve with stepped up economic and commercial ties. From the beginning, India has been a highly desired market for the Sri Lankans and an important source of supply of primary products at a lower cost. Even though Sri Lanka is not economically dependent on India, there are many area in which both the countries can forge a vibrant economic co-operation.[137] India's relation with Sri Lanka date back to the third century B.C. when Emperor Ashoka sent emissaries to the Island Kingdom and Buddhism spread from India to Sri Lanka. In the post-1947 period Indo-Sri Lankan relations weathered many potentially destabilizing storms and even touched the rock bottom in the mid-eighties, but never did they reach a point of saturation or complete disruption.[138] In the summer of 1983, as a result of Sinhala-Tamil ethnic conflict, more than 140,000 Sri Lankan refugees, political immigrants and leaders of Lanka Tamil organisation have settled in the Indian state of Tamilnadu. Colombo's invitations to Pakistani, British and even Israeli military advisers created the danger of internationalizing the conflict. The Indian government repeatedly offered assistance in a peaceful settlement by political means. Finally, on July 29, 1987, in Colombo, Rajiv Gandhi and President J.R. Jayewardene of Sri Lanka signed an agreement.[139] To assist the implementation of this agreement, Jayewardene invited Indian troops (Indian Peace-Keeping Force) into the country and Indian warships began patrolling the coastal area to prevent arms smuggling. India was particularly interested in persuading Colombo not to give the naval base in Trincomali to a third country and to limit the activities of the Voice of America on the island, as well as in the withdrawal of the Pakistani and Israeli military advisers.[140] However, a treaty of the kind envisaged in the draft with a crisis-ridden country would have benefited Sri Lanka more than India. More than anything else, India would have lost its leverage with Sri Lanka on the resolution of the ethnic conflict and found itself co-opted into Colombo's larger military strategy against the Liberation Tigers of Tamil Eelam (LTTE). In sum, the friendship treaty would have created more discord than co-operation between the two countries.[141] The contentious bilateral issues are the stateless problem of the people of Indian origin and sovereignty over Kachchativu Island.[142] There are about two lakh Sri Lankan Tamil refugees in India, whose voluntary repatriation is contingent upon the return of peace in the Island.

India and Nepal have entered a new era of mutual goodwill with the conclusion of the Mahakali treaty. India's interests in Nepal have revolved around its security concerns and economic stakes. Following Communist takeover in China, the Chinese leadership moved its forces into Tibet and laid claims on all the Himalayan Kingdoms, constituting India's northern security tier, as well as on the parts of Indian territory in NEFA (North-East Frontier Agency) and the Aksai-chin region.[143] Accordingly, the possible threat of the Chinese military intrusion in or through Nepal, to weaken India's defence perimeter and the challenge of Communist ideology and subversion to destabilise the feudal political orders in the Himalayan kingdoms could not be ignored by India for ensuring its northern security. Further, in the next century, beyond 2030, India would not be able to meet its energy needs, either by developing all its known potential of hydro-power, or by extracting its fossil fuel deposits. It is, therefore, inevitable that the prospects of harnessing regional hydro-power potential in Nepal[144] and Bhutan for mutual benefit are explored seriously and systematically.[145] Nepal's Mahakali, Karnali and Burni Gandaki rivers offer great promise in the field of hydro-power generation. The only viable Indian approach to meet this future challenge can be through a long-term perspective of building mutual confidence and multi-dimensional economic interdependence with its neighbours. Thus while Nepal offers India a huge source of meeting its expanding energy requirements, India also offers Nepal a huge market for trade along with a promising and dependable source of investments and technology. India in the past had not been able to make proper and effective use of economic factors, but , in future, this challenge will have to be met.[146] As far as Indo-Bhutan relations are concerned, there has been no border problem as it is well defined. The last occasion a question arose about it was in 1855 when a treaty between Bhutan and India defined the boundaries of the Dooars district of Bengal. India helped Bhutan to become a member of the United Nations. Relations between Bhutan and India are close and India is associated with the planned development of the country. Bhutan is an active member of SAARC and has cordial relations will all its members. Bhutan is thinly populated. Foreigners are not allowed to come in large numbers. Bhutan has faced an influx of people of the Nepalese origin into Southern Bhutan. The rapid increase in the population of the Nepalese race has affected the ethnic composition of this part of Bhutan.

Obstructive Factors

The obstructions in the process of regional cooperation are many, including internal, intra-regional and extra-regional. Some of these are inherent in the system, nations had acquired, while the others emerged due to the policies and programmes adopted and pursued for the growth and development of their people and the nation state structure.[147] Over the years, issues of national identity, water resources management, trade and transit, economic pressures, ethnic sensitivities, terrorism and drug trafficking and illegal migrations have acquired emotive overtones.

The troubled Indo-Pak relationship casts a shadow on the prospects of peace and cooperation in the region. There is no gainsaying that a breakthrough in SAARC remains contingent in a qualitative improvement in the atmospherics between India and Pakistan.[148]

The impetus accorded by multi-ethnic, multi-lingual, multi-cultural and multi-religious factors over the past more than two decades or so, has made the process of nation state building further complicated and complex.[149] Almost all the countries of this region have been facing the problem of ethnic conflicts in one or the other forms. Allied with this, is the issue of trans-migration — not only of the peoples and their ethnicities but also of the evils of the terrorist, insurgent and other anti-social activities of the mafias indulged in drugs, narcotics and illicit arms trade activities. The trans-border migrations, pushed either "by war or for work or food or by drives towards ethnic racial ideological or religious homogenisation" tend to not only disturb the internal socio-cultural and politico-economic structure but also "cause complications for interstate relationship", which, sometimes, thwarts the process of regional cooperation.[150]

According to experts, South Asia, one of the poorest and the most populated region of the world, is considered to be the world's dangerous place due to large number of threats to security.[151]

On economic front, the marginality of intra-regional trade makes for a general apathy towards intensified cooperation. All the countries in the region are seeking technology, aid and investment from outside the region. There is apprehension that India's large economy, resource base and level of technological and industrial development would swamp the less developed nascent economies of the other South Asian countries, tilting the balance to their grave disadvantage.[152]

The new trends and compulsions generated as a consequence of globalisation and liberalisation have created new challenges to the states of the region at the individual, bilateral and regional levels. The changing patterns of life, institutionalised and aggravated as a result of consumerism and marketisation, have created new problems for developing states of the South Asian region with regard to the retention and protection of their socio-cultural fabric, the most serious among these problems is a need to retain a balance between the existing traditionalism based value system and the new globalised or universalised one.[153] Joseph Stiglitz, in his book, "Globalisation and its Discontents", emphasised, "There are two things. The first is, life is difficult enough for developing countries, and you should not make it more difficult by having unfair rules of the game. So even with fair trade agreements a level playing field, many developing countries — perhaps most — would not be successful. It would make things easier, but it would not solve their problems. The second is that these countries in the past have looked to the IMF for advice. And the IMF's advice is not just advice...they advised many countries to liberalise their capital markets pre-maturely, and that led to a boom when the capital rushed in and a crisis when the capital rushed out."

However, SAARC summit held in the beginning of 2004, imparted some healthy signs and generated a favour for cooperation among South Asian countries. At the end of summit 'Islamabad Declaration' was adopted, that includes a landmark agreement over SAFTA (The SAFTA Treaty signed by 7 SAARC nations, in Islamabad, will operationalise the free trade area by January 2006), an additional protocol to the SAARC convention on combating terrorism, SAARC social charter etc. This spirit has to be maintained and kept up. The upswinging in bilateral relations is also a noticeable development in South Asia. Now SAARC nations are making serious endeavor to pay more attention to trade and commercial relations.

Although, with Sri Lanka, we have the problem of Tiger terrorism, with Bhutan the issue of insurgency, with Bangladesh the problem of illegal immigrants and so on. So there is a view recently emerged after July 21, 2004 SAARC meet that SAARC is not taken seriously at the international level because it is unable to surmount bilateral problems. On the other hand, ASEAN or the European Union have, far from running away from bilateral issues, boldly grasped the nettle and moved on. Therefore, New Delhi should welcome placing Kashmir on the SAARC table and encourage the neighbors to do the same with like problems. Only then can SAARC become instrumental in creating a stable South Asia.

But, to be honest, almost all bilateral issues in the region can only be resolved with the intervention of the big powers. SAARC's strength lies in the fact that it does not interfere in the sovereign affairs of its member states; instead it tries to address such common problems as poverty, illiteracy, health and human trafficking. SAARC meet should focus on how best to bring about a synergy between its member states. For example, Sri Lanka's advantage lies in its exemplary human development indicators, India's in information technology expertise and Nepal's in surplus power. To SAARC's credit, it has been successful in framing policies binding on all its members on the issue of human trafficking. It is also formulating a framework for free trade. This is just the sort of focus it should maintain.[154]

Further SAARC has already made some progress in establishing contacts with like-minded organisations the most prominent being the European Union. Individually all of the SAARC countries enjoy close bilateral relations with each ASEAN member, but the same is not true for SAARC. India has already graduated to the status of being a full dialogue partner with ASEAN in 1995. India was formally admitted as ARF member (ASEAN Regional Forum) in 1996. In the context of increasing economic global interdependence, prudence dictates, that countries and regional groups should maximise their spread of connections in order to guard against the risks of over-dependency. As co-operation between the South Asian states improves, there will be incremental growth in the co-operation between SAARC and ASEAN. This in turn will have wider implications outside the South Asian subcontinent. Other regional and sub-regional groups have been formed, with which SAARC will surely interact. The Indian Ocean[155] Rim Association for Regional Co-operation (IOR-ARC) groups 14 African, Asian and Gulf countries including two SAARC states — India and Sri Lanka — and three ASEAN states — Indonesia, Malaysia and Singapore — in an economic bloc built on a unique tripartite structure. A new sub-regional grouping known as BIMSTEC brings together for economic co-operation Bangladesh, India, Myanmar, Sri Lanka and Thailand. Both IOR — ARC and BIMSTEC have SAARC and ASEAN states in associations for economic co-operation. This may be a sign of future developments in SAARC–ASEAN co-operation.[156]

Recently Prime Minister Dr. Manmohan Singh took part in the first meeting of BIMSTEC held in Bangkok, which indicated India's increasing closeness with ASEAN. BIMSTEC has been organised to boost economic and commercial cooperation and development among the countries in and around the Bay of Bengal. These countries are heavily dependent on this sea route for their export and import. Members include Bangladesh, SriLanka, Thailand, India, Bhutan, Nepal, Myanmar, Malaysia and other coastal countries of this area. Thailand played a significant role in its formation. It is constituted with the hope to act as a bridge between the two Asian organisations — ASEAN and SAARC.

In Bangkok, Prime Minister also gave a positive signal towards the free trade agreement with Thailand. Thailand visit is significant in other aspects also. Thailand has been a safe home for terrorists active in the north-eastern area of India as well as for under world people. But after 9/11 and with the development of relations with India Thailand changed its attitude towards India. In a way the role of present PM of Thailand is important. His family is reckoned among the country's top commercial and industrial families. His company has a big business in the field of telecom in India. And therefore he is completely aware of India's economic progress. Thus, it is natural for him to improve relations with India. Consequently, Thailand is no longer an old convenient and secure place for ULFA, Naga terrorist or for people demanding Bodoland. Another issue linked with regional development is the underdeveloped transport facilities in the area. The whole region has backward road and rail links. There have been agreements on various plans in this direction, but all plans are at theoretical level. No solid steps have been taken in the direction of implementation. The member countries of BIMSTEC are connected through sea route, where cheap international transport facility is available. But, in the countries like, Bangladesh, Nepal, Bhutan, Myanmar, due to transport related problems, developmental processes are getting obstructed. Especially in north-eastern areas of India, there is a huge problem of transport and for the proper development of the region a good deal of transport facility is inevitable.[157]

Besides, there is an urgent need of the acknowledgement of

the fact that South Asia is an organic whole and therefore regional cooperation is not a matter of choice but a vital necessity. Such innate reality is very difficult to be denied and very costly to be avoided.

The adoption of a widespread and solid framework of various confidence building measures, and ever-greater emphasis upon the formulation of strategies concerning economic regionalism are the two key-threads, a faster and steadier move towards which could only pave a way in the right direction. Undoubtedly, India has to play a natural leadership role here, in carrying all its South Asian neighbors with it in a cooperative framework. Although, the political complexities in the region do not permit easy solutions, but India's visible investment in good neighborly relations has already set the tone for building an organic South Asia.

Notes

1. Michael Brecher, *Nehru: A Political Biography*, OUP, 1959, p. 576.
2. Democracy completely disappered from this country from 1952 to 1988.
3. Lal Bahadur Shastri had a modest, middle-class background.
4. Laloo Prasad Yadav belongs to the Yadav community, which is considered socially backward.
5. Mayawati belongs to the Schedule Caste, which is socially low caste.
6. At the time of the very inception of Pakistan, leaders like M.A. Jinnah, Liaquat Ali Khan and Abdur Rab Nishtar were very keen that the Princely states of India retain their independent status without acceding to India. They felt that if the larger Indian Princely states retained their separate identity, it would prove the validity of the two-nation theory. However, irony is that the political leaders and people of East Pakistan who were passionate advocates of the two-nation theory were the first to question its validity, throw it aside and create Bangladesh.
7. J.N. Dixit, 'Pak's India Policies', *International Studies*, 32, 3, 1995.
8. To get the details of these planned skullduggeries, (which ultimately proved to be abortive) see Field Marshall Mohammad Ayub Khan: *Friends not Masters: A Political Autobiography*, London: Oxford University Press, 1967. Also see Stanley Wolpert: *Zulfi Bhutto of Pakistan : His Life and Times*, Delhi : Oxford University Press, 1993.

9. J.N. Dixit, 'Pakistan's India Policies', *International Studies*, 32, 3, 1995.
10. K.R. Malkani, 'There is no charity in Politics', *Sunday Times*, 15.06.1997.
11. Siddharth Varadarajan, 'Pakistan's predicament — perplexed by the Gujral Doctrine', *The Times of India*, 27.05.1997.
12. *Sunday Times*, 15.06.1997.
13. Gopal, Nehru-III, Nehru to Kennedy, 8 Deccember, p. 256.
14. S.M. Burke, '*Pakistan's Foreign Policy: An Historical Analysis*', London, 1972, p. 16.
15. Except Junagarh, Jodhpur and Hyderabad, where India used force to set right the anomalies.
16. S. Gupta, *Kashmir: A Study in India-Pakistan Relations*, London 1966.
17. *Ibid*., pp. 143-46.
18. Gowher Rizvi, 'Nehru and the Indo-Pakistan rivalry over Kashmir 1947-64', *Contemporary South Asia*, 4, 1, 1995, p. 20.
19. S.N. Mishra, "India and South Asia," in *India : The Cold War Years*, South Asian Publishers Pvt. Ltd., New Delhi, 1994, p. 72
20. S. Gupta, *Kashmir: A Study in India-Pakistan Relations*, London, 1966, p. 160.
21. Zafrullah's Statement cited in *Ibid*., p. 162.
22. R.J. Moore, *Making the New Commonwealth*, Oxford, 1987, p. 79.
23. S. Gopal, *Jawaharlal Nehru: A Biography*, New Delhi, 1975, p. 29.
24. *Ibid*., p. 27.
25. S.N. Mishra, 'India and South Asia II', in *India : The Cold War Years*', South Asian Publishers Pvt. Ltd., New Delhi, 1994, p. 73.
26. S. Gopal, *Jawaharlal Nehru: A Biography*, New Delhi, 1975, p. 116.
27. Gowher Rizvi, 'Nehru and the Indo-Pakistan rivalry over Kashmir 1947-64', *Contemporary South Asia*, 4, 1, 1995, p. 24.
28. *Ibid*.
29. Including the newly formed Jana Sangh, the Hindu Mahasabha, the RSS and Akali Dal.
30. S. Gopal, *Jawaharlal Nehru : A Biography*, New Delhi, 1975, p. 123.
31. Foreign Relations of the United States 1948, Vol. 5. Part 1, p. 292, cited in *Ibid*., p. 117.
32. Abdullah has raised the issue with the US Ambassador at a meeting in Srinagar in 1949 and again with Sir Owen Dixon, the UN mediator in Kashmir in 1950.

33. Gowher Rizvi, 'Nehru and the Indo-Pak rivalry over Kashmir 1947- 64', *Contemporary South Asia*, 1995, Vol. 4, No. 1, p. 25.
34. S. Gopal, *Jawaharlal Nehru: A Biography*, New Delhi, 1975, p. 125.
35. Nehru's Note on interviews with Dulles, 22 may 1953 in *Ibid.* p. 128.
36. S. Gopal, *Jawaharlal Nehru: A Biography*, New Delhi, 1975, pp. 18-82.
37. Gowher Rizvi, 'Nehru and the Indo-Pak rivalry over Kashmir 1947-64', *Contemporary South Asia*, Vol. 4, No. 1, 1995, p. 27.
38. A. Appadorai and M.S. Rajam, *India's Foreign Policy and Relations*, South Asian, 1985, p. 107.
39. Gowher Rizvi, 'Nehru and the Indo-Pak rivalry over Kashmir 1947-64', *Contemporary South Asia*, Vol. 4, No. 11, 1995, p. 27.
40. Ayub was neither a Punjabi nor a Pushtoon but a Hindko Speaker from Hazara, without any ethnic base in the army.
41. Dean Acheson and John Foster Dulles had made clear that India would have been their preferred ally and had only turned to Pakistan because India remained wedded to its policy of non-alignment.
42. 'Mr. Ayub's motives in seeking military alliance had little to do with the country's defences against India and still less with fighting communism: it was primarily to strengthen the army so that he could wrest political power', Gowher Rizvi: 'Riding the tiger: institutionalizing the military regimes in Pak and Bangladesh', in Christopher Clapham and George Philip (Eds.): *The Political Dilemmas of Military Regimes*, London , 1985, p. 203.
43. Ayub Khan, *Friends Not Masters: A Political Autobiography*, Oxford, 1967.
44. The main lines of communications for the defence of Ladakh went through the Kashmir Valley and any weakening of India's control in that region would seriously jeopardise her defence against future Chinese aggression. Mr. Nehru considered it as 'outrageous and beyond the pale of consideration any proposal to hand over Ladakh, although a deliberate red herring, to Pakistan' — *National Herald*, 16 June 1963, cited in Gopal: Nehru III, p. 260.
45. Gopal, Nehru-III, p. 256.
46. Burke, *Pakistan's Foreign Policy*, p. 283.
47. There can be no doubt that Ayub's high level diplomacy was a factor in the Soviet Union's opting for a pronouncedly even-handed treatment of India and Pakistan in the next three or four years. N.C. Mehrotra (Ed): *Problems of India's Foreign Policy*', Atma Ram & Sons, Delhi, 1984.

48. William J. Barnds, 'India, Pakistan and the Great Powers', pp. 199-200.
49. N.C. Mehrotra (Ed.), *Problems of India's Foreign Policy*, Atma Ram & Sons, Delhi, 1984, p. 90.
50. Arnold Smith , Commonwealth Secretary General , has stated that Lal Bahadur Shastri, during his visit to Canada, told the Canadian Foreign Minister in June 1965 that "he was anxious for a settlement and was prepared to make concessions, but this would be politically impossible for him...unless he came under pressure from the Soviet Union and the United States, as well as Commonwealth Countries." Arnold Smith: *Stiches in Time: The Commonwealth in World Politics*, p. 25.
51. N.C. Mehrotra (Ed.), *Problems of India's Foreign Policy*, Atma Ram & Sons , Delhi, 1984, p. 98.
52. William J. Barnds, *India, Pakistan and Great Powers*, Praeger Publishers, New York, 1972, p. 201.
53. *Ibid.*, p. 203.
54. Ayub derived this conviction, according to Asghar Khan, the former chief of the Pakistan Air Force, from the advice of his Foreign Minster, Bhutto (the First Round, p. 6). Bhutto in turn claimed that his assessment was based on the analysis of Indian psychology and strategy by the Chinese Foreign Minister Chen Yi. (*Ibid.*, p. XVI).
55. *Ibid.*, pp. 74-75.
56. *China, India, Pakistan:Documents*, pp. 428-31.
57. N.C. Mehrotra (Ed.), '*Problems of India's Foreign Policy*', Atma Ram and Sons, Delhi, 1984, p. 108.
58. *Ibid.*, p. 112.
59. *Ibid.*, p. 113.
60. Already been analysed in Chapter 2.
61. N.C. Mehrotra (Ed.), *Problems of India*'s *Foreign Policy*', Atma Ram and Sons, Delhi, 1984, p. 145.
62. In addition, the integration of Sikkim, which was an unfinished task of the national revolution, was accomplished in 1974-75. This was in a way the high watermark of Mrs. Gandhis's pragmatic and vigorous external policy.
63. B.M. Jain, 'Indo-Pak Relations in the Post-Cold War Period', *Indian Journal of Asian Affairs*, Vol. 6, No 1-2, , 1993, p. 105.
64. The group's origins go back to at least 1971, when it came into prominence through the hijacking of an Indian airliner.
65. M.Y. Malik, A.M. Wani, S.A. Hamid and Javed A. Mir.

66. Edward Desmond, 'The insurgency in Kashmir', *Contemporary South Asia*, 4, 1, 1995, p. 6.
67. *Ibid.*
68. *Ibid.*, p. 7.
69. *Ibid.*, p. 8.
70. They are taken in police jeeps-usually with scarves obscuring their faces — and positioned at major road crossings. Every passing bus is stopped and the passengers are forced to dismount and walk in front of the jeep. The 'cat' fingers colleagues he recognises, who are immediately seized and taken in for questioning.
71. Edward Desmond, 'The Insurgency in Kashmir', *Contemporary South Asia*, 4, 1 1995, p. 11.
72. Benazir Bhutto, in an interview with Edward Desmond in late 1990s, claimed that senior army officers asked for her backing in a plan that would give her a place in history as the 'Conqueress of Kashmir.' Mrs. Bhutto, who was under intense US pressure to dissociate Pak from the uprising, claimed that she refused to go along. *Ibid.*, p. 10.
73. Alexander Kalashnikov, the inventor of A.K. Rifles.
74. It is now internationally accepted that the Pak army and the ISI Directorate are providing military training, weapons, military equipment , ammunition and explosives to the militants, besides financial support . The ISI spends approximately Rs. 5 Cr. per month for its proxy war campaign. The Pak Army also actively supports the militants.
75. Seminar, 479, July 1999.
76. *The Times of India*, Mumbai: 'People-to-people Contact will Build Goodwill' (Editorial), November 29, 2004.
77. Excerpts from a seminar held in Beijing on August 27th and 28th, 1996 on the relationship between India and China, in which scholars, academicians, diplomats and researchers from both the countries took part.
78. *India Today*, June 1, 1998.
79. Sahdev Vohra, 'India's Foreign Relations Part-I' in U.I.I. *Journal*, Vol. 126, No. 525, July — September , 1996.
80. J. Dasgupta and J.K. Ray, 'The web of International Relations', *Progressive* 1961, p. 178.
81. S.N. Misra, *India : The Cold War Years*, South Asian Publishers Pvt. Ltd. , New Delhi, 1994, p. 84.
82. *Ibid.*, p. 76.
83. 'India was required to maintain 11 mountain divisions on the border

with China and each mountain division was three times more costly to support than an ordinary infantry division.' Sandy Gordon: 'South Asia after the Cold War', *Asian Survey*, Vol. 35, No. 10, October 1995.

84. B.M. Kaushik and O.N. Mehrotra, 'Pakistan's Nuclear Bombs', New Delhi, 1980, p. 50; This attitude was evident in Ambassador Agha Shahi's speeches during the UN General Assembly session discussion on the NPT and speeches by other Pakistani leaders, like Foreign Minister Arshad Hussain, of that time.
85. Z.A. Bhutto, *Awakening the People — Speeches of Zulfiquar Ali Butto* 1950-69, Pakistan Publications, Rawalpindi, 1970, p. 21
86. Karan R. Sawhny, 'Sino-Pakistani Nuclear alliance — Prospect and Retrospect', *Mainstream*, April 22, 2000 p. 21.
87. *The Pakistan Times*, Rawalpindi, June 8, 1974.
88. A global network of clandestine purchases through dummy companies was organised. This network purchased various components needed for the nuclear military efforts. Abdul Quadeer Khan, is supposed to have master minded this covert operation. *Ibid.*
89. This amendment mandates the termination of assistance to any state that imported uranium enrichment equipment or technology after 1977 and refused to place it under IAEA insection. Pakistan contravened these provisions in 1979, by importing equipment for its secret uranium – enrichment plant at Kahuta.
90. Karan R. Sawhny, 'Sino–Pakistani Nuclear alliance', *Mainstream*, April 22, 2000, p. 22.
91. A 1983 US State Department analysis declared that there was "unambiguous evidence that Pakistanis actively pursuing a nuclear weapons development program." *Ibid.*
92. R.G. Sawhney, 'Zia's Pakistan', New Delhi, 1985, p. 136. The $ 3.2 billion American aid package for this purpose facilitated Pakistani nuclear enterprise. General Zia had the blessings of Ronald Reagon and CIA Director William Casey.
93. Following the death of President Bhutto, Beijing temporarily suspended its nuclear assistance.
94. P.L. Bhola, 'Pakistan's Nuclear Policy', New Delhi, 1993, p. 133.
95. According to Pakistan's former Army chief, General Aslam Beg, the US administration had from 1987 to 1990. facilitated Sino-Pakistani collaboration by continuously issusing misleading certifications to the US Congress about Pakistani nuclear explosive capability, thus , permitting Pakistan to continue to receive economic and military aid.

96. K. Subrahmanyam, 'Sino-Pak nuclear deal: New light on an old Alliance', *The Times of India*, New Delhi, August 30, 1995.
97. Nilofar Suhrawardy, 'The Sino-Pak nuclear Axis', *The Pioneer*, New Delhi , February 12, 1996.
98. Harold Hough, 'Pakistan's Nuclear status — Confusion or strategy?', *Jane's Intelligence Review*, London, Vol. 7, No. 6, June 1995, p. 270.
99. Cameron Binkley, 'Pakistan's Ballistic Missile development — The sword of Islam?' in William C. Potter and Harlan W. Jencks (Ed.) : "The International Missile Bazaar — A New suppliers Network', Boulder, West view Press, 1994, p. 93.
100. Brahma Chellaney, 'Pak Fuel, Chinese Bomb', *The Hindustan Times*, New Delhi, May 1, 1995, p. 12.
101. *Ibid.*
102. 'The Vice-President of China National Nuclear Corporation (CNNC) said that this sale did not violate any domestic or international laws as the magnets sold to Islamabad were not magnetised'. — 'China admits selling ring magnets to Pakistan: Report', *The Times of India*, New Delhi, April 16, 1996.
103. Seema Sirohi, 'China supplying extra heavy water to Pak', *The Telegraph*, Calcutta, September 12, 1997; also 'China to export nuclear power equipment to Pak', *The Hindu*, New Delhi, September 21, 1997.
104. 'China to sell nuke control room to Pak', *The Pioneer*, New Delhi, September 30, 1997.
105. In fact the test firing the Ghauri missile in April 1998 provoked India to conduct nuclear tests at Pokharan in May 1998.
106. Matin Zuberi, "Pokharan II and Chagai", *World Focus*, June-July 1998, p. 13.
107. *Ibid.*
108. *Ibid.*
109. Mr. Samar Mubarak Mand of PEAC who led the team for the tests claimed that all six tests were conducted by scientists belonging to his organistion and Kahuta 'had nothing to do with it.' Dr. A.Q. Khan, however, asserted that since only Kahuta provided enriched uranium, "without Kahuta nothing can be done."
110. Amit Baruah, 'Pakistan also detonates five nuclear devices,' *The Hindu*, New Delhi, May 29, 1998, p. 1.
111. *World Focus*, April, 2000.
112. R.R. Subramanian, 'A Minimum and Credible Deterrence for India', *World Focus*, April, 2000.

113. *Ibid.*
114. C.V. Ranganathan, 'India-China Relations — Retrospect and Prospects', in "Indian Foreign Policy-Agenda For the 21st Century", Konark Publishers, 1998.
115. Raghu Dayal, 'Speeding Dragon-Chinese Railways leaves Indian Counterpart behind', *The Times of India*, Mumbai, December17, 2004).
116. Excerpts of the interview of Wang Jinzhen, Assistant chairman of the China Council for Promotion of International Trade (CCPIT), who visited India as a part of 100-member Chinese business delegation, *The Times of India*, Mumbai, August 7, 2004.
117. For details see Sujata Bose and Ayesha Jalal, *Modern South Asia–History, Culture and Political Economy*, Oxford University Press, Delhi, 1998.
118. Although, a large number of developing countries tried to emulate the European endeavour, but with little success.
119. Sumitra Chishti, 'Regionalism, Multilateralism, and the Developing Countries since the End of the Cold War,' *International Studies*, Vol. 32, No. 4, 1995.
120. The same period witnessed a tremendous growth of Trans-national Companies, which are considered the main agents of regional grouping.
121. Norman D. Palmer, *New Regionalism in Asia and the Pacific*, Lexington Books, 1991.
122. Paul Krugman, "Regionalism *Vs* Mutilaterism", Washington, DC: Mimeographed, 1992.
123. Sumitra Chishti, 'Regionalism, Multilaterism and the Developing Countries since the End of the Cold War,' *International Studies*, Vol. 32, No. 4, 1995.
124. Varun Sahni, 'India as a Global Power', in *Indian Foreign Policy*, Vol. 1, FSI, New Delhi, 1997.
125. Nancy Jetley, 'SAARC: Looking Ahead,' in *Indian Foreign Policy*, Vol. 2, FSI, New Delhi, 1998.
126. See K.K. Bhargava, *et. al*, *South Asia-Towards Dynamism and Cooperation*, Popular Prakashan, Bombay, 1994.)
127. Shelton U. Kodikara (ed), *External Compulsions of South Asian Politics*, Sage Publications, New Delhi, 1993.
128. See Navika Kumar, "WTO made easy, Cancun Edition", *The Sunday Express*, September 7, 2003.
129. The 'World Economic Situation and Prospects 2004' report says both India and China grew at a rate of more than twice the world

average last year and continued strong growth in these "low income" countries will benefit the world economy as a whole, reduce global poverty and serve as an incentive for other developing nations.

130. Excerpts from the interview of Joseph Stiglitz, "IMF variant of market economy is a mythical version, that is why it has failed", *The Indian Express*, Pune, Jauary 15, 2004.

131. *Ibid.*

132. As India grows more powerful in the coming decades, the insecurity of its neighbours is bound to increase. However, each of the countries in South Asia, is an independent, Sovereign political entity, Nothing will alter that fact today and it is indeed far from Indian policy.

133. Maj. Gen. Dipankar Banerjee, 'The End of the Cold War', in *Indian Foreign Policy* , Vol. 1, FSI, 1997, p. 98.

134. Nancy Jetley, 'SAARC: Looking Ahead', in Indian Foreign Policy, Vol. 2, FSI, 1998.

135. *Ibid.*

136. An enclave of West Bengal in Bangladesh called Tin Bigha was given to Bangladesh in the interest of goodwill.

137. V.R. Panchamukhi, etal.: 'Indo – Sri Lanka Economic Co-operation: An operational programme', New Delhi, Interest Publications, 1993.

138. P. Sahadevan, 'India and Sri Lanka', in Indian Foreign Policy, Vol. 2, 1998.

139. It was considered to be a tangible success for Indian diplomacy , a formal recognition of India's high prestige in the region and the establishment of a regional approach to the solution of regional problems.

140. Verinder Grovers (Ed.), 'Introduction to India's Foreign Policy and International relations', Deep & Deep Publications, New Delhi, 1992.

141. P. Sahadevan, 'India and Sri-Lanka', in *Indian Foreign Policy*, Vol. 2. 1998 (for India, the IPKF operation turned out to be a thankless job).

142. From a military angle, the Island did not hold any staregic value for India at the time when Mrs. Indira Gandhi entered into an agreement with Sri Lanka to recognise its sovereignty over a tiny barren Island in the Palk Straits in 1974. But, today, its importance has increased considerably in view of the expanding maritime activities of the people of the coastal Ramnad and the steady rise in the commercial value of marine products, especially prawns. It was unfortunate that the Indian leadership looked at the Kachchtivu dispute entirely in a territotrial context and ignored the future commercial importance of the Palk Bay region. As such, it did not forsee the problems which Indian fisherman are facing today. This was probably one of the very

few instances of India surrendering a small portion of its territory over which it enjoyed a rightful claim of ownership. *Ibid.*

143. Such claims were laid by Mao accusing the British that they had taken over these territories from China and such territories will be liberated. A theory of Tibet being China's palm and other Himalayan Kingdoms being its five fingers was advanced. Selected works of Mao-Tse-Tung as cited in Leo E. Rose, *Nepal: Strategy for Survival*, University of California Press, Berkeley. 1971.
144. Some 6,000 rivers and streams of Nepal carry a total potential of generating 83,000 MW of hydro-power, of which an estimated 40,000 MW can be harnessed, economically and without much difficulty.
145. *Water Nepal* Vol. 4, No. 1, September 1994, see contributions of U.K. Verma and Rajendra D. Joshi.
146. S.D. Muni, 'India and Nepal', *Indian Foreign Policy*, Vol. 2, 1998.
147. For further details see Justus Richter and Christian Wagner, Regional Security, Ethnicity and Governance, New Delhi, 1998, p. 8. Also see K.S. Sidhu, "Srilanka as a factor in South Asian Security", Indian Journal of Strategic Studies, Vol. XXIV, Allahabad, 2003.
148. See Swarna Rajgopalan, *State and Nation in South Asia*, Lyne Riener Publishers, London, 2001. Also see S.L. Sharma, T.K. Oommen (eds), *Nation and National Identity in South Asia*, Orient Longma, India 2000.
149. Manik De Silva, "Ethnicity and Conflict in South Asia", *International Studies*, 38, 1, New Delhi 2001.
150. Partha S. Ghosh, **Regional Security and Cross-***Border Population Movements in South Asia.*
151. Ashley Tellis, *Stability in South Asia*, Santa Monica, 1997, p. 11.
152. See Burton Stein and Sanjay Subrahmanyam (ed.), *Institutions and Economic Challenges in South Asia*, Oxford University Press, Delhi, 1996.
153. For details see, J.N. Dixit, "Future of Security in South Asia", *South Asian Survey*, Vol. 8, January-June, 2001, New Delhi.
154. *The Times of India*, Mumbai, July 24, 2004.
155. It is of great importance to India's national security. India consistently advocates the idea of turning the Indian Ocean into a Zone of peace with emphasis on the reduction of all foreign military presence in the region and the creation of conditions that would enable India to control developments in the Zone.
156. Lakshman Kadirgamar, 'S.A. Co-operation in the Twenty–First Century', *South Asian Survey*, Vol. 5, No. 1, 1998.
157. *Sahara Samay*, Lucknow, November 6, 2004.

5

External Forces and India

The disintegration of the Soviet Union drastically changed the power configuration in the world, but immeasurably added to the complexities of the international situation. Thus the world faces a new situation and so did India. Many of the old hypotheses had become victims of the march of history. The economic struggle had become far more crucial than before, with palpable consequences for foreign policy. United States with its overwhelming power became the chief architect of all the major decisions in the post Cold War era. US, to establish its supremacy in the world has played the dangerous game of wars. Gulf War1 and Gulf War 2 were imposed upon the innocent people of the West Asia. Terrorism became the widespread phenomenon across the globe. Even the US could not escape from the clutches of terrorism. Worldwide expansion of technology and possession of nuclear weapons by many countries made easy accessibility of lethal weapons in the hands of terrorists. Globalisation made national boundaries irrelevant. Flow of capital did not see any barrier. Besides, the rich countries tried to marginalise the poor through the institutions of WTO, IMF and World Bank. In the era of democratic and representative institutions, there is UNO, which is pursuing the principle of hegemonism and inequality. Rich countries dominate this world body. Interdependence, competition and technology are today's ideologies. In this atmosphere, countries have to formulate their foreign policy. For India, this task is even more challenging for the obvious reasons inherent in its history, polity and economic potential, which place it among the leading nations of the world.

THE UNITED STATES AND MULTI-PLAYER WORLD

From the ashes of the old world order did not rise any clearly discernible contours of a new world order. In fact world power is more diffused now than in the past. But, one thing is very much clear and that is the pre-eminent role of the United States for many years in the future. Following is the reality of the current world order:

(a) USA is a single surviving super power, its political influence, military strength and continuing economic importance is matchless.

(b) A relative decline of the economic clout of United States and emergence of many players at world stage: Japan,[1] China, EU, and ASEAN, INDIA.

(c) USA's current pre-eminence in the world and its continuance in the near future.

Russia's current heavily dependent economic status has reduced its political position and has denied it a leading role at least for now.[2] This would leave the USA, the EU and China as the three leading political powers of today. To retain and enhance its position China would need to maintain a tension free environment around its periphery. In all likelihood USA's role will continue to be pre-eminent for some years yet.[3] However, in today's world economic and technological capabilities go together and count as one major element of power. In fact, the economic struggle has come to occupy centre-stage. Even the political struggles in the international community are revolving around the economic struggle, which simply means that the economic struggle had taken primacy over the political struggle.[4] The clear economic leaders are USA, the EU, Japan and China. On the other hand there are clear signs of the USA's relative economic decline even though its influence will continue to be substantial for several decades more. The technological component of power will, however, strongly favour USA and Japan for several decades more. While pure military capability will be of diminishing importance in global affairs in the coming era. Here again it is the USA that alone will possess the capability to project power around the globe. This is unlikely to change for many years. The only element of power that Russia currently enjoys its strategic nuclear arsenal. The other power in this category is clearly China. Its large military is modernizing though slowly. It has the third significant nuclear weapons force, which too is seeing a steady upgradation in capability.[5]

United States power posture enhanced in the post-Cold War period. But, how? United States doesn't bother about it. Nevertheless, its prestige declined considerably with the Gulf war 2. US pursued a double standard policy in the case of Iraq. It has links with the un-democratic/authoritarian regimes of Middle East, it has favored Musharraf's regime in Pakistan but at the same time, it went on to wage war against Iraq to uproot Saddam's dictatorship and to establish democracy there. The logic is not easy to digest. The 9/11 commission report said that both Clinton and Bush governments did little to stop Pakistan, even though there were belief in the State Department and the NSC that Islamabad was behaving like a rogue state in two areas, backing Taliban/Bin Laden terror and provoking war with India.[6] Instead, USA concluded an agreement with Musharraf for using Pakistan's territory to launch operation against Iran. Earlier it did the same for launching operation against Afghanistan. No nation could dare to stop America, not even the United Nations. $40m were spent in Gulf war1, in which $10m was shared by US. While the total cost of Gulf War 2 was estimated to be $80m, which was afforded by United States. Besides, till date America has spent $200 b in Iraq. No country can afford such huge money to be spent in a futile and mass destructive activity like war. But, the economic interests of America took it to Iraq and compelled it to play a dangerous game of firing and killing. Still America is spending around $4 billion per month in Iraq. In fact it has used marketing techniques to alter Muslims in Middle East.[7]

Nevertheless, US can foster a decent government in Iraq if every day it turns a little more power over to Iraqis and creates the economic conditions where Iraqis can be successful. The more US empowers Iraqis, the less humiliated they will feel, the more time US will have to help them and the less they will need its help. What the US needs most in Iraq is a strategy of "dehumiliation and re-dignification".[8]

The post-Cold War multi-player world marks China in the rank of the world's leading nations. Other player such as, Japan has become too powerful economically to be sidelined, or allow it to be sidelined, (politically) for very long. It has the second largest Gross National Product (GNP) in the world. It is the largest creditor nation in the world as well as the largest donor nation. A unique position of Europe and its steady and time bound process of integration increasingly make it one single entity rather than three or more major countries. Separately they do not feature among the top few nations. Also together they are not quite the sum of their combined potential. With steady European unification Germany has emerged as the leading member of the community.

In the year 2003, India's economy was the fastest growing in the world, at 7.4 per cent and the 'world economic situation and prospects 2004' report says both India and China grew at a rate of more than twice the world average last year and continued strong growth in these 'low income' countries will benefit the world economy as a whole, reduce global poverty and serve as an incentive for other developing nations.

One long-term possibility is the resurgence of Russia. Again and again in history Russia has risen and fallen and risen again. With its resources, its scientific pool and its educated population, Russia will not remain down and out for too long. It is one country with whom India has no basic conflict of national interests, nor any major divergence of perceptions. India has not only to keep this perspective open but also be helpful whenever possible.[9]

Beside, there are other significant players. Argentina, Brazil, South Africa, Nigeria, Egypt, and Indonesia are potential players that have capabilities to affect developments in their vicinity.

Further, an important development is the formation of number of regional groupings or organisations, most of which aim at promoting economic co-operation. The rapid rise of East Asia, ASEAN and Asia-Pacific region proved great economic potential.

Moreover, an annual growth rate in GDP of less than 7 per cent cannot hold the nation together any more. Actually, the national growth rate of near 10 per cent may be the minimum that is needed to ensure social stability.[10] The foreign policy should be aimed to achieve this objective. It will then need to encompass a whole range of new activities including ensuring access to natural resources at affordable prices, keeping sea lanes of communication open, developing relations with prosperous regional organisations and ensuring flow of foreign investment in the country.[11] To ensure continued economic prosperity India will need to globalise speedily, with special emphasis on regions like ASEAN, East Asia and the larger Asia-Pacific that offers maximum scope.

Since USA remains the pre-eminent player in the world, good relations with it will be important to India for many years to come. Actually there are numerous areas where there is already a high degree of co-operation. Most of these are in vital economic and investment sectors.

President Clinton during his visit to India demonstrated in his pronouncements that the US has now carried out a reassessment and has arrived at the conclusion that India is an independent factor to be reckoned with in international politics. Thus, it did not take long for the US administration to accept the inevitability of a nuclear India. The Jaswant-Talbott talks helped to evolve over a period of time the US acceptance of the Indian nuclear arsenal. The Indian leadership came out with its doctrine of no first use and credible minimum deterrent. Two years after the Shakti tests India and the US were able to sign a vision statement during the visit of President Clinton in March 2000.[12] Therefore, the Indian nuclear arsenal and the Indian nuclear doctrine are not today very serious irritants in the Indo-US relations. There are other related issues, such as the Comprehensive Test Ban Treaty and fissile materials production cut off. On the CTBT the Indian government has declared a unilateral moratorium on the tests and the Prime Minister made it clear that India would sign and ratify the CTBT only if the nuclear weapon powers ratified the treaty without any caveats. The US Senate has rejected the treaty and the question of the CTBT coming into force does not arise at present. There is no precedent of the US Senate adopting and ratifying a treaty, which it has once rejected. In the case of chemical weapons convention the US senate ratified it with a number of caveats.

USA did not allow economic relations with India to grow beyond a certain limit. It has lifted sanction, which it imposed in 1998 after Pokharan II, but the sanctions imposed in 1970s, still continue. In this atmosphere, there is only limited scope for economic relations to grow. Beside, the major irritants between the two democracies are Pakistan, nuclear non-proliferation and outsourcing issues. Politicians were playing up the issue of jobs being outsourced to other countries. The US Ambassador to India David Mulford said at a FICCI meeting, "US has about $57 billion in its services account which means that the country was still an e porter of services to the rest of the world and the number of jobs being outsourced is very small in the economy which creates and destroys millions of jobs every year. Describing outsourcing as a hard political issue, he said it was not a problem between India and US but a global phenomenon tied with globalisation.[1] very year thousands of young Indians go abroad, especially USA for education and jobs. In US universities, majority of students are foreigner. But, with the outsourcing issue coming into force the number of foreign students in American universities is declining. As a result many universities are running in loss.

Besides, bilateral relations with other nations around the globe need to be given a further boost. reater integration into the dialogue process in ast Asia should lead to an improvement in relations with China. An approach of constructive engagement is the most appropriate posture. Moreover, to deal with this leading global player India should continue and strengthen relations with countries on China s borders. ussia s importance to Indian policy would continue to remain valid in this conte t.

GLOBALISATION/GEO-ECONOMICS

The gap between the legacy of Bretton Woods and the economic and political demands of the modern world is growing. Much of this change is driven by rapid advances in and thus lower costs of, communications, information flows and travels. Official policy, much of it American, has played its part by reducing barriers to the movement of goods and capital across national boundaries. The result has been more intrusive and intense economic interaction — including the explosive growth of world capital markets, which led to the demise of fixed exchange rates — between a large and growing number of entities outside government control, a phenomenon that has come to be called "globalisation".[14]

It is being claimed, "the present surge of globalisation is in a way a resumption of the previous trend". The process of globalisation accelerated from the mid-19th century to the outbreak of the First World War and the cross-border flows of goods, capital and people proceeded on larger and larger scale. The factors behind them were crumbling trade-barriers as the doctrine of free trade gained ascendancy and sharp fall in transportation costs because of the development of railways and steamships. However, between 1914 and 1991, the process of globalisation slowed down. Two world wars, the Bolshevik Revolution, the emergence of the Soviet Bloc, the end of colonialism and a number of former colonies like India trying to reserve their markets and resources for their indigenous industries and the cold war hampering globalisation. During this period trade barriers and restrictions on capital flow became the order of the day. During the 1930s the US imposed high tariffs and, in retaliation, other countries too did the same thing. This aggravated the Great Depression and the volume of world output and that of trade fell. International capital flows more or less dried up as countries after countries clamped restrictions. These restrictions were continued even after the Second World War as the allied powers wanted to maintain fixed exchange rates. The Bretton Woods agreement also aimed at this. They, however, agreed to reduce trade barriers for their own economic recovery and to this end they brought in the GATT. During the early years of the 1970s the Bretton Woods system collapsed as the US failed to maintain the value of dollar, at which it was fixed when the system was born. Not only the dollar but other currencies too were allowed to float freely against one another at the rates determined by market. This heralded the rebirth of the global capital market. The revolution in the field of information technology, economic liberalisation and the formation of WTO has contributed a lot towards accelerating globalisation.[15]

Today in the world system, in the name of globalisation volatile and uncontrollable global financial market conditionalities imposed by multinational corporations are challenging the exclusive authority of the state. Thus the state sovereignty is under siege. The basic rules, monitoring systems and punitive mechanisms of this international economic regime are being set by the advanced Western states and by transnational corporate actors and institutions whose interests though not congruent with these states are largely convergent with them. Further the rise and growing strength of these transnational economic agents, mechanisms and institutions *e.g.*, TNCs, GATT/WTO, IMF/WB, international money markets with their astronomical levels of financial capital flows, is central to the consolidation of a global neo-liberal economic system.[16]

The period following the Second World War saw the birth of comparably successful economic institutions — such as the International Monetary Fund, the World Bank, the General Agreement on Tariffs and Trade — designed to promote long-term prosperity through stable exchange rates, worldwide development and open trade. Today these institutions[17] are increasingly subject to criticism. The World Trade Organisation was formed in 1995 as the result of American calls for a body to resolve market-access disputes.[18] In fact, the basic model for globalisation is flawed. Its principal function is the upward mobility of wealth from the poor to the rich within a country and from the poor to the rich countries. Further, globalisation in its present form is working at the cost of the people for the benefit of the national and international elites.[19]

The world's financial systems have been converted into one

big casino. Hot money moves freely from country to country on the international computer networks manipulating the stock exchanges, currency markets and bringing to a grinding halt, the economies of unpliable nations. The resulting surpluses are transferred to the controlling centres. This trillion dollar-a-day game is becoming a bane of the countries, which have fallen into this trap. Those who have escaped are now the target of opening up their systems to fall in line.[20] Globalisation also involves control of international institutions of money and finance. And overnight these can bring about economic changes and make the difference between bread and starvation. These casino-style operations, moving trillions of dollars, are a hit, kill and run operation and have undermined the economies of many countries and threaten many more.[21]

Furthermore, there is a deliberate orchestration of pressure on developing countries including India from rich countries as well as the multilateral institutions like IMF and the World Bank, which they control. In this regard following aspects can not be ignored:[22]

(a) The United States threatens to use Super 301 and Special 301 to force developing countries to reduce their tariff rates and levels of protection given to domestic economies, while the US decides to pursue restrictive policies on imports from developing countries.

(b) The US has succeeded in forcing India to sign the Multilateral Investment Guarantee Agency (MIGA) Convention. Under this foreign investors must secure a guarantee from the MIGA against political risks in investing in India. A guarantee from the sovereign government of India is not enough.

(c) The establishment of the WTO, it is feared, will function as a potential centre for destroying the basic domestic interests of developing countries particularly when it is going to collaborate with the IMF-World Bank twins. These three institutions are now devising powerful instruments of cross conditionalities and cross retaliations to subjugate the weak and poor in the comity of nations and protect the interests of the rich and the MNCs.

(d) The present world economic order is iniquitous as it assumes the existence of a level playing field and equal partners. It applies the same set of rules on the international exchange of commodities, services, capital, technology and manpower to all countries whether they are rich or poor, strong or weak, developed or under-developed, industrialised or non-industrialised. In such a world order the game of unequals will be heavily loaded against the basic interests of the poor and the weak.

(e) A major difficulty that India is likely to face is the problem of market access. This is particularly true in the case of India's export of textiles and leather, two commodities that have shown a strong export growth. The principle of open international trade must apply to all countries who subscribe to WTO.

(f) Another significant are in which India has a strategic and economic interest is oil and new and renewable energy sources. The fact that the bulk of the energy demand and consumption is from the developed countries who also and appear to 'influence' the behaviour of oil prices and supplies, is inevitably going to affect the interests of the developing countries.

(g) Other serious impediments to India's growing competitiveness and market share in some sectors could be in the form of the so-called 'social clause' (core labour standards and child labour) and concern for 'environmental degradation'.

(h) Developing countries will continue to face major hurdles and inequalities even in the simple matter of seeking a fair representation in international decision-making bodies.

India will have to take the lead to give greater economic content to flora like NAM, G-77, G-15, UNCTAD, WTO etc. so that their role in catalyzing and co-ordinating common positions of developing countries is made effective. India will have to ensure, that developing countries are able to resist pressures where their vital economic interests are involved.

The Fifth WTO Ministerial Conference was held in Cancun, Mexico from 10 to 14 September 2003. The main task was to take stock of progress in negotiations and other work under the Doha Development Agenda. The Ministerial Conference is the organisation's highest-level decision-making body. It meets "at least once every two years", as required by the Marrakech Agreement Establishing the World Trade Organisation — the WTO's founding charter. Other WTO Ministerials include Doha 9-14 Nov. 2001, Seattle 30 Nov. 3, Dec. 1999, Geneva 18 & 20 May 1998 and Singapore 9-13 Dec. 1996. The Cancun Ministerial Conference ended on 14 September without consensus after Chairperson Luis Ernesto Derbez concluded that despite considerable movement in consultations, members remained entrenched, particularly on the "Singapore" issues. (<http://www.documents.wto/min/03.org>)

Recently the Geneva trade talks in July 2004 were not conclusive, but they have achieved two things. One, they have kept the door open for further negotiations, scheduled for 2005. Two, they have forced rich nations — the US and EU — to concede to important demands of poorer countries like India. The main sticking point in most trade negotiations among the World Trade Organisation's member nations is farm trade: the rich West subsidises farmers, as do most poorer nations. However, rich countries insist that developing ones open up markets and drop sops faster than they do. During the marathon, 10-year long Uruguay Round trade negotiations, rich nations made certain commitments to phase out subsidies and opening up markets. Instead of keeping their commitments, they keep coming back to negotiate, offering to do what they were supposed to do years ago in return for more concessions from developing nations. That's can't work. Broadly, history shows that freer trade and investment flows lead to greater competitiveness, faster growth and higher incomes for each economy. But freer trade has costs in the short run: protected crops become unprofitable, people get laid off in sectors opened up to low-cost competitors, unions take to the warpath.

What India and other developing nations have succeeded in doing now is commendable: instead of digging in stubbornly and refusing to open up, they have forced the US and EU to agree that dismantling their domestic sops is necessary to keep talking. That is not as insignificant as it sounds.

This is election year in America, spooked by Iraq, terrorism- and the specter of jobs disappearing to Bangalore. There is no doubt that the US is in no position to talk serious trade reform till November, when elections are over. So the Geneva talks couldn't have achieved more than what they have: to keep talking without burying issues vital to poor nations. Nothing has been set. And it is one we can live with.

Even as the mantra of the day is 'globalisation' and 'integration', the major economic powers appear to be rapidly consolidating themselves into regional groupings (geo-economic) and arrangements, which may appear to contradict their commitment to meaningful 'multilateralism' and free trade. There is NAFTA in North America. The European Union, at present a grouping of 15 countries of Western Europe, is expanding eastwards towards Central and Eastern Europe. The Asia-Pacific Economic Community (APEC), though not an entity in the sense of EU, is also gradually defining an area for itself. ASEAN, looking ahead, is not averse to integrating itself with APEC and to working out arrangements with other groupings. The nascent Indian Ocean Rim Initiative, likewise, is an effort to carve out a geo-economic space for purposes of exploring and optimizing supra-regional co-operation among littoral and hinterland states of the Indian Ocean. Moreover, SAARC seeks to promote sub-regional economic and trade co-operation mainly through the SAPTA and the SAFTA. Even as India build and strengthen SAARC, it will continue to need to consolidate and evolve a special relationship with ASEAN and seek an entry into APEC on the eastern side. The Indian Ocean Rim Initiative would need to be fully explored and operationalised along with sub-regional co-operation agreements like BIMSTC (involving Bangladesh, India, Myanmar, Sri

Lanka and Thailand) and BBNI (involving Bangladesh, Bhutan, Nepal and India). At the same time India cannot overlook the fact that nearly a third of its trade at present is with the European Union and a fifth of its trade is with the US. Both the US and the EU, are also a major source of investment and technology for India. This is true also of Japan and perhaps Russia.[23]

The challenge for Indian diplomacy will be to reconcile both the trends towards inevitable long term globalisation and the consolidation of regionalism and sub-regional co-operation in such a manner that India is able to take advantage of both at the same time even as it strengthen SAARC and its ongoing and expanding links with South East Asia, the Pacific Rim and the Indian Ocean.

THE NUCLEAR FACTOR AND DISARMAMENT

"Today a nuclear weapon is not a weapon you can use, but it is a weapon you can threaten to use, to coerce a country to change its foreign policy. We don't think that the US or China is going to drop a bomb on us, what Pakistan does is another issue, but I can cite at least 37 occasions where the nuclear weapons have been used to coerce a country to change its foreign policy. Way back in 1971 they were used against India. The US aircraft carrier Enterprise with nuclear weapons aboard, entered the Bay of Bengal through the Malacca Strait, not for fishing, but came to coerce us."[24] The International Court of Justice, in its landmark judgment, ruled that it is not possession or proliferation of nuclear weapons that violates international law, but their use in situations other than the survival of a country is in threat. In other words, the military doctrines of at least four of the nuclear-five are illegal as they envisage first use. The Court also ordered the nuclear states to disarm as per the requirements of Article VI of the NPT. That the ICJ is powerless to implement its decisions is another matter altogether.[25]

As early as in the 1950s Jawaharlal Nehru wrote several letters to the American and Soviet leaders, urging them to accept the goal of nuclear disarmament. As an initial step, he proposed a 'standstill agreement' in 1954 to ban nuclear testing, which is also referred to as Nehru's proposal for CTBT.[26] Later in 1963[27], when the US and Soviet Union signed the Partial Test Ban Treaty (PTBT), India became signatory to it. However, India refused to sign the NPT, which became operational in 1970, on the grounds of it being unequal and discriminatory and also on security grounds. The NPT was extended indefinitely in 1995 amidst Indian opposition. Continued practice of nuclear apartheid by the nuclear weapon states as one of the reasons for India's nuclear tests (Pokhran-II).[28]

Further, Arundhati Ghosh says, "I don't believe that weapons, nuclear, or otherwise, are for prestige. Weapons give us security and our nuclear weapons will give us security in a world where nuclear weapons exist and as long as the five nuclear weapons states retain them as a currency of power to coerce any country. What else do you think gives these five countries the power to sit in Geneva and tell us how we should run our foreign policy, how we should look after our security interests."[29]

The significance of CTBT[30] lies not so much in the area of nuclear weapon development, which is going to continue, as in the meek surrender by 153 non-nuclear weapon nations of their sovereignty. While the international law says a sovereign state cannot be compelled to sign treaties against its will.[31] The fear of coercion stems from Art.14 (of CTBT) which makes the treaty's entry-into-force conditional on India's ratification. By voting for the infamous Art.14 of the CTBT in contravention of the Vienna Convention, these nations have accepted that nuclear hegemons are entitled to impose their will on the rest of the world.[32]

However, there is a change, after Pokhran-II that the US desires to engage India constructively on important issues about which there are differences of opinion between the two countries. The frequency and number of high-level discussions between India and the US indicate a mutual desire to transcend differences of opinion on some basic issues and to establish a practical and working relationship. Although it is clear that the US is now on a weaker wicket to pressurise India on signing the CTBT, the US Senate having shelved the treaty by non-ratification.[33]

Further, pressure is pressure only if you feel it. India has agreed to join the negotiations in the Conference on Disarmament (CD) in Geneva, as India has always been committed to a nuclear weapon free world, which the five nuclear weapons states never accepted. "Countries always found our stand on disarmament very irritating when we had nothing to disarm. Today when we say we have weapons, we are going to be heard more carefully."[34]

Furthermore, NAM countries have been with India all through, but they are weak countries. They were compelled to become party to the NPT indefinitely. They feel trapped and look towards India to keep up the fight for disarmament. And having been one of them and believing in them, India's signing the CTBT will be a betrayal of their trust.[35] However, India has remained committed to non-discriminatory and comprehensive test ban arrangements. If Indian scientists and strategic experts remain convinced, that giving a general endorsement to the CTBT will not harm India's security interests, India must consider signing the CTBT, but not ratify it till all the other nuclear weapons powers do so.[36] May be, India, as a signatory to the CTBT would be in a position to bring round the nuclear weapon states to a time-bound programme of nuclear disarmament.[37]

UN SECURITY COUNCIL

It is a fact that the agenda for the UNO is set by the USA and not by it's 191 members. Washington acts as a supremo of all that the UNO stands for. Nothing happens against its wishes. So powerful is the hold of the Americans on the World body. The USA acts as a global policeman and uses the UNO to impose its will on the rest of the world.[38] The occurrence of two wars in the Gulf region is the latest testimony to this fact.

After the end of the Cold War, there was widespread talk of the need for restructuring the world organisation on a more rational, realistic and equitable basis. So that the developing countries could also get their representation in the world body and could make it more just, truly representative and democratic. A large majority of member states already support the expansion of the permanent and non-permanent membership of the UN's Security Council, as well as the inclusion of both developing and developed countries in the expanded permanent membership. It is clear that the Security Council of today does not fully reflect the realities of the international community as it has entered the 21st century.[39] In order to enhance the legitimacy of the UNO, it is urgently necessary to reform the Security Council.[40]

Here, India's claims could find avenues for fulfilment. India has a long-term interest in a permanent seat consistent with its importance as an active and functional member of the UNO. Following is the objective criteria, which testify to its eligibility for permanent membership of the Security Council.[41]

- India's commitment to the UNO charter and its ideals,
- India's size and population,
- India's emergence as a regional power in its own right,
- India's contribution to all major UN peacekeeping operations,
- India's advocacy of dialogue and discussion as a means of settling conflicts,
- India's sacrifices in the cause of the success of the peacekeeping missions, reflected in the death of a large number of Indian soldiers,
- India's good and honorable record as a regular and non-defaulting payer of its dues to the UN funds,
- India is a world's largest democracy with a track record, which can be the envy of any civilised nation,
- As a leader of the non-aligned world, it has played a critical role in establishing peace and all round human growth and development,
- Today, India has acquired special importance in the market-driven global politics. India has a market comprising a billion people, with the second biggest

middle class in the world. All these make positive signal for India,

- India's nuclear power status is a reality,
- India served the UN as a non-permanent member of Security Council not less than six times, a distinction no country of the world possesses.

Besides, a large number of countries, back Indian claim for UN Security Council seat including — Britain, France, Russia, Czech Republic, Vietnam etc. The American attitude has also changed considerably. Many countries support permanent Council membership for Japan and Germany, the second and third highest contributors to the UNO respectively. But Italy has organised medium-size nations to oppose this move, which would leave Rome as the only large European nation without a permanent seat.[42]

New Delhi should not be apologetic about the country's legitimate claim. In today's global setting, India is a power to reckon with. It cannot be equated with Pakistan. If anything, India has to be seen vis-à-vis China. If China can be a permanent member of the Security Council, there is no reason why India should be denied the position it deserves.

After all, no one realises better than India that a new world order is in the making and if countries like India which have a global vision and global perspective, which believe that world peace and harmony are vital for the enrichment of the human mind and human progress, which are committed to doing good to others while doing good to themselves, do not support and preserve the United Nations, the world will become rudderless and lose direction. It may be a trite statement, but in reality the world is at the crossroads and humanity's needs and wants are so many and the resources are so few and scattered and unevenly distributed that if there was no world organisation to mobilise human energy and endeavor into constructive channels it would become necessary to invent such a body.[43]

UNO-Threats, Challenges and Change

In his address to the General Assembly in September 2003, United Nations Secretary-General Kofi Annan warned Member

States that the United Nations had reached a fork in the road. It could rise to the challenge of meeting new threats or it could risk erosion in the face of mounting discord between States and unilateral action by them. He created the High-level Panel on Threats, Challenges and Change to generate new ideas about the kinds of policies and institutions required for the UN to be effective in the 21st century.

In its report, the High-level Panel sets out a bold, new vision of collective security for the 21st century. Now world is full of new and evolving threats, threats that could not have been anticipated when the UN was founded in 1945 — threats like nuclear terrorism, and State collapse from the witch's brew of poverty, disease and civil war. In today's world, a threat to one is a threat to all. Globalisation means that a major terrorist attack anywhere in the industrial world would have devastating consequences for the well-being of millions in the developing world. Anyone of 700 million international airline passengers every year can be an unwitting carrier of a deadly infectious disease. And the erosion of State capacity anywhere in the world weakens the protection of every State against transnational threats such as terrorism and organised crime. Every State requires international cooperation to make it secure.

There are six clusters of threats with which the world must be concerned now and in the decades ahead: (1) war between States; (2) violence within States, including civil wars, large-scale human rights abuses and genocide; (3) poverty, infectious disease and environmental degradation; (4) nuclear, radiological, chemical and biological weapons; (5) terrorism; and (6) transnational organised crime. The good news is that the United Nations and its collective security institutions have shown that they can work. The World Health Organisation helped to stop the spread of SARS before it killed tens of thousands, perhaps more.

But these accomplishments can be reversed. There is a real danger that they will be, unless nations act soon to strengthen the United Nations, so that in future it responds effectively to the full range of threats that confront them.

Policies for Prevention

Meeting the challenge of today's threats means getting serious about prevention; the consequences of allowing latent threats to become manifest, or of allowing existing threats to spread, are simply too severe. Development has to be the first line of defence for a collective security system that takes prevention seriously. Combating poverty will not only save millions of lives but also strengthen States' capacity to combat terrorism, organised crime and proliferation. Development makes everyone more secure.

There is an agreed international framework for how to achieve these goals, set out in the Millennium Declaration and the Monterrey Consensus, but implementation lags. Biological security must be at the forefront of prevention. International response to HIV/AIDS was shockingly late and shamefully ill-resourced. It is urgent that we halt and roll back this pandemic. But we will have to do more. Global public health system has deteriorated and is ill-equipped to protect people against existing and emerging deadly infectious diseases. The report recommends a major initiative to build public health capacity throughout the developing world, at both local and national levels. This will not only yield direct benefits by preventing and treating disease in the developing world itself, but will also provide the basis for an effective global defence against bio-terrorism and overwhelming natural outbreaks of infectious disease.

Preventing wars within States and between them is also in the collective interest of all. If we are to do better in future, the UN will need real improvements to its capacity for preventive diplomacy and mediation. We will have to build on the successes of regional organisations in developing strong norms to protect Governments from unconstitutional overthrow, and to protect minority rights. And we will have to work collectively to find new ways of regulating the management of natural resources, competition for which often fuels conflict. Preventing the spread and use of nuclear, biological and chemical weapons is essential if we are to have a more secure world. This means doing better at reducing demand for these weapons, and curbing the supply of weapons materials. It means living up to existing treaty commitments, including for negotiations towards disarmament. And it means enforcing international agreements. It urges negotiations for a new arrangement which would enable the International Atomic Energy Agency to act as a guarantor for the supply of fissile material to civilian nuclear users at market rates, and it calls on Governments to establish a voluntary time-limited moratorium on the construction of new facilities for uranium enrichment and reprocessing, matched by a guarantee of the supply of fissile materials by present suppliers.

Terrorism is a threat to all States, and to the UN as a whole. New aspects of the threat-including the rise of a global terrorist network, and the potential for terrorist use of nuclear, biological or chemical weapons require new responses. The UN has not done all that it can. The report urges the United Nations to forge a strategy of counter terrorism that is respectful of human rights and the rule of law. Such a strategy must encompass coercive measures when necessary, and create new tools to help States combat the threat domestically. The report provides a clear definition of terrorism, arguing that it can never be justified, and calls on the General Assembly of the UN to overcome its divisions and finally conclude a comprehensive convention on terrorism.

The spread of transnational organised crime increases the risk of all the other threats. Terrorists use organised criminal groups to move money, men and materials around the globe. Governments and rebels sell natural resources through criminal groups to finance wars. States' capacity to establish the rule of law is weakened by corruption. Combating organised crime is essential for helping States build the capacity to exercise their sovereign responsibilities and in combating the hideous traffic in human beings.

Response to Threats

Of course, prevention sometimes fails. At times, threats will have to be met by — military means. The UN Charter provides a clear framework for the use of force. States have an inherent right to self-defence, enshrined in Article 51. Long-established customary international law makes it clear that States can take military action as long as the threatened attack is imminent, no other means would deflect it, and the action is proportionate. The Security Council has the authority to act preventively, but has rarely done so. The Security Council may well need to be prepared to be more proactive in the future, taking decisive action earlier. States that fear the emergence of distant threats have an obligation to bring these concerns to the Security Council. The report endorses the emerging norm of a responsibility to protect civilians from large-scale violence — a responsibility that is held, first and foremost, by national authorities. When a State fails to protect its civilians, the international community then has a further responsibility to act, through humanitarian operations, monitoring missions and diplomatic pressure — and with force if necessary, though only as a last resort. And in the case of conflict or the use of force, this also implies a clear international commitment to rebuilding shattered societies. Deploying military capacities — for peacekeeping as well as peace enforcement — has proved to be a valuable tool in ending wars and helping to secure States in their aftermath. But the total global supply of available peacekeepers is running dangerously low. Just to do an adequate job of keeping the peace in existing conflicts would require almost doubling the number of peacekeepers around the world. The developed States have particular responsibilities to do more to transform their armies into units suitable for deployment to peace operations. And if we are to meet the challenges ahead, more States will have to place contingents on stand-by for UN purposes, and keep air transport and other strategic lift capacities available to assist peace operations. When wars have ended, post-conflict peace building is vital. The UN has often devoted too little attention and too few resources to this critical challenge.

A UN for the 21st Century

To meet these challenges, the UN needs its existing institutions to work better. This means revitalizing the General Assembly and the Economic and Social Council, to make sure they play the role intended for them; and restoring credibility to the Commission on Human Rights.

It also means increasing the credibility and effectiveness of the Security Council by making its composition better reflect today's realities. The report provides principles for reform, and two models for how to achieve them —

- one involving new permanent members with no veto,
- the other involving new four-year, renewable seats.

It argues that any reform must be reviewed in 2020. We also need new institutions to meet evolving challenges. The report recommends the creation of a Peace building Commission — a new mechanism within the UN, drawing on the Security Council and the Economic and Social Council, donors, and national authorities. The report recommends strengthening the Secretary-General's critical role in peace and security. To be more effective, the Secretary-General should be given substantially more latitude to manage the Secretariat, and be held accountable. He also needs better support for his mediation role, and new capacities to develop effective peace building strategy. He currently has one Deputy Secretary-General; with a second, responsible for peace and security, he would have the capacity to ensure oversight of both the social, economic and development functions of the UN, and its many peace and security functions.

The way forward

The report is the start, not the end, of a process. The year 2005 will be a crucial opportunity for member states to discuss and build on the recommendations in the report, some of which will be considered by a summit of heads of State. But building a more secure world takes much more than a report or a summit. It will take resources commensurate with the scale of the challenges ahead; commitments that are long-term and sustained; and, most of all, it will take leadership — from within States, and between them.[44]

TERRORISM

According to the precise definition provided by the world book CD-ROM, terrorism is the use or threat of violence to create fear and panic. The aims of the terrorists differ from those of ordinary criminals. Most criminals commit crimes for personal profit. But most Terrorists commit crimes in support of political causes: to focus international attention on a neglected problem; or to strike fear amongst the people; or to strike at the perceived oppressors, their installations, or installations identified with them. The world terrorism first appeared during the French Revolution (1789-1799).[45]

Terrorist tactics have been used for hundreds of years. The modus operandi of terrorists is well known. Terrorists kidnap and assassinate people, set off hand grenades and bombs, hijack airplanes, blast trains and commit other heinous crimes.

Terror, terrorism and terrorist connote the relationship among 3 'I's — Instrument, Ideology and Individual (Intriguer). Terrorist is an individual, who plots something secretly, for the attainment of particular set(s) of goals, espouses the ideology of terrorism and performs it through the instrument of terror. In a broad sense, it seems, the modern terrorism is a by-product of the policy of peace and development. In fact with the advent of nuclear weapons in 1940s, with its hasardous and overkill element, world witnessed an awe and terror policy, pursued by both the Super Powers. A huge and horrid clamour would have been made all around that the Super Powers had acquired MAD (Mutually Assured Destruction) level. In this dreadful environment, war, being an utmost ruinous, deadly and costly affair, had lost all its meaning and became futile. Thus, maintenance of peace was given primacy to all. It was stressed that peace had to be preserved at all costs. As a result, the notion of 'peace before justice' came to dominate the world. Justice had been placed on back seat, which culminated in the large number of unsettled disputes. Consequently, small disputes became big disputes, local conflicts turned into universal ones and so on. At one hand, war as a classical means of settlements of disputes couldn't last long, at the other, absence of any other appropriate and peaceful means of settlement of disputes marked an era, which saw a new world — full of dissidents. Allied with this is the mien of development — the new advancements in the field of science and technology. The dissidents after getting mingled with these modern, sophisticated scientific and technological tools (in the form of arms-ammunitions, weapons, information network etc.) reproduced an offspring — the terrorist — a new variety of non-state actors.

The twin incidents in the year 2001 (9/11 and 12/13) not only shocked the two biggest democracies but the whole world and brought the issue of terrorism center stage in all international activities. A feigned attempt was made to unite and integrate the whole world against terrorism. US in its crusade against terrorism, targetted the nation (Afghanistan) which is the most backward and underdeveloped nation in the world. But got dismal result in the mission, so far. This task is yet to accomplish. But the business of international politics is so intricate that no one could espouse a straight forward equation. One has to go through a multiple set of equations to get a proper understanding of it.

USA had been adamant on its stand to wage war against Iraq while the principal actors like — France, Germany, Russia, China are in the opposition? Being the only surviving Super Power, USA has to maintain its superpowerdom in the mutli-player world. For this, it does not want to let the regions, strategically very important for US interest and influence, to get out of its hand. Especially where the US meets an incompatible government the outcome becomes crises (Iraq). But there has always been a gap between the interpretation and intention of a country in international politics. Weapons in the hands of Iraq are unsafe and therefore dangerous. The dangerous game of war was pushed for the sake of avoiding future danger. This was the logic placed by USA George Bush, any how, wants to wage war against Saddam Hussain, even keeping aside the authority of Security Council.[46] What would he get out of this war? Safe, secure or peaceful world? Everyone knows the answer. Because war can not resolve any problem today, it would only escalate the crisis (through destruction and innocent killings) instead of its dilution. Besides, whether it was Vietnam or Afghanistan, war had always been futile. Even in the course of containing USSR in Afghanistan US had fed and armed those fundamentalists (follower of Islam) which now have become dragon and eager to emit fire against its feeder.

Terrorism — History, Meaning, Nature and Kind

For the history of terrorism, the credit goes to the French Revolution (1789-1799) during which the Word 'terrorism' for the first time appeared. Some of the revolutionaries, who seised power in France, used terror tactics as a policy against their enemies. Throughout their rule they adopted the policy of violence, hence their rule was known as the 'Reign of Terror'. Terrorist tactics have been used for hundreds of years. After the end of the American Civil War in 1865 and during the 1900s, an American group, the Ku Klux Klan, used violence to terrorise blacks.[47] In the 1930s, the dictators Adolf Hitler of Germany, Benito Mussolini of Italy and Joseph Stalin of the Soviet Union used terrorism to discourage opposition to their governments. Before the independence of Israel in 1948, a Jewish group used terror to speed the end of British rule in Palestine and create a Jewish homeland. Since the 1960s, various Palestinian groups have carried out a campaign of terrorism aimed at the destruction of Israel and the establishment of an independent Palestinian State. In Northern Ireland, Roman Catholic and Protestant extremists have used violence to push for, respectively, the end of, or the continuation of, British rule.

Terrorists are deeply motivated individuals committed to their goals. They commit crimes in support of political causes, to focus international attention on a neglected problem, or to strike fear amongst the people; or to strike at the perceived oppressors.[48] But, a new dimension to the world of terrorism has been added by the emergence of Islamic fundamentalists.[49] The goal of these fundamentalists has been, unlike the other terrorists, to establish Islam all over the world and especially to liberate regions, which were once ruled by Muslims.

This liberation movement, better known as 'jehad', is the chief moving force behind the militancy in Kashmir. Besides, there are numerous local battles, being fought by these jehadis to accomplish the goal of establishing Islamic Supremacy, from Sudan, Egypt, Kosovo, Chechnya, much of Central Asia, Afghanistan, Pakistan to Indonesia. Everywhere jehadis are performing their well-knitted and well-appointed job. Which is definitely the outcome of well equipped training institutions and camps, carrying the business of teaching Islam and preparing the innocent people for staging jehad all over the globe. The ability of the militants to handle Stinger anti-aircraft missiles, the use of multi-barrel rocket launchers and other sophisticated weaponry found its genesis in the training camps in Islamabad with funding from those who now fear Osama Bin Laden.[50] The militant recruits in Pakistan consisted of Tunisians, Algerians, Egyptians, Saudis, Sudanese and several others financed by those who wanted the erstwhile USSR defeated in Afghanistan.[51] Despite the break-up of USSR, the jehad had not ended. Apart from private financiers, the jehad was riding on a wave of 'narcomania'. This is another aspect of terrorism — 'Narcoterrorism'. It is alleged that Afghanistan liberation camps in Pakistan were turned into centers of 'narcomania'. Drugs were smuggled into Pakistan and abroad to finance the jehad. Vast fields of opium and poppies on both sides of the Afghanistan-Pakistan border sprang up overnight to earn funds for financing extremists across the world.[52]

Besides, Pakistan becomes a burning example of state sponsored terrorism, which, by means of these training centres, used to instill poison against India and has been creating an atmosphere for its entrants that assists them to develop a mindset, which sees India as an evil, as a foe. Even for this purpose, they have altered India's history, norms and culture and projected India as an ill-hearted, ill-doing, and ill-thinking nation.

As far as Kashmir is concerned, jihadis are primarily located in two organisations. Earlier known as the Harakat-ul-Ansar, Harkat-ul-Mujahidin (HuM) was designated a foreign terrorist organisation by the US government in October 1997. It is HuM, which was responsible for the hijacking of Indian Airlines Flight 814. It is an Islamic militant group based in

Pakistan, that operates primarily in Kashmir. Its leader Fazlur Rehman Khalil has been linked to Bin Laden. HuM operates terrorist training camps in eastern Afghanistan. It conducted a number of operations against Indian troops and civilian targets in Kashmir and is liked to the Kashmiri militant group Al-Faran that kidnapped five Western tourists in Kashmir in July 1995.

Other is Lashkar-e-Taiba (LeT). The parent organisation of LeT is Markaz-Ad-da' Wah Wal Irshad which claims to be committed to Islamic education and Jihad. At a congregation in Lahore, Lashkar leader spewed venom against India and the United States. Significantly, nearly all of the terrorist "spectaculars" that have taken place recently (with the exception of the Oklahoma bombing) have been linked to the Afghanistan-Pakistan region. From here "terrorist" — well armed, trained, under some command and control — appears to move with surprising ease across national boundaries. Terrorism is therefore unequivocally a transnational enterprise, and, much what is today called "international terrorism" emanates from our immediate neighborhood. Killing of innocents is a part and parcel of their strategy. The list of popular terrorist organisations comprises Al-Qaeda, Hizbul Mujahideen, Hamas, Lashkar-e-Taiba, Jaish-e-Mohammed, Jamaat-e-Islami, Harkat-ul-Ansaar, LTTE, to name the few only. These people are violence loving individuals, life has no meaning to them. They could go to any extreme to secure their ends. They are just like an omnipotent and omnipresent virus. Having procured strong information network based on highly modern and best technologies, they have reached to that point, from where they can ensnare the whole world.[53] In this sense, they are omniscient, able to know and get the thing even at much faster rate and in shortest span of time than that of any state actor. What was the outcome of 'war against terror'? So far, USA didn't get success. Osama Bin Laden was reported to had gone to nowhere, but some unknown places in Tora Bora Hills in Afghanistan, with his 500 Cavalier Commandos equipped with latest technological instruments and other requisites, at the time, when the strongest state actor went on an unended mission of getting him alive or dead. US's all efforts to search him went in vain. Osama remains inaccessible.[54]

This new phase of terrorism is probably the most dangerous and to combat it will require a huge co-operative effort across continents. The first step is to introduce a Global Convention on Terrorism, which makes it incumbent on states, that provide a hospitable area for terrorist operations, to clean up their act or face international enforcement action. Until then states like India and the United States must also evolve joint strategies to crush this international menace.

In this regard the statement of former Secretary of State of US is significant. She says, "I don't feel that we have really made enough advances in fighting terrorism. The real problem is the way the United States is viewed in the world. I think the number one issue is national security. I don't think we are more secure than we were four years ago. Then terrorism, Iraq, unfinished business of Afghanistan are the other issues. While the administration is saying that they have caught a lot of terrorists, we don't know how many new terrorists are being created. I don't feel that we have really made enough advances in fighting terrorism."[55]

UN Convetions on Terrorism

United Nations has a number of conventions preventing the act of terrorism. The problem lies with the implementation level. As regards the UN conventions on terrorism, the first ever text was adopted on 18th December, 1972. The subject of the text was described as the 'Measures to prevent international terrorism which endangers or takes innocent human lives or jeopardises fundamental freedoms, and study of the underlying causes of those forms of terrorism and acts of violence which lie in misery, frustration, grievance and despair, and which cause some people to sacrifice human lives, including their own, in an attempt to effect radical changes.'[56] In 1976 the UN General Assembly decided to establish an ad hoc committee to draft an International Convention Against the Taking of Hostages which came into effect on 29th November, 1978. However, by 1981 international community had realised that terrorism is sponsored by nation states and its prevention is not possible unless such activities are restricted. Thus, on 4th December, 1989 an International Convention against the Recruitment, Use, Financing, and Training of Mercenaries was adopted. Moreover, no definition of terrorism could evolve until 1987 when the UN General Assembly adopted an important resolution, with overwhelming majority, which condemned all acts of terrorism except those fighting for right to self-determination against foreign and racist regime as 'criminal' wherever and by whomever committed, including those which jeopardise friendly relations among states and their security. Furthermore, on 9th December, 1994, a Declaration of Measures to Eliminate Terrorism, was adopted. The Declaration expressed concern over linkage of drug traffickers and money launders with para military gangs which resort to all types of violence and endanger constitutional order of states by violating human rights. The importance of this declaration could be analysed from the fact that coordination and cooperation among states to combat terrorism was given utmost priority. The need for extradition treaty among nations and efforts at regional and bilateral level was reiterated. In 1997 an International Convention for the Suppression of Terrorist Bombings was adopted. On 19th October, 1999, Security Council also adopted a resolution (1269) and called for co-operation among member nations.[57] On 9th December, 1999, yet another International Convention for the Suppression of the Financing of Terrorism was adopted by the United Nations General Assembly. For the first time, the Convention especially targets the financial sponsors of terrorist activity, rather than simply the actual perpetrators of the specific acts. Under this law, it is not even necessary that an act of terrorism has taken place; according to article 2 of this convention, the intention or knowledge or the use of the funds collected or provided is sufficient.[58] Besides, the convention sets new limits on the banking secrecy.

Normally the conventions do not receive the requisite number of ratification for its enforcement. This makes a great problem in the implementation of these conventions. In

October, 2001, UN Security Council has passed a much-awaited resolution (1373) which states that if any nation is found guilty of aiding, sponsoring and instituting training camps for terrorists, it would have to face economic, political and military sanctions.

However, there were provisions like collective defence and collective security, in the United Nations Charter, to deal with the aggressor. The collective defence provides a right to self defence to each country outside the United Nations (military alliances like NATO, WARSAW Pact, SEATO, CENTO had been serving the same purpose), while the collective security operates under United Nations and on the principle 'one for all and all for one', which means attack on one nation would be considered as an attack against all. But, both these devices are unlikely to yield positive results as far as fight against terrorism is concerned. Nevertheless, the resolutions on terrorism can strengthen the device of collective security, provided the members might ready to use it purposefully.

Peace and the Genesis of Collective Security

The period extending from the end of Nepoleonic wars (1815) to the commencement of First World War has been regarded as the classic era of peace. This classic peace was due to the preponderance of power and this preponderance of power had been in the hands of England and France, especially England. Their chief motive was not the preservation of peace but to form alliances so that the growth of power in other alliances could be prevented.

It is only after the First World War that the idea of collective security came into being, which was, in fact the conversion of ever-changing preponderance of power into the permanent preponderance of power of law abiding nations, through the League of Nations. But this world organisation was not ripe enough, so that it could contain the turbulence carrying the seeds of war.

The dream of collective security turned into reality only under the aegis of the United Nations. Although this organisation was powerful enough and was considered to be making peace effectively, as had been evident in the Korean Crises, Suez Crisis, Congo Crisis and the like. But at the same time the factor that had been contributing the most to the maintenance of peace, was the emergence of Nuclear Weapons, a fruit of development, indeed. With the advent of Nuclear Weapons emphasis was given upon the maintenance of peace, even more than ever, as these weapons did possess the capacity of overkill.

Consequently, the world witnessed the concept of peace before justice followed by enumerable unsettled disputes, small disputes became big disputes, local conflicts turned into universal conflicts. By this time, one can recall the Rousseau's dictum that 'man is born free, but everywhere he is in chains'. Which means, earlier man was living a very cheerful, comfortable and peaceful life, but the fruits of development and science had spoiled man's life.

Development and Terrorism

The development in the field of science and technology, took place especially in the twentieth century, played a major role in the creation of these dangerous people. Having obtained the sophisticated technological know-how and lethal weapons, they have become a peril to all. Misusing the boon of Science and exploiting the power of Kalashnikov, like superman, they have been planning strategies and turning them into concrete action successfully, thereafter.

Besides, what happened, with the end of Cold War, the World underwent drastic changes. Virtually capitalist block became victorious with its democratic system, liberal norms and market economy — which came to buzz the world. Liberalisation and globalisation became the pass-words, economy saw no boundary in the execution of capital. The whole world was brought under single domination and one system. The repercussion of all these changes had profound for the very people under discussion. As globalisation increases, the countries having poor world economic competitiveness index, face a lot of trouble in satisfying local people.[59] This is, what happened in most of the countries of West Asia, they opened their economy under global pressure, but with the introduction of new technology, the local people, with their customary type of education, found themselves in miserable conditions, as they were facing difficulty in getting jobs now, in the new circumstances which required modern and dextrous education (of course much costlier).[60] In other words, government was not able enough to provide job for its youths. In despair, with no option in sight, the unemployed youths, joined jehad.[61] They have joined jehad because they were not satisfied with the policies of the government and the jehadis grabbed the pulse of these youths and attempted to instigate their discontent still further. They developed a strong aversion for United States too. Since, in the aftermath of end of the Cold War, USA emerged as a single and strongest power — able to influence the World events. It played an important and dominating role in the Gulf War.

Even, after the war had stopped, US ground troops were remained there. This created outrage among the local people, especially because USA was found guilty of stationing its troops on the land of holy Islamic cities — Mecca and Medina. Once USA had provided a huge aid to the countries of this region and now came to that point where it is in the receiving end and has been receiving utter wrath.

Conversion of Conventional war into Proxy War

War as a means of settling disputes, no longer stood valid, as was the case in the past when it was regarded as a means of settling disputes and the maintenance of peace. Today war has no meaning at least in the sense, it lacks the element of Winnability. Furthermore, unlike the wars in the past when society had been kept aloof from it and it was an extremely exclusionary activity, fought by the state with its armed forces, often in a particular battle zone, now war came not only into society but was indistinguishable from it.[62]

The non-existence of any other appropriate means of settlement of disputes, gave rise to a large number of dissidents all over the world, comprising a different category of non-state actors-the terrorists. What followed as a further degeneration downwards into proxy war — where a patron state supplied the favored regime with the weapons that were the most appropriate to fight an 'irregular' war. This was often not a war at all but a series of conflagrations and bush fires that swept across Africa, South Asia, East Asia or West Asia or wherever the great powers found their interests clashing. Thus billions of dollars of weapons flowed into the hands of various non-state actors who variously espoused a dubious and poorly understood left or right wing ideology.[63] The option of 'proxy war' (low level war) thus became the favored option for those countries who had already tried and failed at achieving their objectives through conventional war. Thus, proxy war was launched as an extension of war by other means. Today terrorism has spread to parts of Russia, Tajikistan, Uzbekistan, China, Saudi Arabia, Egypt, Algeria, parts of Africa, South Asia, South East Asia and United States, there is hardly any part of the globe which has remained untouched.

For the adoption of appropriate strategy/mechanism, to uproot this scourge, the correct way is to go by the United Nations route. Each and every nation should contribute willingly. Undoubtedly, USA has an indispensable role to play, but it would have to rise above partisan practices and to move towards the welfare of whole world community in a truly democratic manner. Other major actors like Britain, Russia, Germany, France, and India are also exhibiting their velour in dealing with terrorism. However, it is still in question, up to what extent, they are going to employ the services of UNO, further up to what extent, they are going to follow and implement resolutions, adopted by UNO. Because Pakistan has been transgressing the resolution in both letter and spirit and in spite sufficient evidences have come up against Pakistan, USA is not only not willing to recognise it as 'terrorist state' (while Saddam Hussein's Iraq was punished) but even keeping it at par with India in dealing with Kashmir problem, altogether ignoring the fact that it was Pakistan, that had been irresponsibly giving air to terrorist activities in Kashmir by aiding, abetting and providing training.

Huge investment in military is not the solution, instead investment to improve human development indicators (per capita income, education, health, longevity), is the cry of the hour.

The segregation of what is happening in Kashmir from September 11, terrorist attacks, will take USA to inconclusive results only, under its 'War against Terrorism' crusade. In the beginning it appeared, as if USA is coming forward genuinely and looking the problem as an indivisible whole. But soon it becomes spurious. To get justice requires doing justice first.

In the ultimate analysis, nations should try to co-operate collectively under United Nations to get positive results, as in their individual capacity they can't do more, to put an end to this malice. Furthermore, since the notion of national interest has come under severe challenge due to various reasons. Thus, now one can't sever national and international interests. There are a number of phenomenons, which are worldwide in nature and no one can limit them in boundaries. Yet, if we follow the reasoning of realists that to perceive national interest is extreme morality, then, for the sake of preserving national interest we should co-operate collectively, or otherwise if we want to go by idealist thought, they also used to say the similar line of reasoning, at least, in this regard. They believe in world peace and one world and for them, to go for it, is extreme morality.

Therefore, come forward, nations of the world unite, work for the cause, combinely and get the ultimate peace for humanity.

MILLENNIUM DEVELOPMENT GOALS AND WOMEN'S EMPOWERMENT

The year 2004 marked the twenty-fifth anniversary of the General Assembly's adoption of the Convention on the Elimination of All Forms of Discrimination against Women. Nevertheless, the mistreatment of women and girl children continued, including through trafficking, sexual abuse and domestic violence. Despite concerted international efforts to eradicate all forms of violence against women, gender-based violence had increased in many parts of the world.

Violence against women was a clear violation of basic political rights and was an infringement of international human rights. Obstacles to women's full participation in social life and the political arena must be removed. Many women continued to live in circumstances of extreme poverty, armed conflict, discrimination, violence and illiteracy. Thus, the 10-year review of the Beijing World Conference must serve as an opportunity for the international community to recommit to the promotion of equality, development and peace for women, enshrined in the Beijing Platform for Action. There is an emerging consensus that the road to achieving the Millennium Development Goals ran through Beijing, where the World Conference on Women was held in 1995. Many countries reaffirmed the Millennium Declaration's call for women's empowerment as an inalienable component of sustainable development and — in particular — the global quest to push back the frontiers of poverty and hunger, noting that it drew upon the recognition, enshrined in the Beijing Platform for Action, that poverty could not be eradicated through anti-poverty programmes alone, but would require democratic participation and reform of economic structures to ensure access for all women to resources, opportunities and public services.

All the points in the Beijing Platform for Action (BPFA) are in goal 3 of the UN's Millennium Development Goals (MDGs) — promote gender equality and empower women, so it makes the BPFA less important. But, MDGs won't work without the BPFA. Because the Goal 3 is a prerequisite for the other seven MDGs —

(1) eradicate extreme hunger and poverty
(2) achieve universal primary education
(3) reduce child mortality
(4) improve maternal health
(5) combat HIV, malaria and other diseases
(6) ensure environmental sustainability
(7) develop a global partnership for development

These goals cannot be attained unless gender equality and empowerment is attained or worked upon. The MDGs are the new language now. One has to see how the BPFA and the MDGs can fit together.

Patricia Licuanan, chaiperson of the Asia-Pacific NGO Forum on Beijing+10, spoke about the gains made and new challenges that call for a rethink on some key strategies and issues.[64]

Microcredit

It is time to confront old favorite strategies. Microcredit was seen as a big thing at the Beijing conference — everyone hailed it as an initiative for women in poverty. But now there are mixed reports from different countries. It has benefited some, but microcredit is not working everywhere (Bangladesh, for example). One has to see in what circumstances microcredit works, one needs empirical data. There is a case for deeper analysis. Perhaps skills and capacity-building are necessary to ensure that microcredit actually helps those it is supposed to. Critics feel microcredit has its limitations, that it does not lead to long-term change in women's lives. That microcredit equals micro-impact. It's time now to a new level of microcredit.

Gender Mainstreaming

It has led to tokenism and become distorted. Some institutions think gender-mainstreaming means just the appointment of women. They are missing the point that the goal of gender mainstreaming is gender equality and empowerment. More and more people now feel it would be better to go back to the rights-based approach. Put simply, this approach means that women are entitled to equal treatment and empowerment; it's our right, not something that is dependent on anything or anyone.

Globalisation and Women

Globalisation has winners and losers. But the downside is so strong, particularly with poor women. Women need safety nets for low-level jobs, women's occupations and women dominated industries that are being affected by imports. New information technologies also have a downside — they are being used for the sex trade. Globalisation is partly responsible for increased trafficking in women and children. There is an increased feminisation of overseas labour, in the Philippines, for instance.

Gains since the Beijing Conference

Nearly 800 activists converged in Bangkok recently at the Asia-Pacific NGO Forum on Beijing+10, to take a hard look at what has been accomplished in the region and what remains to be done.

In many countries institutional mechanisms are more or less in place. All signatories to the BPFA have a focal point for women-gender plans, a body to implement the BPFA. The major breakthrough has been in the area of women's rights and laws on violence, mainly because of legislations. The progress has been uneven but at least it is recognised that these are problems. A lot of mechanisms and structures have been set up. Reproductive health issues have been given importance. There is also a recognition of HIV/AIDS by some countries that were in denial some years ago.

ASEAN Committee on Women coordinated implementation of the Regional Programme on Women and Skills Training, and was in the process of preparing a work plan on women's advancement and gender equality to address gender integration, research and policy development, promoting the employability of women, and preparing women for the challenges of globalisation.

Venezuelan Government had established a broad and solid platform from which women could exercise their rights and pursue development and participation. Among other initiatives, the Government had implemented a series of measures including establishment of a microfinance fund, community kitchens, a network for the supply, distribution and sale of staple foods at a low cost and an inner-city mission to give comprehensive medical care to the poor, among others. The National Institute for Women had implemented a programme of economic rights for women and had highlighted the value of production, training and technological training and employment for them.

Burkina Faso had adopted a national policy for promotion of women (2005-2015), which served as a guideline for action by the Government, and all its partners, to empower women. Among its aims were stabilisation of women's social and legal status and promotion of their access to decision-making, education, technical expertise, health and poverty reduction. Implementation of the national policy was to be monitored and executed through action-oriented plans and the mainstreaming of the gender perspective in sectoral policies and programmes.

In Mali the measures taken by Government to improve the economic status of women included the development of facilities to grant credit to women to enable them to conduct income generating activities. Hundreds of women were being trained in the agri-food industry, and a national committee had been established to eliminate harmful practices to mothers and children and programmes initiated to combat HIV/AIDS and malaria. Efforts were also underway to eliminate illiteracy and increase the enrolment of women and girls in schools, and legal clinics had been created in various administrative regions aimed at promoting and protecting women's rights.

Gender equality was connected to development and the eradication of poverty, in Philippines. For that reason, Government had mainstreamed gender issues in all areas called for in the Beijing document, and in the context of the Millennium Goals. The 30-year Philippine Plan for Gender-Responsive Development had been translated into an operational plan, and the National Commission on the Role of Filipino Women, in collaboration with Government agencies, NGOs and academia, had been tasked to oversee implementation of commitments in three major areas: promotion of economic empowerment, protection and fulfillment of women's rights, and promotion of gender responsive governance.

Myanmar Government recognised that violence against women was a serious concern for women's health and their advancement, and Myanmar authorities had taken integrated measures to prevent and reduce such violence. Studies had been carried out to determine the causes and consequences of violence against women and the effectiveness of preventive measures. Counselling training workshops had been held, and support centres established in various states. An education campaign had also been launched to inform the public about violence against women and laws protecting them.

Yet, despite these and other examples of progress in women's empowerment, the consensus remained that full implementation of the Beijing objectives for gender equality and advancement of women had yet to be achieved. The occasion of the 10-year review must be seised as an opportunity to identify obstacles impeding implementation of the commitments undertaken at Beijing, and its five-year review, and to formulate an integrated national and international strategy for their realisation.

The implementation of the Beijing Declaration and Plan of Action was intrinsically linked to the implementation of Millennium Development Goals. It was urgent and imperative to mobilise financial resources at national, international and multilateral levels especially for the least developed countries that were already overwhelmed with debt.

Carolyn Hannan, Director of the Division for the Advancement of Women, noted that several topics had recurred throughout the review of the Millennium Goals, including the need for increased attention to gender perspectives in peace and security; the challenges faced in relation to increasing women's participation in decision making; and the need to identify gender perspectives in poverty eradication initiatives. She now looked forward to finalizing preparations for the 10 year review of the Beijing Platform for Action, promising that all the points raised would be taken into account.

Women also suffered especially from armed conflict and terrorism. Countries welcomed the strategies of the United Nations Development Fund for Women (UNIFEM) to promote women's participation in peace-building processes. Security Council Resolution 1325 and ECOSOC resolution 2004/12 were crucial in this regard.

A high-level inter-governmental review of regional implementation of the Beijing Platform for Action had been held in Bangkok, Thailand, in September 2004. The Bangkok Communiqué had set forth the achievements made over the past ten years and identified gaps remaining to be filled. Those gaps included the need to increase the accessibility, availability and affordability of quality reproductive health services; to reduce the vulnerability of women and girls to HIV/AIDS; to support and institutionalise gender mainstreaming as a systematic approach to ensure gender-responsive implementation of programmes and policies; to reduce poverty and to support community and independent media attempts to counter negative and stereotypical portrayals of women and girls as sexual objects.[65]

Notes

1. Japan and Germany (within EU) have risen as new economic power houses with incommensurate military power. It is a common myth that they are not spending on defence. Japan is the fourth largest military spender and Germany too is no babe in the military woods. But they have not assumed crushing military burdens and global policing responsibilities that would have a crippling impact on their economic growth. V.P. Dutt: 'Post-cold war scenario', *World Focus*, 1996. (Oct.-Nov.-Dec.).
2. The cold war was waged with great intensity and at enormous expense. The Soviet Union's disintegration was a direct consequence of its inability to bear the cost of this arms race. The USA too suffered enormously as a consequence. About three trillion dollars were spent on its nuclear weapons programme alone. George F. Keenan: 'Who Won the cold war? Ask instead what was lost,' *International Herald Tribune*, 29 October 1992.
3. Maj. Gen. Dipankar Benerjee: 'The End of the cold war', in *Indian Foreign Policy*, Vol. 1, 1997.
4. V.P. Dutt, 'Post-cold war scenario', *World Focus*, Oct.-Nov.-Dec., 1996.
5. Maj. Gen. Dipankar Banerjee: 'The End of the cold war', in *Indian Foreign Policy*, Vol. 1, 1997.
6. *Times of India*, Mumbai, July 24, 2004.
7. Excerpts from the interview of Hamid Ansari and Brahm Chennai, in a TV show on DD News channel, 28-01-2005.
8. Thomas L. Friedman, 'The Humiliation factor,' *The Indian Express*, November 11, 2003.

9. *World Focus*, Oct.-Nov.-Dec., 1996.
10. Maj. Gen. Dipankar Banerjee: 'The End of the Cold War,' *Indian Foreign Policy*, Vol. 1, 1997.
11. *Ibid.*
12. K. Subrahmanyam, 'Nuclear Factor in Indo-US Relations', *World Focus*, June-July 2000.
13. *Times of India*, Mumbai, April 22, 2004.
14. Richard N. Hass and Robert E. Litan, 'Globalisation and its Discontents', *Foreign Affairs*, May / June 1998.
15. Girish Mishra, 'Globalisation and India,' *World Focus*, Oct.-Nov.-Dec., 1999.
16. Achin Vanaik, 'Rethinking India's Foreign Policy', *Indian Foreign Policy*, Vol. 1, 1997.
17. The IMF, for instance, has come under attack for imposing drastic conditions in its "rescues" of Mexico in 1995 and Asia today.
18. Richard N. Haass and Robert E. Litan, 'Globalisation and its Discontents', *Foreign Affairs*, May/June 1998.
19. *World Affairs — Some Challenges of the future*, Vol. 3, No. 4, Oct.-Dec., 1999.
20. *Ibid.*
21. *Ibid.*
22. K. Raman Pillai (Ed.). 'Indian Foreign Policy in the 1990', Radiant Publishers, New Delhi, 1997.
23. A.N. Ram, 'India's Economic Diplomacy', *World Focus*, Oct.-Nov.-Dec., 1999.
24. Arundhati Ghosh, 'India's objections to CTBT', *World Focus*, June-July, 1998.
25. Treaty Coercion and International Law, *Times of India*, March, 1997.
26. P.S. Jayaramu, 'India's Security and CTBT diplomacy,' *Mainstream*, Feb. 27, 1999
27. Following the Cuban missile crisis of 1962.
28. Sec Vajpayee's interview published in *India Today*, May 25, 1998. See also Vajpayee's statement in Parliament on the opening of the Budget session, *Mainstream*, May 30, 1998.
29. Arundhati Ghosh, 'India's Objection to GBT,' *World fours*, June-July, 1998.
30. Comprehensive Test Ban Treaty, whereas it is neither comprehensive, nor a Test Ban — 'How would India be different from these five rogue

states? And, India is what India is — a nuclear weapon state. India has not violated any law or treaty signed. US can say that having tested nuclear weapon does not make you a member of the club, India don't' want to be member of any club. Nor is India asking for the privileges that they have taken upon themselves through coercion'. *World Focus*, June-July, 1998.

31. Article 34 of the Vienna convention on the Law of Treaties, 1969, states that 'a treaty does not create obligations or rights, for a third state without its consent.' Article 52 declares void treaties concluded through force or the threat of force.
32. Treaty Coercion and International Law, *Times of India*, March 1997.
33. J.N. Dixit, 'Indo-American Relations', *World Focus*, Oct.-Nov.-Dec., 1999.
34. Arundhati Ghosh, 'India's Objections to CTBT,' *World Focus*, June-July, 1998.
35. *Ibid.*
36. J.N. Dixit, 'Indo-American Relations,' *World Focus*, Oct.-Nov.-Dec., 1999.
37. P.S. Jayaramu, 'Post-Pakhran India and CTBT, *Mainstream*, Feb. 27, 1999.
38. Hari Jaisingh, 'UN Council seat for India and US,' *World Focus*, June-July, 2000.
39. *The Navhind Time*, 9.8.2000, Goa.
40. *Ibid.*
41. S. Viswam, 'India and the United Nations,' *World Focus*, Oct.-Nov.-Dec. 1996.
42. Japan, Germany and Italy, as Axis powers during World War II were excluded from membership in the UNO. The five permanent Council members were considered the main war victors in 1945. *The Navhind Times*, Goa, September 9, 2000.
43. S. Visvam, 'India and the United Nations,' *World Focus*, Oct.-Nov.-Dec. 1996.
44. <http://www.globalpolicy.org>
45. Walter Reich (Ed.), 'Origins of Terrorism', The Woodrow Wilson Centre Press, 1998.
46. Kofi A., Annan in The Wall Street Journal Special, 'Maintain UN unity at all costs', *The Indian Express*, March 12, 2003. 'If the Security Council fails to agree on a common position, and some members take action without the council's authority, the legitimacy of

that action will be widely questioned. On the other hand, if they agree on a common course of action, the Council's authority will be enhanced and the world will be a safer place'.

47. Amitabh Mattoo, 'Terrorism in Kashmir', *World Focus*, January, 2000.
48. For details Omar Malik, 'Enough of the definition of Terrorism', A Royal Institute of International Affairs Book, Brookings Institute Press, 2001.
49. For further details see Mark Juergensmeyer: 'Terror in the mind of God — The Global Rise of Religious Violence', University of California, 2001.
50. Walter Laquer, 'The New Terrorism — Fanaticism and the Arms of Mass Destruction',Oxford University Press, 1999. Also see Research paper on 'Pakistan, Kashmir and the Trans-Asian Axis', by Yossef Bodansky: 'Islamabad's Road Warrior', Freeman Center for Strategic Studies, Houston, Texas, USA, 1995.
51. 'Pakistan's Kashmir Strategy', a research paper by Yossef Bodansky, Freeman Center for Strategic Studies, Houston, Texas, USA, 1995.
52. Sendero Luminoso Gabriela, 'The Threat of Narcoterrorism', New York, Praeger, 1990.
53. For further details see Jeffrey D. Simon, 'Terrorist Trap', Indiana University Press, 2001.
54. For details see Yossef Bodansky, 'Bin Laden — The Man Who declared War on America', Prima, 2001.
55. Excerpts from the Interview of Madeleine Albright, Former US Secretary of State, *The Times of India*, Mumbai, July 23, 2004.
56. K.R. Gupta (Ed.), *International Terrorism: Conventions, Resolutions, Legislations, Terrorist Organisations and Terrorists*, Vol. 2, New Delhi, Atlantic Publishers and Distributors, 2002.
57. *Ibid.*, Vol. 1. Also see UN Conventions and Resolutions Against Terrorism, Quaker United Nations Office, New York.
58. *Ibid.*
59. Raimindo Strassoldo, 'Globalism and Localism — Theoretical Reflections and some Evidence', in Zdravko Minar (Ed.): 'Globalisation and Territorial Identities', Aldershot, Avebury, 1992.
60. Sandra Braman, 'Interpenetrated Globalisation — Scaling, Power and the Public Sphere', in Sandra Bbraman and Annabelle Sreberny Mohammadi (Ed.): 'Globalisation, Communication and Transnational Civil Society', Cresskill, New Jersey, Hampton Press, 1996.
61. Bassam Tibi, 'Religious Fundamentalism, Ethnicity and the Nation-State in the Middle East', T.K. Oommen (Ed.), 'Citisenship and

National Identity — From Colonialism to Globalism', New Delhi, Sage, 1997. Also see Girijesh Pant: 'Terrorism and West Asia', *World Focus*, January, 2002.

62. Tara Kartha, 'Terrorism — A New Face of War?', *World Focus*, January, 2000.

63. *Ibid.*

64. Excerpts from the Interview, *The Times of India*, Bombay, July 16, 2004.

65. <http://www.documents.uncommittee.org>

6

Power Acquisition and India in the New Millennium

An American think tank made a forecast that by 2050 India will become world's No. 1 player in the field of economy. However, for achieving this status the growth rate, which is expected from India, does not seem to be possible in the long run. The observation of a British Institute appears a little bit close to the reality. The Global Investment Banking and Securities of Britain in its report, said that in the next 15 years India will become world's fifth economic power and in further 15 years India will be the third economic power of the world. Thus, if we accept the findings of this report, it's clear that after 30 years or so, there will be three major powers in the field of economy — America, China and India. The report says, the way India's economy is growing and its market is spreading, there is no doubt that India will leave behind Germany, France and Brazil in coming ten years and Japan and Britain in the next twenty years. Goldman Sax of Global Investment Banking and Securities, says, "in the contemporary world economy there are six major players, viz. America, Japan, Britain, Germany, France and Italy. According to Goldman, except America all other economies have come to stability. The dangerous element in the countries like Britain, Japan, France, Germany and Italy, is that they all have got 'stagnancy level' in their production and services sector. While, China and India have now started paying attention to these sectors. The need is to enhance the pace of the developmental policies.

India will be the super power in the field of computers. India is reckoned among the top software manufacturers in the world and the consumption of our hardware product is increasing these days. Indians have reached up to the world level in the field of automobile engineering. India is exporting purely Indian car to west European countries. India is continuously trying to make hydrogen car. These days with the successful flight of 'Saras', India has stepped into the field of airoplane manufacturing. It has made good progress in biotechnology too.

With the use of new scientific and technological methods agricultural production is increasing. Which in turn will lead to the economic prosperity of farmers. And thus agriculture could be brought to the state of industry. Patents of 146 medicines are available in the field of pharmaceuticals and drugs. India is trying to catch the figure of 200. India is top player in outsourcing and manufacturing. There will be growth in automobile, leather and textile industries. With the use of science and technology, India's production and export would increase many times.

Today India is the youngest nation of the world. Its 50 crore population is below 25 years. In the next two years, there will be 40 crore workforce in India, which need direction and facility. Empowerment of this workforce is inevitable for India to progress.

India is the only country with a dedicated ministry for non-conventional energy sources. Indian government has expressed its commitment to renewable energy sources in the Electricity Act, 2003 and its draft national electricity policy. Biomass and waste account for 40% of total primary energy supply and 85% of residential energy usage. The IEA has positively noted the government's intention to actively promote use of renewable energy in remote areas that cannot be connected through the grid and encourage decentralised power generation and distribution based on renewables. India is one of the world's largest producers of wind energy. About 11% of its electricity is generated from hydropower. India is especially active in promoting bio-fuel consumption. More accelerated, large-scale deployment of renewable technologies will also depend on their affordability.

Coal will remain the dominant commercial energy source in India through 2030, though its share of total commercial primary energy supply will decrease to 44% and the share of coal in power generation to 64% by 2030. Total installed nuclear capacity will more than triple between 2002 and 2030 while its share of overall installed capacity will remain constant at 4%. A long-term solution is needed for disposing of nuclear waste. (Excerpts of an interview of Claude Mandil, executive director of the Paris-based International Energy Agency, *The Times of India*, Mumbai, November 29, 2004).

Further India's latest defence systems comprise Prithvi, Agni-I, Agni-II, Mobile Terminus System, ICV BMP-II, ALH, Tonguska-400, Anti-air craft (Vijay), Brahmos-Cruise missile (range-200 Km), Samyukta-electronic warfare system (Interception Analysis Communication), Brahmos Commad Post, Pinaca-multi-barrel Rocket launcher etc.

Undoubtedly, the economic dimension is the most important dimension of foreign policy now. Economic potential and growth can no longer be separated from the measure of influence one exercises in the world. Further, only participating players can influence collective decisions and the larger their stake in the game and the stake others have in them, the greater their influence. The first priority of Indian diplomats should be to enhance all forms of economic relationships with their host countries and the first priority of the Indian government should be broad based economic development with increased interdependence. As India enlarges its share of world trade, its voice in world councils will also gather weight.

A large country can exercise economic power in the international system in two different ways. In terms of economic attractiveness (e.g. China) and economic competitiveness (e.g. Japan). Country's investment potential or market or both, constitute the basis of economic attractiveness. In this sense India's economic power stems from its attractiveness. However, in order to have a global economic presence a country must be economically competitive.

Since economics is now being regarded as the "new concept of security", which means, in order to become a major power today, a country does not have to be a military power (e.g. Japan. This is due to fungibility of money power, by which one type of power resource can be converted into another type of power resource in the international system). Therefore, the inability of India to compete economically in the capitalist world system cannot be compensated by any other power resource.

Over the next thirty years, India must aim for growth rates of 10 to 12 per cent per annum. However, even with a far more modest growth rate of 7 per cent per annum, national income will double every ten years. Therefore, strategy should be to maintain peace and grow strong economically.

Furthermore, economic links should be established with as many countries as possible and existing linkages with capital-surplus economies deepened. The aim should be to consolidate association with ASEAN, APEC etc. Efforts to promote increased trade, economic and other forms of co-operation among the members of the SAARC countries should continue. India should also explore linkages between SAARC and other regional organisations such as ASEAN, the EU. New ideas for co-operation among Indian Ocean Rim countries and with the newly independent but landlocked Central Asian Republics need to be explored. Thus emphasis should be on both glocalisation (integration with world economy, while managing local economic conditions) and regionalism, so that India could get maximum advantage.

A nuclear deterrent is of utility to India only if it enhances its security. Undoubtedly, it is an important asset that India possesses, at least in today's world. But nuclear weapons are unlikely to be a "currency of power" for very much longer. So, they will contribute only marginally to Indian power in the next century. A broad national consensus has emerged on a 'no first use' policy and the need to develop a 'credible minimum deterrent'. The categorical and unambiguous commitment to no first use of nuclear weapons in case of conflict determines the contours of India's nuclear posture. Further, India should also campaign for an international treaty banning the first use of nuclear weapons. Such a treaty could be the first stage in the process of delegitimisation of nuclear weapons. If all nuclear weapon powers subscribed to such a treaty, it would be tantamount to a complete ban on any use of nuclear weapons. Besides, India should have in place modest nuclear arsenals to achieve minimum and credible deterrence and also sway future negotiations of START III or perhaps START IV. The modest nuclear weapons capability is seen as a means to force general and complete disarmament. With India's nuclear neighbours, nuclear arms control, as well as confidence-building measures can increase transparency and reduce the dangers of an open-ended nuclear arms race.

India needs to maintain good, co-operative relations with all neighbours on the basis of mutuality, reciprocity, while trying not to benefit or equally, provided, of course, the neighbours are willing to play a fair game. Certainly, this is a difficult e ercise in respect to a istan, which suffers from paranoia in respect to India but gradually over a period India needs to continue to promote a balanced relationship. India should do three things to face the reality of ashmir issue

First, India has to maintain its urisdiction and necessary levels of law and order to give the people of ammu and ashmir a sense of security against the depredations of terrorism and secession.

Second, India has to underta e substantive and profoundly innovative political initiatives to structure a political solution the aim of which should be restoration of genuine democratic and appropriately autonomous political arrangements, which would be responsive to the aspirations of the people of ashmir.

Third, India should nip a istani sponsored violence

and terrorism in the bud by all means possible without getting enmeshed in an open military conflict with Pakistan.

Clearly, a sponsorship of terrorism across the Line of Control, or elsewhere, is a violation of the Line of Control, as indeed of Shimla Agreement and Lahore Declaration. There is a need to acknowledge the current Line of Control in Jammu and Kashmir as an international border, stabilise the situation and then allow normal intercourse between Kashmiris on both sides. This is what Z.A. Bhutto reportedly assured Mrs. Gandhi in Shimla in 1972.

Further, trust is not built by engaging in dialogue in winter and committing aggression in summer. A senior serving Pakistani diplomat in a discussion on the intractability of the problems of Jammu and Kashmir stated that, "The only way is to convince the people of both India and Pakistan, that the Kashmir problem alone should not be the central point of interaction between them. We must convince them, that it is a small problem which should be submerged by the logic of many larger issues and larger interests on which India and Pakistan could co-operate for the welfare of millions of our people".

Furthermore, for India, its foreign policy has not been fixated on Pakistan, but that has been a significant preoccupation of it. India needs to re-examine this in detail. Globally, India has to move purposefully towards realizing its true dimensions — as a major civilisational state, with its own strategic autonomy and strategic space, born out of its economic and political interaction with other countries particularly in the Asia-Pacific community. In 1820, Asia contributed 58 per cent of the world GDP; today it is at 37 per cent; by 2020, expectations are that it could regain the level of 200 years ago. India has a signal role to play in the coming decades.

India's relations with the major powers will also determine its power posture in the world. U.S.A. remains the greatest power with immense capacity to influence world events. The prospects for greater economic and commercial co-operation and India's new advances in the Information Technology and other knowledge-based industries have created a very positive environment in which Indo-US differences can now be managed with greater confidence and in a more relaxed manner. Possible, through economy both democratic countries come closer in other spheres and India and the US achieve durability of their relationship. Whether it is the question of India's Security Council membership, or conditionalities of global economic institutions, a lot will depend on the USA.The high-level talks between the US and India facilitated the US administration to accept the inevitability of a nuclear India. Moreover, US Administration cannot overlook India's economic potential and its nuclear status.

India needs to continue to maintain a balanced relationship between and among the major powers — notably between the US and now Russia, despite the latter's weakened power, for a variety of reasons, especially for India's need for Russian arms supply. The weakest leg of India's relationship with Russia continues to be trade. However, during Russian President Vladimir Putin's October, 2000 visit effort was made to boost relation in areas like information technology. But there needs to be a major surge in private investment, especially in setting up joint ventures. Further, a possibility of Strategic Alliance among Russia/ China /India is taking shape. The three countries are the world's largest multi-religious and multi–ethnic nations. There are a range of interests spanning Islamic terrorism to countering American hegemony, that these three countries can informally work in tandem in the international arena. However, India needs to be conscious of the likely pulls/pressures from the other two.

As far as bilateral relations between India and China are concerned, the best course of action for India is an approach of constructive engagement — to engage China in a continuing process of co-operation with the goal of strengthening and expanding an across-the-board mutually interdependent relationship. Further, peace and development are indivisible, it will not be possible to sustain the required levels of socio-economic development without durable peace and co-operation among the states. It is in this context that India and China should work for the consolidation of a peaceful environment, only then, they can profit in socio-economic terms. It may also be reasonably hoped that common prosperity will create its own vested interests in peace in both countries, as it has done in the case of France and Germany. As economic development continues apace many animosities will die a natural death and continuing conflict and tension might appear to be too high a price to pay for peace and economic well-being. But India must never stop being watchful.

Besides, India cannot have a "good foreign policy" irrespective of the quality of a state's domestic policy and standing. The Indian state has failed not only to deliver the goods, it has not even been able to prevent its own degeneration. Decaying political institutions, corrupt political behaviors, criminalised political culture — the marks of an unhealthy polity are evident for all to see. Elections alone do not make democracy to work. Political process should be truly democratic, that could promote interests of common man. While, what is actually happening is the consolidation of North within the South e.g. the establishment of a significantly sized elite in Southern countries like India which is enjoying western living standards and whose income and wealth differentials vis-à-vis the vast majority of the population continues to grow. At the other hand India remains a "survival society" in which a vast number of people face absolute deprivation and degradation. Besides, prosperity for all, India must pay attention to social cohesion as a fundamental security need for India, which is challenged by caste conflict and communal tensions.

Further, the deeper institutionalisation of political liberty and of egalitarian democratisation is the need of the hour, which means the ever-greater empowerment of ordinary people. The concept of 'humane governance', which puts people at the centre of all governance policies, strategies and actions, should be adopted. Even more to increase the capability of all human beings by assuring good health, adequate education, greater longevity and the ability to influence the political decisions, so that India could use its greatest asset — human resources maximally. Further, development requires the removal of major sources of unfreedom: poverty as well as tyranny, poor economic opportunities as well as systematic social deprivation, neglect of public facilities, as well as intolerance, or overactivity of repressive states.

Moreover, government should be strong and stable, so that it could pay considerable attention to more important affairs — to make and implement developmental policies rather than busy in making strategies for how to save the government.

For sound foreign and security policies, proper co-ordination among departments of home, finance, defence and external affairs is needed. Establishment of a National Security Council is a welcome development. It should be empowered by law and not by an executive order and should be composed of a dedicated group of professionals, often drawn from outside the routine bureaucracy, with a lifetime of specialisation in their subjects. Further, it must be consciously designed as an instrument that can produce coherent policy in a parliamentary democracy.

Other Important Points:

- The battle against demographic growth has barely begun. As the growing numbers of people who are young, energetic, talented yet unemployed, results in growing frustration and alienation in society. This challenge cry out for a concerted response.
- India has to create conditions to harness its own resources for productive purposes and to provide adequate opportunities to the country's brilliant scientists, technologists, engineers, doctors and skilled labour so that India can march forward. India should not lose faith in its people and must pursue the objective of self-reliance.
- India has a society where only 10 to 15 per cent of the population has benefited. This itself in real terms is

large and provides a huge market that attracts foreigners. India has to cater to the needs of the remaining 80 to 85 per cent of the masses who have been neglected.

- Often an excuse is given that India has a huge middle class. Therefore to fulfil its demands new economic policies (or for that matter globalisation), were introduced, but at the same time India also has a population, 40 per cent of whom lives below the poverty line. Why not policies were introduced for their upliftment. This point was raised by Nobel Laureate Dr. Amartya Sen, who focusses on improving the quality of life and prioritizing distributive justice. He righty points out that economic take-off requires an educated, healthy and socially secure population.
- In asserting the performance of the economy, the condition of the vast masses should be the criterion and not that of tiny few at the top.
- If any one possesses money by adopting dubious means, his black money should be seised. Also an upper limit of possession of money should be introduced (ceiling of money).
- It is estimated that India is likely to become one of the largest markets in the world, with a middle class estimated to be in the region of 500 million by the year 2025. The World Bank has predicted that India's share of world trade and output will double in the next two decades and that this will fundamentally alter the way the world does business by the year 2015. Other global economy watchers have predicted that by the year 2015, India will emerge as the fourth largest economy in the world. India should remain confident and make necessary arrangements so that this prediction will come true.
- Everyone has seen and been impressed by the manner in which the economic integration of Europe, steadfastly and patiently pursued, has taken the bloody battlefield of 1945 and transformed it into an economic miracle

that today stands on the threshold of full fledged political union. Latin America, South East Asia, Southern Africa are witness, in varying degree, to similar economic process. Thus regional economic cooperation has in a way become the password to the modern age today. And only then, South Asia could emerge from the shadows of conflict and hostility to take its rightful place among the comity of nations. Regional co-operation in South Asia could materially improve the lives of over a billion of the world's most impoverished people, while at the same time offering an escape route from the conflict and hatreds that history has burdened us with. Further, as and when regional co-operation in South Asia does take off, the resultant joins to each country and to the subcontinent will be immense. For example, while India is energy deficient, its neighbourhood is not. Pakistan, Bangladesh and Nepal are all surplus in energy and if India was able to commercially access these surpluses, India may be able to significantly moderate its energy bill. In a similar manner, opening its trade, transportation and communication links in the subcontinent will greatly reduce costs in all SAARC countries, bringing increased benefits to all citisens, in particular the poor and the deprived sections of society on whose back the present inefficiencies are mainly sustained.

- Regarding stability, to ensure that a Government so constituted would last for a reasonable period and would not always be on its toes fighting a grim battle for its survival all the time and having no time or interest left for the service of the people, certain steps may be suggested : The existing Lok Sabha rule of procedure 188(vi) which bars revival of discussion "of a matter which has been discussed in the same session" would be amended in its application to a No-Confidence motion that a fresh No-Confidence motion can not be discussed before the expiry of one year or more than, twice during the five-year term of the House; Rule 198 laying down of the procedure for moving a Motion of No-Confidence may be slightly amended that the motion shall also contain the name of the proposed new leader of the House who shall take over and head the new Council of Ministers in case the motion of No-Confidence in the existing council is passed. This would in effect bring into our system the German constructive vote of no-confidence device; the practice of standing from more than one constituency must be ended forthwith; parties with an overall score of less than ten per cent should be eliminated. The others should be allotted seats according to their respective percentages in the total vote.

Select Bibliography

Books

Aiyar, Mani Shankar. *Pakistan Papers*, New Delhi: UBS Publishers & Distributors Ltd., 1994.

Appadorai, A. *Select Documents on India's Foreign Policy and Relations*, 1947-1972, Volume II, Delhi: Oxford University Press, Oxford New York, 1985.

Archibugi, Daniele and David, Held (Ed.). *Cosmopolitan Democracy: An Agenda for a New World Order*, Cambridge: Polity, 1995.

Arnett, Eric (Ed.). *Nuclear Weapons After the Comprehensive Test Ban — Implications for Modernization and Proliferation*, Oxford: Oxford University, 1996.

Asianand, Sri. *1996...Whither India? Whither Mankind*? New Delhi: Educational Publishers and Distributors India Ltd., 1996.

Attar, Chand. *Nehru's Vision of Nation Building*, New Delhi: Indus Publishing Company, 1989.

Azad, Maulana Abul Kalam. *India Wins Freedom*, Longman's, Green, 1960.

Bahera, Navnita Chadha, et al. *Beyond Boundaries: A Report on the State of Non-official Dialogues on Peace, Security and Co-operation in South Asia*, Canada: University of Toronto-York University, 1997.

Bandopadhyaya, J. *The Making of India's Foreign Policy: Determinants, Institutions, Processes, Personalities*, New Delhi: Allied Publishers, 1970.

Basham, A.L. *The Wonder that was India*, New York: Grove Press, 1954.

Berks, R.N. and Bedi, M.S. *The Diplomacy of India: Indian Foreign Policy in the United Nations—California*, Stanford University Press, 1958.

Bernard, K. *The Dimensions of Conflict in South Asia*, Englewood Cliffs, N.J. Prentice Hall, 1966.

Bhagwati, Jagdish. *India in Transition: Freeing the Economy*, Oxford: Clarendon Press, 1993.

Bhutani, Sudarshan. *A Clash of Political Cultures: Sino-Indian Relations (1957-1962)*, New Delhi: Roli, 2004.

Bidwai, Praful and Achin, Vanaik. *Testing Times: The Global Stake in a Nuclear Test Ban*, 1996.

Bidwai, Praful and Anuradha, Chenoy, et al. *India Under Siege: Challenges Within and Without*, New Delhi: Wiley Eastern Limited, 1995.

Blinkenberg, Lars. *India-Pakistan: The History of Unresolved Conflicts*, Darsk Uderrigs Politisk Institute, Denmark, 1972.

Brecher, Jeremy and Tim, Costello. *Global Village or Global Pillage: Economic Reconstruction From the Bottom Up*, St. Boston: South End Press, 1994.

Brecher, Michael. *India's Foreign Policy: An Interpretation*, Institute of Pacific Relations, 1957.

——. *India and World Politics: Krishna Menon's View of the World* (Recorded Interview), London: Oxford University Press, 1968.

——. *Nehru: A Political Biography*, London: Oxford University Press, 1959.

Brodie, Bernard. *Strategy in the Missile Age*, Princeton, N.J.: Princeton University Press, 1979.

Butwell, Richard (Ed.). *Foreign Policy and the Developing Nations*, Lexington: University of Kentucky Press, 1969.

Chakravarti, P.C. *India's China Policy*, Indiana University Press, 1962.

Chari, P.R. and Others. *Nuclear Non-Proliferation in India and Pakistan*; South Asian Perspective, 1996.

Chatterjee, Partha. *A Possible India: Essays in a Political Criticism*, Delhi: Oxford University Press, 1997.

Chellaney, Brahma (Ed.). *Securing India's Future in the New Millennium*, New Delhi: Orient Longman, 1999.

Chitkara, M.G. *Indo-Pak Relations: Challenges Before New Millennium*, New Delhi: APH, 2001.

Chopra, H.S.; Robert, Frank and Jurgen, Schroder (Ed.). *National Identity and Regional Cooperation: Experiences of European Integration and South Asian Perceptions*, 1999.

Chopra, J.K. *India As a Regional Power*, Jaipur: Sublime, 2000.

Chopra, Pran, et al. *India — The Way Ahead*, New Delhi: Har Anand Publications, 1998.

Chopra, V.D. (Ed.). *New Trends in Indo-Russian Relations*, Delhi: Kalpaz Pub., 2003.

Chopra, V.D. (Ed.). *Pakistan and Asian Peace*, New Delhi: Patriot Publishers, 1985.

Choudhary, G.W. *Pakistan's Relations with India*, 1947-1966, London: Pall Mall Press, 1968.

Clark, Ian. *Globalization and International Relations Theory*, New York: OUP, 1999.

Claude, Luis L. *Power and International Relations*, New York: Random House, 1962.

Cohen, Stephen P. *India, Emergent Power*? Crane, Russia, 1978.

Cortright, David and Amitabh, Mattoo (Ed.). *India and the Bomb: Public Options*, 1996.

Craig, Baxter; Yogendra, K.; Malik, Charles, H.; Kennedy and Robert, C. Oberst. *Government and Politics in South Asia*, Vanguard Books Pvt. Ltd., 1988.

Dass, Tania. *Beyond Cold War: Security Council and International Politics*, Kolkata: Minerva Publications, 2004.

Dewitt, David; David Haglund and John Kirton. *Building A New Global Order: Emerging Trends in International Security*, Oxford University Press, 1993.

Dhar, Pannalal. *India, Her Neighbours and Foreign Policy*, New Delhi: Deep and Deep Publications, 1993.

Dibb, Paul. *Towards a New Balance of Power in Asia*, Oxford University Press, for the International Institute for Strategic Studies, 1995.

Dixit, J.N. *Across Borders: Fifty Years of India's Foreign Policy*, 1998.

—— (Ed.). *External Affairs — Cross Border Relations*, New Delhi: Roli Books, 2003.

——. *India's Foreign Policy and Its Neighbours*, New Delhi: Gyan Publishing, 2001.

——. *India's Foreign Policy Challenge of Terrorism: Fashioning New Interstate Equations*, New Delhi: Gyan, 2002.

——. *Makers of India's Foreign Policy: Raja Ram Mohun Roy to Yashwant Sinha*, New Delhi: Harper Collins Publishers India, 2004.

Doctor, Adi H. *Essays on India's Foreign Policy*, New Delhi: National Publishing House, 1977.

Doody, Agnes G. *Words and Deeds: An Analysis of Jawaharlal Nehru's Non-Alignment Policy in the Cold War 1947-1953*, Pennsylvania State University Thesis, 1961.

Ferguson, Y.H. and Weiker, W.F. (Ed.). *Continuing Issues in International Politics*, Pacific Palisades, Good year Pub. Co., 1973.

Frankel, Francine P. (Ed.). *Bridging the Non-Proliferation Divide: The United States and India*, New Delhi: Konark, 1995.

Freedman, L. *The Evolution of Nuclear Strategy*, London: Macmillan, 1981.

George, Timothy, et al. (Ed.). *India and the Great Powers*, London: Gower, 1984.

Ghoshal, Baladas (Ed.). *ASEAN and South Asia: Development Experience*, 1998.

Giri, V. Mohini. *Emancipation and Empowerment of Women*, Delhi: Gyan Publishing House, 1999.

Goray, W.H. *The Interrelations Between India's Foreign Policy and Defence Policy*, Compendium of Papers read at the Seminar held on 23-28 October, University of Poona, 1967.

Grarem Frederic and Amitabh, Mattoo (Ed.). *India and ASEAN: The Politics of India's Look East Policy*, New Delhi: Manohar, 2001.

Grover, Verinder (Ed.). *Encyclopaedia of SAARC (South Asian Association of Regional Cooperation) Nations*, 7 Vols., 1997.

Grover, Verinder (Ed.). *International Relations and Foreign Policy of India*, Vol. 1, New Delhi: Deep & Deep Publications, 1992.

Gujral, I.K. *Continuity and Change: India's Foreign Policy*, New Delhi: Macmillan, India, 2003.

Gupta, M.G. *Indian Foreign Policy — Theory and Practice*, Agra (U.P.) India: Y.K. Publishers, 1985.

Gupta, R.C. *US Policy Towards India and Pakistan*, Delhi: B.R. Publishing Corporation, 1977.

Gupta, Shekhar. *India Redefines its Role*, Oxford University Press for the International Institute for Strategic Studies, 1995.

Gupta, Sisir. *Kashmir: A Study in India-Pakistan Relations*, New Delhi: Asian Publishing House, 1966.

Habibullah, E. and Narayan, K.B. *The Sinews of Indian Defence*, New Delhi: Lancers, 1981.

Hardgrave, Robert L. Jr. *India Under Pressure — Prospects for Political Stability*, Westview Press/Boulder and London, 1984.

Heimsath, Charles H. and Surjit Mansingh. *A Diplomatic History of Modern India*, Bombay: Allied Publishers, 1971.

Jacob Louis A. (Ed.). *American Understanding of India: A Symposium* (Papers read at a conference held at the Library of Congress, 23-25 October 1986; Convened in conjunction with the Festival of India 1985-1986), New Delhi: Manohar, 2001.

Jain, B.M. *Nuclear Politics in South Asia: In Search of an Alternative Paradigm*, Jaipur/New Delhi: Rawat Publications, 1994.

——. *South Asia, India and the United States*, Jaipur: R.B.S.A. Publishers, 1987.

—— (Ed.). *International System and The Great Power Relationship* (US, China and India), Jaipur: Ina Shree Publishers, 1998.

Jaishanker, S. *Nuclear Factor in Post-war Diplomacy*, New Delhi, 1977. (JNU dissertation)

Jayapalan, N. *Foreign Policy of India*, New Delhi: Atlantic Publishers and Distributors, 2001.

Jha, Nalini Kant (Ed.). *South Asia in Twenty-First Century: India*, Her Neighbours, and the Great Powers, New Delhi: South Asian Pub., 2003.

Kalam, A.P.J. and Y.S. Rajan. *India 2020—A Vision for the New Millennium*, India: Viking, 1998.

Kapur, Ashok. *The Foreign Policy of India and Her Neighbours*, 1996.

Kapur, Ashok, Y.K. Malik, Harold A. Gould and Arthur G. Rubinoff (Ed.). *India and the United States in a Changing World*, New Delhi: Sage, 2002.

Kapur, Harish. *India's Foreign Policy*, 1947-92, Shadows and Substance, Sage Publications, New Delhi/Thousand Oaks/London, 1994.

Karanjia, R.K. *The Mind of Mr. Nehru*, Recorded Talk, London: Allen and Unwin, 1960.

Karunakaran, K.P. *India in World Affairs*, 1947-50, I.C.W.A., 1952.

——. *India's Foreign Policy*, 1956, World Press.

Kavic, Lorne J. *India's Quest for Security*, Defence Policies 1947-65, Berkeley and Los Angeles University, California Press, 1967.

Kennedy, Paul. *The Rise and Fall of the Great Powers Economic Change and Military Conflict from 1500 to 2000*, New York: Random House, 1988.

——. *Preparing For the Twenty-first Century*, Harper Collins, 1993.

Khanna, V.N. *India's Nuclear Doctrine*, New Delhi, 2000.

Khera, S.S. *India's Defence Problem*, Bombay: Orient Longmans, 1968.

Khilnani, Niranjan M. *New Dimensions of Indian Foreign Policy*, (P.M. Narasimha Rao's Era X-rayed), New Delhi: Westvill Publishing House, 1995.

Khurshid, Salman. 'Beyond Terrorism: New Hope for Kashmir', New Delhi: U.B.S. Publishers Distributors, 1994.

Kothari, Rajini. *Footsteps into the future, diagnosis of the present world and a design for an alternative*, New York: Free Press, 1974.

Krepon, Michael and Amit Sevak. *Crisis Prevention: Confidence Building and Reconciliation in South Asia*, 1996.

Krishen, Rajbans. *Kashmir and the Conspiracy Against Peace*, Bombay: Peoples' Publishing House, 1951.

Kumar, Dhrub. *Impact of Indira Gandhi on Indian Political System*, New Delhi: Deep and Deep Publications, 1993.

Kumar, Satish (Ed.). *Yearbook on India's Foreign Policy*, 1987/1988, New Delhi: Sage, 1988.

Kundra, J.C. *Indian Foreign Policy 1947-1954*, J.B. Wolters, Groningen, Netherland, 1955.

Macridis, Roy C. (Ed.). *Foreign Policy in World Politics*, 2 Edn., Englewood Cliffs, N.J., 1962.

Mallik, D.N. *The Development of Non-alignment in India's Foreign Policy*, Allahabad: Chaitanya Publishing House, 1967.

Mann, Poonam. *India's Foreign Policy in the Post Cold War Era*, Delhi: Harman, 2000.

Mansingh, Surjit (Ed.). *Nehru's Foreign Policy*, Fifty Years of Independence, New Delhi: Mosaic Books, 1998.

——. *India's Search for Power*, Delhi: Sage Publications, 1984.

Margolis, Eric. *War at the Top of the World: The Struggle for Afghanistan, Kashmir and Tibet*, New York: Routledge, 2000.

Mathur, Vibha. *India: Foreign Trade Policy and WTO 1991-2003*, Delhi: New Century, 2003.

Mattoo, Amitabh (Ed.). *India's Nuclear Deterrent: Pokhran II and Beyond*, 1999.

Mc Gowan, P.J. and H.B. Shapiro. *Comparative Study of Foreign Policy: A Survey of Scientific Findings*, Beverly Hills: Sage, 1973.

Mellor, John W. (Ed.). *India: A Rising Middle Power*, Boulder, Colo. Westview Press, 1979.

Mishra, Keshav. *Rapprochement Across the Himalayas: Emerging India-China Relations in Post Cold War Period — (1947-2003)*, Delhi: Kalpaz, 2004.

Misra, K.K. *Kashmir and India's Foreign Policy*, Allahabad: Chugh Publications, 1979.

Misra, K.P. *Foreign Policy and its Planning*, New Delhi: Asia Publishing House, 1970.

——. *Studies in Indian Foreign Policy*, Delhi: Vikas, 1967.

——. *Foreign Policy of India: A Book of Readings*, New Delhi: Thomson Press, 1977.

Misra, S.N. *India—The Cold War Years*, New Delhi: South Asian Publishers Pvt. Ltd., 1994.

Mohanty, Bidyut, Girish Kumar (Ed.). *Women and Political Empowerment 2000*, Institute of Social Sciences, New Delhi, 2002.

Murthi, V.K. *In the Larger Personal Interest: An Investigation into Indian Politics Since 1947*, New Delhi: Allora, 1978.

Murthy, R.K. *Cult of the Individual: A Study of Indira Gandhi*, New Delhi: Sterling, 1977.

Muttam, John. *Regional Conflicts and Arms Race: A Study of U.S. Role in the Arms race between Pakistan and India*, New Delhi: Sindhu, 1974.

Nagar, K.S. and Gautam Sharma (Ed.). *India's Security: Super Power Threat*, New Delhi: Reliance Publisher, 1990.

Nanda, B.R. *Indian Foreign Policy: The Nehru Years*, New Delhi: Vikas Publishing House, 1975.

Nanda, J.N. *Foreign Policy of Coexistence-India*, New Delhi: Ashish Varma Publication, 1997.

Nanda, Ravi. *India and the Emerging Multipolar World*, New Delhi: Lancer's, 2001.

Narsimham, M. *World Economic Environment and Prospects for India*, New Delhi: Sterling, 1988.

Nasenko, Yuri. *Jawaharlal Nehru and India's Foreign Policy*, New Delhi: Sterling Publishers, 1977.

Nayar, Kuldip. *India After Nehru*, New Delhi: Vikas Publishing House, 1975.

Nehru, Jawaharlal. *Speeches* 1949-1953, Calcutta, 1954.

——. *India's Foreign Policy, Selected Speeches — September 1946-April 1961*. Publications Division, Government of India, Bombay.

——. *Speeches — March 1953 — August 1957*, Publications Division, Government of India.

——. *The Discovery of India, Jawaharlal Nehru Memorial Fund*, Oxford University Press, 1995.

Nelson, Barbara and Najma Choudhury. *Women and Politics Worldwide*, New Haven and London: Yale University Press, 1994.

Norman, Dorothy (Ed.). *Nehru — The First Sixty Years*, 2 Volumes, London: Bodley Head, 1965.

Odegard, Peter H. *Political Power and Social Change*, New Delhi: Oxford and IBH Publishers Co., 1969.

Ohmac, Kenichi. *The End of the Nation State: The Rise of Regional Economics*, London: McKinsey & Company Inc., Harper Collins Publishers, 1995.

O' Leary, Michael K. and William D. Coplin. *Quantitative Techniques in Foreign Policy Analysis and Forecasting*, New York: Praeger, 1975.

Palsokar, R.D. *Minimum Deterrent: India's Nuclear Answer to China*, Bombay: Thacker, 1969.

Panda, Pramoda Kumar. *Making of India's Foreign Policy: Prime Ministers and Wars,* Delhi: Raj Publications, 2003.

Pant, H.G. *India's Foreign Policy*, Jaipur: Panchsheel, 1971.

Pastor, Robert A. (Ed.). *A Century's Journey: How the Great Powers Shape the World*, New York: Basic Books, 1999.

Patel, R.M. *The Defence of India*, Poona: The Gokhale Institute of Politics and Economics, 1963.

Patel, S.R. *Foreign Policy of India — An Enquiry and Criticism*, Bombay, 1960.

Perkovich, George. *India's Nuclear Bomb: The Impact on Global Proliferation*, Berkeley: University of California Press, 1999.

Pillai, K. Raman (Ed.). *Indian Foreign Policy in 1990s*, New Delhi: Radiant Publishers, 1997.

Pillai, S. Devadas (Ed.). *Aspects of Changing India*, Bombay: Popular Prakashan, 1976.

Poplai, S.L. *Select Documents India 1947-56*, Vol. I, Internal Affairs, Oxford University Press, 1959, I.C.W.A. Publication.

——. *Select Documents, India 1947-56*, Vol. II, External Affairs, Oxford University Press, 1959, I.C.W.A. Publication.

Poulose, T.T. *The CTBT and the Rise of Nuclear Nationalism in India*, 1996.

Power, Paul F. *India's Non-alignment Policy*, Boston: D.C. Heath, 1967.

Prajapati Vishnu (Ed.). *South Asia: Power and Politics: Studies in Political Identity and Regional Resurgence*, 3 Vol., 1998.

Qurong Shen and Bhabani Sen Gupta (Ed.). *China Looks at the World*, 1999.

Radhakrishnan, N. and N. Vasudeven (Ed.). *A Nation in Transition: India at 50*, New Delhi: Gandhi Media Center, 1998.

Raghavan, R.K. *Policing A Democracy: A Comparative Study of India and the US*, 1999.

Raghvan, V.R. Lt. Gen. (Retd.). *India's Need for Strategic Balance: Security in the Post–Cold War World*, 1996.

Raja Mohan, C. *Crossing the Rubicon- The Shaping of India's New Foreign Policy*, New Delhi: Viking, 2003.

Rajan, M.S. *India and International Affairs: A Collection of Essays*, 1999.

Rajan, M.S. *India's Foreign Relations During the Nehru Era*, Bombay: Asia Publishing House, 1976.

——. *Non-alignment: India and the Future*, Mysore: University of Mysore Press, 1970.

Rajkumar, N.V. (Ed.). *The Background of India's Foreign Policy*, Delhi: Navin Press, 1952.

Rana, A.P. *The Imperatives of Non-alignment — A Conceptual Study of India's Foreign Policy Strategy in the Nehru Period*, New Delhi: Macmillan, 1976.

Range, Willard. *Jawaharlal Nehru's Worldview: A Theory of International Relations*, Athens: University of Georgia Press, 1961.

Rao, Nitya, Luise Rurup (Ed.). *A Just Right*, Friedrich Ebert Stiftung, India,1997.

Ray, Prakash; Vanita, Ray and Sanjay Ambatkar (Ed.). *India and ASEAN: Economic Partnership in the 1990s and Future Prospects*, 1996.

Rizvi, Gowher. *South Asia in a Changing International Order*, New Delhi: Sage Publications, 1993.

Rosenau, James N. *Scientific Study of Foreign Policy*, New York: Free Press, 1971.

—— (Ed.). *International Politics and Foreign Policy: A Reader in Research and Theory*, New York: The Free Press, 1969.

Rosgotra, M. (Ed.). *The UN in the Twenty-First Century*, Rajeev Gandhi Foundation, 1997.

Rosgotra, M.K. (Ed.). *Rajiv Gandhi's World View*, Vikas Publishing House Pvt. Ltd., 1991.

Roy, Ajit. *Political Power In India: Nature and Trends*, Calcutta: Naya Prakash, 1975.

Sahgal, Nayantara. *Indira Gandhi's Emergence and Style*, Delhi: Vikas, 1978.

Saighal, Vinod. *Third Millennium Equipoise*, New Delhi: Lancer Publishers, 1998.

Saraf, R.P. (Ed.). *Political and Social Realities in Modern India*, Delhi: Indian Bibliographies Bureau Co-Publisher Balaji Enterprises, 1990.

Sathe, Vasant. *National Government — Agenda For A New India*, New Delhi, 1991.

Saxena, K.C. *Pakistan and Her Relations with India 1947-66*, New Delhi: Vir Publishing House, 1966.

Saxena, Rekha. *Indian Politics in Transition, from Dominance to Chaos*, New Delhi: Deep and Deep Publications, 1994.

Schleicher, Charles P. *International Relations: Cooperation and Conflict*, Prentice-Hall of India (Prentice-Hall, USA, 1962).

Sengupta, Bhabani (Ed.). *Regional Cooperation and Development in South Asia*, New Delhi: South Asian Publishers, 1986.

Shah, A.B. (Ed.). *India's Defence and Foreign Policies*, Bombay: Manaktelas, 1966.

Shams-Ud-Din (Ed.). *India and Russia: Towards Strategic Partnership*, New Delhi: Lancer's Books, 2001.

Sharma, S.R. *US Iraq War. An Erosion of UN Authority*, New Delhi: Mohit Publications, 2003.

Sharma, S.R. *Foundations of Indian Foreign Policy*, New Delhi: Omsons, 2002.

Sharma, V.B. *The Strategic Aspects of India's Foreign Policy*, London, University Ph.D. Thesis, 1958.

Shashi, Bhushan. *Non-alignment-legacy of Nehru*, New Delhi: Progressive People's Sector Publishers, 1976.

Sheen, Vincent. *Nehru the Years of Power*, London, Victor Gollanez. 1960.

Shivam Ravinder K. *India's Foreign Policy Nehru to Vajpayee*, New Delhi: Commonwealth, 2001.

Singh, Iqbal. *Between Two Fires: Towards an Understanding of Jawaharlal Nehru's Foreign Policy*, Vol. II, 1998.

Singh, Jaswant. *Defending India*, 1999.

Singh, M.P. and Rekha Saxena (Ed.). *Ideologies and Indian Politics*, New Delhi: Deep and Deep Publications Pvt. Ltd., 1998.

Singh, Patwant. *India and the Future of Asia*, London: Faber and Faber Ltd., 1966.

Singh, R.K. Jasbir (Lt. Gen.) (Ed.). *Indian Defence Year Book 1998-99*, Dehradun: Natraj Publishers, 1998.

Sinha, P.C. (Ed.). *50 Years of United Nations and World Affairs*, 10 Volumes, 1997.

Sinha, Rameshwar P. and Surya Dandekar (Ed.). *China and Japan in Asian Power Politics: Studies in People, Power and Political Development*, 1998.

Smith, Steve (Ed.). *International Relations, British International Studies Association*, Lawrence Freedman's Strategic Studies, 1985.

Sondhi, M.L. and Ashok Kapur. *US and India: Changing Strategic Parameters*, Delhi: Manak, 2002.

Sondhi, M.L. and K.G. Tyagi (Ed.). *Asia-Pacific: Security, Globalisation and Development*, New Delhi: Manas, 2001.

Sondhi, M.L. and K.G. Tyagi (Ed.). *India in the New Asia-Pacific*, New Delhi: Manas, 2001.

Spannier, John. *Foreign Policy Since World War-II*, University of Florida, 1988.

Spear, P. *India and Pakistan and the West*, New York, 1949.

Stein, Arthur. *India and the Soviet Union*. The Nehru Era, Chicago University Press, 1969.

Subramanyam, K. and Jasjit Singh (Ed.). *Security Without Nuclear Weapons*, New Delhi: Lancer International, 1986.

Sukhwal, B.L. *India, A Political Geography*, New Delhi: Allied Publishers, 1971.

Sulaiman, Naushad Anwar. *India, Germany and European Union: Partners in Progress and Prosperity*, Delhi: Kalinga, 2002.

Surhadi, Ajit Singh. *India's Security in Resurgent Asia*, New Delhi: Heritage, 1979.

Suyder, Glenn H. *Stockpilling Strategic Materials: Politics and National Defence*, San Francisco: Chandler Publishing, 1966.

Swamy, Subramanian. *India's China Perspective*, Delhi: Konark, 2001.

Tahir-Kheli, Shirin R. *India, Pak and the United States: Breaking with the Past*, Council of Foreign Relations Press, New York, 1997.

Thakur, Janardhan. *Indira Gandhi and Her Power Game*, Delhi: Vikas, 1979.

Tiwari, Sanjeev Kumar. *Indian Ocean Rim-Association for Regional Cooperation* (IOR-ARC): Problems and Prospects, Delhi: Abhijeet Pub., 2004.

Travis, Thom A. *India, Pakistan and the Third World: In the Post-Cold War System*, 1997.

Van, Eekelen W.F. *Indian Foreign Policy and the Dispute with China*, Martinus Nijhoff, The Hague, 1964.

Vanaik, Achin. *The Painful Transition — Bourgeois Democracy in India*, London: Verso, 1990.

Verma, Sudhir. *Women's Struggle for Political Space-From Enfranchisement to Participation*, New Delhi: Rawat Publications, 1997.

Vivekanandan, B. and D.K. Giri (Ed.). *Contemporary Europe and South Asia*, New Delhi: Concept Publishing Company, 2001.

Waters, Malcolm. *Globalization*, London: Routledge, 1995.

Wohlforth, William Curti. *The Elusive Balance: Power and Perceptions during the Cold War*, Ithaca, New York Cornell University Press, 1993.

Yadav, R.S. (Ed.). *India's Foreign Policy Towards 2000 A.D.*, New Delhi: Deep & Deep Publications, 1993.

Zakaria, Fareed. *From Wealth to Power: The Unusual Origins of America's World Role*, Princeton: Princeton University Press, 1998.

Zuckerman, S. *Nuclear Illusion and Reality*, London: Collins, 1982.

Articles and Journals

Aiyar, Swaminathan S.A. "Towards a Global Recession?", *World Focus*, Vol. 19, No. 9, September 1998.

Anand, Vinod. "India's Strategy in Operation Vijay", *World Focus*, Vol. 20, No. 6-7, June-July, 1999.

Bagchi, Kishore N. "Double Standard Double Issues: Security Assurances of the NPT and the Comprehensive Test Ban Treaty", *Asian Studies*, Vol. 14, No. 1, 1996.

Balasubramaniam, V. "Defence in a Dangerous World", *Eastern Economist*, July 25, 1980.

Bandopadhyaya, J. "Economic Basis of Foreign Policy", *India Quarterly*, Vol. 25, No. 4, Oct.-Dec., 1969.

——. "Dynamics of India's Strategic Environment", *International Studies*, July-December, 1978.

Basu, Jyoti. "Challenges of the 21st Century", *World Focus,* Vol. 19, No. 10-11-12, Oct.-Nov.-Dec., 1998.

Bhambhri, C.P. "Political Process and Foreign Policy", *World Focus*, Vol. 20, No. 10-11-12, Oct.-Nov.-Dec., 1999.

Bhattacharya, Sudipta. "Economic Liberalization in India", *Mainstream*, March 18, 1995.

Brown, Seyom. "Changing Essence of Power", *Foreign Affairs,* Vol. 55, No. 2, Jan. 1973.

Brucan, Silviu. "Power and World Politics", *Pacific Community,* Vol. 3, No. 4, July 1972.

Bull, H. "Strategic Studies and Its Critics", *World Politics*, Vol. 20, No. 4, 1968.

Bundy, William P. "Elements of Powers", *Strategic Digest*, Vol. 8, No. 2, Feb. 1978.

Burlatsky, Fyodor M. "Halting the arms race and planning for World peace", *Strategic Digest*, August 1972.

Bagchi, Kishore N. "Double Standard Double Issues: Security Assurances of the NPT and the Comprehensive Test Ban Treaty", *Asian Studies*, Vol. 14, No. 1, 1996.

Chari, P.R. "Emerging Strategic Balance", *China Report*, Vol. 14, No. 3, May / June 1978.

Chhabra, Hari Sharan. "Foreign Policy in Information Age", *World Focus*, Vol. 19, No. 2, Feb. 1998.

Chirappanath, A.K. "Modern Search for Peace: The Gandhian Way", *Journal of Gandhian Studies*, April 1978.

Chopra, M.K. "Building India's Defence for Today and Tomorrow," *Organizer*, August 10, 1980.

Cohen, Stephen P. "Indian Strategy and Decision Making: A Means to Achieving Great Power Status", *Strategic Studies*, August 1978.

——. "India's Role in the New Global Order: An American Perspective", *Indian Journal of Asian Affairs*, Vol. 6, No. 1-2, 1993.

D'costa, Anthony P. "The long march towards Capitalism", *Contemporary South Asia*, Vol. 4, No. 3, November 1995.

Desmond, Edward. "The Insurgency in Kashmir", *Contemporary South Asia*, Vol. 4, No. 1, March 1995.

Dixit, Aabha. "Indo-Pak Relations Today", *World Focus*, Vol. 19, No. 6-7, June-July, 1998.

Dixit, J.N. "Pakistan's India Policies: Role of Domestic Political Factors", *International Studies*, Vol. 32, No. 3, July-Sept., 1995.

Dubey, Muchkund. "Minimum Nuclear Deterrence", *World Focus*, Vol. 19, No. 6-7, June-July, 1998.

Dutta, V.P. "Post–Cold War Scenario", *World Focus*, Vol. 17, No. 10-11-12, Oct.–Nov.–Dec., 1996.

Gallios, Pierre M. "India's Nuclear Explosion and India's Security", *Foreign Affairs Reports*, June 1975.

Gonsalves, Eric. "Fifty Years of Foreign Policy", *World Focus*, Vol. 17, No. 10-11-12, Oct.-Nov.-Dec., 1996.

Gray, Christopher M. "The Character, Wealth and Power of Nations", *Orbis*, Vol. 42, No. 4, Fall, 1998.

Gujral, I.K. "Vision of India", *World Focus*, Vol. 19, No. 10-11-12, Oct.-Nov.-Dec., 1998.

Jain, B.M. "Indo-Pakistan Relations in the Post-cold War Period", *Indian Journal of Asian Affairs*, Vol. 6, No. 1-2, 1993.

Jervis, Robert. "Co-operation Under the Security Dilemma", *World Politics*, Vol. 30, No. 2, Jan. 1978.

Kochan, Ran. "Changing Emphasis in the Non-Aligned Movement", *World Today*, Vol. 28, No. 11, Nov. 1972.

Mahapatra, Chintamani. "Clinton's Visit to India", *World Focus*, Vol. 21, No. 6-7, June–July, 2000.

Mates, Leo. "Non–alignment", *Foreign Affairs*, April 1970.

Mattoo, Amitabh. "Kargil and Kashmir", *World Focus*, Vol. 20, No. 6–7, June–July, 1999.

Mishra, Girish. "Globalisation and India: Some Implications", *World Focus*, Vol. 20, No. 10-11-12, Oct.-Nov.-Dec., 1999.

Nambiar, Satish. "The Security Dimensions", *World Focus*, Vol. 21, No. 6-7, June-July, 2000.

Narayanan, K.R. "India and the World Today", *World Focus*, Vol. 19, No. 10-11-12, Oct.-Nov.-Dec., 1998.

Palit, D.K. "India's Quest for Security, 1947-77", *Mainstream*, July 28, 1979.

——. "India as an Asian Military Power", *India International Centre Quarterly*, Jan. 1975.

Palkhivala, Nani A. "India and the Nuclear Issue", *Indian and Foreign Review*, Nov. 1-15, 1979.

Pardesi, Ghanshyam. "Economic Development and Foreign Policy: A case study of India", New Delhi, JNU Dissertation, 1976.

Radovanovic, Ljubomir. "Economic Factor in Non-Aligned Policy", *Review of International Affairs*, April 20, 1974.

Rajan, M.S. "India as a Global Power", *World Focus*, Vol. 19, No. 10-11-12, Oct.-Nov.-Dec., 1998.

Ransom, Harry Howe. "Strategic Intelligence and Foreign Policy", *World Politics*, Vol. 27, No. 1, Oct. 1974.

Roberts, Richard B. and Mc Clure, Frank T. "Arms, Arms Control and Foreign Policy", *Journal of Arms Control*, Vol. 1, No. 3, July 1963.

Roberts, William H. "Non–violence and the Conduct of Foreign Policy", *World Affairs*, Jan.-Mar., 1966.

Singh, Swaran. "Sino–Indian Relations", *World Focus*, Vol. 19, No. 1, Jan. 1998.

Smyth, Henry De Wolf. "Nuclear Power and Foreign Policy", *Foreign Affairs*, Vol. 35, No. 1, Oct. 1956.

Stojanovic, Radoslav. "Interdependence in International Relations", *International Social Science Journal*, Vol. 30, No. 2, 1978.

Subrahmanyam, K. "Nuclear Factor in Indo-US Relations", *World Focus*, Vol. 21, No. 6-7, June-July, 2000.

——. "India and the Security of the Sub-continent," *India Quarterly*, July-Dec., 1980.

Subramanian, R.R. "Minimum and Credible Deterrence", *World Focus*, Vol. 21, No. 4, April 2000.

Thomas. "A Grand Strategy For India", *Indian Defence Review*, Jan. 1990.

Viswam, S. "India's Look — East Policy", *World Focus*, Vol. 18, No. 6, June 1997.

Walli, R.L. "International Relations and the Problem of Development", *Journal of Political Studies*, Vol. 8, No. 2, September 1975.

Wisner, Frank G. "From Confrontation to Reconciliation:

India and Pakistan at the Crossroads", *Journal of the United Service Institute of India*, Vol. 126, No. 525, July-Sept., 1996.

Zuberi Matin. "Pokhran-II and Chagai", *World Focus*, Vol. 19, No. 6-7, June-July, 1998.

——. "The Proposed Nuclear Doctrine", *World Focus*, Vol. 21, No. 4, April 2000.

Publications (Government of India)

Foreign Affairs Record, New Delhi, Ministry of External Affairs.

Foreign Policy of India, Texts of Documents 1947-59 (Second Edition, New Delhi, Lok Sabha Secretariat, 1966).

Foreign Policy of India, Texts of Documents 1947-64 (Third Edition, New Delhi, Lok Sabha Secretariat, 1966).

India's Foreign Policy. Selected Speeches, September 1946-April 1961 Jawaharlal Nehru (New Delhi, The Publications Division, Ministry of Information and Broadcasting, Government of India, 1961).

Selected Speeches of Indira Gandhi, January 1966-August 1969 (New Delhi, The Director, Publications Division, Ministry of Information and Broadcasting, Government of India, 1971).